Public Interests

Public Interests

Media Advocacy and
Struggles over U.S. Television

ALLISON PERLMAN

Rutgers University Press

New Brunswick, New Jersey, and London

Library of Congress Cataloging-in-Publication Data
Perlman, Allison, 1975–
     Public interests : media advocacy and struggles over U.S. television / Allison Perlman.
        pages cm
     Includes bibliographical references and index.
     ISBN 978–0–8135–7230–7 (hardcover : alk. paper) — ISBN 978–0–8135–7229–1 (pbk. :
alk. paper) — ISBN 978–0–8135–7231–4 (e-book (epub)) — ISBN 978–0–8135–7232–1 (e-book
(web pdf))
     1. Television broadcasting—Social aspects—United States. 2. Television and politics—United
States. 3. Social movements—United States. I. Title.
     PN1992.6.P473 2016
     302.23'450973—dc23
     2015032498

A British Cataloging-in-Publication record for this book is available from the British Library.

Visit our website: http://rutgerspress.rutgers.edu

Manufactured in the United States of America

Contents

Acknowledgments

This book is a history of media advocacy, but it was informed by the remarkable work of people currently committed to media reform. Since 2005 I have attended a number of conferences and workshops in which hundreds of people engaged in media activism and advocacy gathered to discuss their work, share tactics and strategies, and find common cause in the fight to reform the media. I am so appreciative of what they do, grateful for the conversations about media advocacy, and inspired by their commitments to fight for media justice and media democracy.

The research for this book was especially aided by the kindness, interest, and generosity of archivists and librarians across the country. Sincere thanks go to the amazing staffs at the Library of Congress, the National Public Broadcasting Archives, the Wisconsin Historical Society, the Schlesinger Library, the Alabama Department of Archives and History, Special Collections at Ohio State University, Special Collections at the University of California–Los Angeles, the Tamiment Library at New York University, Special Collections at George Washington University, and the Birmingham Public Library.

I was honored to be at the University of Virginia for a year as the Verklin Fellow in Media Ethics and Policy. Thank you to David Verklin for creating this wonderful opportunity and to the media studies department at the University of Virginia—Hector Amaya, Aniko Bodroghkozy, Jennifer Petersen, Andrea Press, Siva Vaidhyanathan, and Bruce Williams—for including me in their intellectual community. It would be hard to overstate how important that year was to the development of this book or how much I learned from this remarkable group of scholars. In addition, I was thrilled to be a part of the inaugural Phil Zwickler Memorial Writing Workshop for Historians of Gender and Sexuality. Thanks go to Gill Frank for inviting me, and to him, Alison Lefkowitz, Erica Ryan, Tim Stewart-Winter, and Stacie Taranato for their insightful comments on my work.

Over the years, as this project has evolved, many friends, colleagues, and mentors read chapters, offered important feedback, talked me through difficult stages, and provided much-appreciated guidance and moral support. Thank you so much Hector Amaya, Miranda Banks, Kyle Barnett, Aniko Bodroghkozy, Steve Classen, Janet Davis, Jonathan Gray, Hollis Griffin, Andrew Hartman, Michael Kackman, Becky Lentz, John McMurria, Jeff Meikle, Julia Mickenberg, Chon Noriega, Mike O'Connor, Jennifer Petersen, Victor Pickard, Alex Russo, Gautham Rao, Avi Santo, Tom Schatz, Stephanie Schulte, Josh Shepperd, Mark Smith, and David Uskovich. Thanks also go to the two reviewers for Rutgers University Press, whose insightful and incisive comments were crucial as I revised the final manuscript.

I completed this book at UC Irvine, where I have a split appointment in history and film and media studies. I am so grateful to all my colleagues in both departments for making UCI such a supportive, collegial academic home. I owe special thanks to Alex Borucki, Sharon Block, Kristen Hatch, Lucas Hilderbrand, Bliss Lim, Vicky Johnson, Nancy McLoughlin, Jessica Millward, Bob Moeller, Rachel O'Toole, Fatimah Tobing Rony, and Jon Wiener, who have been important allies, friends, and mentors since I arrived at UCI. Sincere gratitude goes to UCI Humanities Commons for providing me with a generous publication subvention grant to publish this work.

I could not have asked for a better editor than Leslie Mitchner, and I am grateful for her interest in my work and for her patience and generosity as I finished this book. Big thanks also go to the wonderful people at Rutgers University Press, especially Lisa Boyajian and Marilyn Campbell, and to Joe Abbott for his skillful copyediting of the manuscript.

I am so appreciative of my family—Alan Perlman, Nancy Zivitz, Adam Perlman, Beverly Perlman, Stuart Gould, Amy Goldfrank, and Lauren Gould—for their support, their love, and their willingness to refrain from asking "how's the book coming along?" at key moments. Thanks also to my long-standing surrogate family—Jami Bartlett, Kim Hewitt, Chris Jennings, Lisa Loeffler-Kaplan, Maria Magaña, Aaron Miller, Mike O'Connor, Kevin Strait, and Michele Solberg—for being the most wonderful, loyal, and generous friends that a person could ever hope for.

Though Trevor Griffey entered my life over twenty years ago, he became the most important person in it about two years ago. He stood by me and supported me as I finished this book, provided excellent feedback on my manuscript, and talked me through a number of issues as I completed it. I am awed by and thankful for his intelligence and his integrity, as well as for his compassion and kindness. But perhaps most importantly, I am grateful for the home we have built together, for the love that I feel when I'm in it, and for the joy of sharing it with him.

Abbreviations

ACNO Advisory Committee of National Organizations

AETC Alabama Educational Television Commission

AETN Alabama Educational Television Network

ALJ Administrative Law Judge

BEST Black Efforts for Soul in Television

CURB Citizens United for Responsive Broadcasting

EEO Equal Employment Opportunity

EEOC Equal Employment Opportunity Commission

ETFA Educational Television Facilities Act

ETRC Educational Television and Radio Center

FAE Fund for Adult Education

FCC Federal Communications Commission

FRC Federal Radio Commission

GLAAD Gay and Lesbian Alliance against Defamation

HBC Hispanic Broadcasting Corporation

HBLP Hispanic Broadcasting Limited Partnership

HBS Hispanic Broadcasting Systems

JCEB Joint Council on Educational Broadcasting

JCET Joint Committee (Council) on Educational Television

LULAC League of United Latin American Citizens

MRC Media Research Center

NAACP National Association for the Advancement of Colored People

NAB National Association of Broadcasters

NAEB National Association of Educational Broadcasters

NARTB National Association of Radio and Television Broadcasters

NBMC National Black Media Coalition

NCCET National Citizens Committee for Educational Television

NCF National Conservative Foundation

NDEA National Defense Education Act

NEA National Educational Association

NET National Educational Television

NETRC National Educational Television and Radio Center

NHMC National Hispanic Media Coalition

NHPI National Hispanic Policy Institute

NOW National Organization for Women

PBS Public Broadcasting System

PTC Parents Television Council

PTI Perenchio Television Inc.

SECA Southern Educational Communications Association

SICC Spanish International Communications Corporation

SIN Spanish International Network

SREB Southern Regional Education Board

WEAL Women's Equity Action League

Public Interests

Introduction

American social movements have been bound up with television since the earliest years of the medium. In the 1960s, television famously brought images of police dogs attacking young people in Birmingham, Alabama; tear gas and police batons brutalizing marchers in Selma, Alabama; and Martin Luther King Jr.'s soaring oratory in front of the Lincoln Memorial into living rooms across the country, defining for viewers the stakes and struggles for African American civil rights. Second-wave feminist concerns found their way into the prime-time programming of the 1970s in numerous ways, including Maude Findlay's decision to get an abortion on *Maude*, Mary Richards's choice to stake out a life on her own as a career woman on *The Mary Tyler Moore Show*, and Ann Romano's struggles to raise two daughters as a divorced woman on *One Day at a Time*. Vice President Dan Quayle's attack in 1992 on fictional Murphy Brown's decision to have a child out of wedlock, and her retort to him within the show's narrative, was one of the hallmarks of the culture wars, the battles in the 1980s and 1990s between conservatives and progressives over American culture and American values. Television has popularized and ignored, advocated and contained, celebrated and mocked social movements, and its ability to bring public struggles into the intimacy of private spaces has made it a crucial component of campaigns for social and political change.

Less well known, however, have been the offscreen battles over television regulation. Throughout the second half of the twentieth century, struggles over broadcasting policy were critical parts of campaigns for social justice and political reform in the United States. As American social movements responded to an increasingly mass-mediated society, they tried to mold television to reflect their moral and political beliefs. And as television specifi-cally became the locus of a shared public culture, reformers understood that their successes or failures would be tied to the narratives presented in, faces and voices appearing on, and values and perspectives circulating in the televi-sual public sphere. Of the many strategies deployed to effect change—which included boycotts of offending sponsors and stations or negotiations with net-work executives—were campaigns to alter the legal and regulatory structures that underpin how television works in the United States. This book is a his-tory of these efforts.

Public Interests offers an alternate lens on the relationship between televi-sion and U.S. social movements by focusing not on how television represents or reports on social or political change but on how social movements have sought to transform the way television operates. Through case studies, *Public Interests* demonstrates that broadcasting policy has been understood by social and political reformers as an important instrument that allocates cultural and economic resources, defines the boundaries of inclusion and exclusion of the polity, and confers political legitimacy on communities across the nation. By exploring the television reform efforts of education reformers, African Ameri-can civil rights activists, feminists, social conservatives, and Latino rights advo-cates from 1950 to 2007, *Public Interests* investigates how and why social move-ment actors have sought to shape regulations often presumed to be of interest only to technocrats or the media industries, from television license allocation schemes to media ownership restrictions.

Television reform has been about television, but it has also always been about more than television. Campaigns to transform broadcasting policy have sought to change the possibilities for television programming. Reformers have presumed a correlation between what audiences see onscreen and their cultural dispositions and political beliefs, their recognition and comprehension of the nation's diversity, and their views of—and their capacity to identify with—people like and unlike themselves. An end goal of television reform efforts continually has been to transform who and what is visible on the small screen. Television reform battles thus have been struggles to expand the parameters of what public culture should mean in a multicultural and multiracial society.

If struggles over broadcasting policy have sought to alter what appears on television screens, they also have been fights for social citizenship rights. In his seminal *Citizenship and Social Class* (1950), T. H. Marshall offers a framework of citizenship hinged on a triad of rights: civil (rights connected to individual freedoms, like freedom of speech, property rights, and due process under the law), political (the right to participate in the institutions of power and gover-nance), and social (the right to fully share in the heritage and life of the collec-tive).[1] Media reformers have demonstrated consistently that social citizenship requires both a media system responsive to people's needs and a definition of the "public" inclusive of them and their interests. As *Public Interests* illustrates, television reform campaigns thus have involved the politics of distribution and the politics of recognition.[2] They have been efforts both to reallocate resources in the form, for example, of broadcast licenses and employment opportunities and to demand that the nation's diversity be recognized not only within television narratives but also in broadcasters' perceptions of their publics and in regulators' understanding of the public interest.

In focusing on these struggles over television regulation, *Public Interests* highlights the important intersections between American social movements and broadcasting policy. It provides an alternate lens through which to view television's relationship to the Cold War, the long civil rights movement, second-wave feminism, and the culture wars. It examines how television has mattered to American social movements and interrogates how media advocacy has complemented their larger projects for social change. In sum, it explores how demands for a more inclusive conception of the public, for an expansion of what David Hollinger has called "the circle of the we," have been enacted in an age of television.[3]

Social Movements and Broadcasting Policy

The difference between print and broadcast media adds complexity to the age-old claim that independent media is central to social change. For instance, in 1827 Samuel Cornish and John Russwurm, the founders of *Freedom's Journal*, the nation's first African American newspaper, stated, "We wish to plead our cause. Too long have others spoken for us. Too long has the public been deceived by misrepresentations in the things that concern us dearly."[4] This sentiment underlines the tremendous importance that all social reformers have attached to access to the media—to the ability to shape the conditions of one's representation and to contribute to the national dialogue in one's own voice. Or, as poet, playwright, and activist Amiri Baraka put it more than a century later, "if you give me a television station, we won't need a revolution."[5]

While both of these sentiments underline the tremendous importance attached to access to the media, the difference between them is important. Cornish and Russwurm did not require a government license to start their paper. The First Amendment, and the freedom of the press that it guarantees, protects newspapers from prior restraint, from the capacity of the government to restrict in advance what is published or to require government permission to publish in the first place. While Cornish and Russwurm evinced tremendous political courage by circulating their paper in both northern and southern states in the 1820s, their ability to "plead our cause" was protected by the Constitution and unimpeded by any federal licensing requirement.

Such was not the case for radio and television—the dominant communication forms of the twentieth century. When radio, or "wireless" in the parlance of the day, emerged in the United States in the first decades of the twentieth century, it functioned primarily as a point-to-point form of communication. It also operated mostly outside the bounds of federal regulation until 1912, when the tragedy of the *Titanic* spurred Congress to pass a law regulating this communications medium. Not only was there a widespread public perception that radio amateurs had circulated devastating misinformation about the scale and scope of the disaster, but ships that may have been able to aid the sinking *Titanic* failed to receive its distress call. The Radio Act of 1912 provided federal mandates for maritime uses of radio and created the radio license, a federal permit to use the airwaves to be distributed by the Commerce Department.[6] And with a licensing process came the inevitability that government would be involved in the structuring of speech, of the press, and of other media.

As radio increased in popularity, the government became more involved in determining the conditions of its use. In the 1920s the Radio Act of 1912 no longer seemed sufficient since when it was devised, legislators could not have imagined that radio would become a popular mass medium bringing public entertainments into people's homes. The 1912 Act was replaced by the Radio Act of 1927, itself the culmination of four national radio conferences convened by Secretary of Commerce Herbert Hoover. In this newer law Congress deemed the airwaves themselves a public resource and constituted a new temporary agency, the Federal Radio Commission (FRC), to allocate broadcast licenses. Congress instructed the FRC that the "public interest, convenience, and necessity" should guide its licensing decisions. Seven years later, the 1934 Federal Communications Act reiterated the foundational elements of the 1927 act, replacing the temporary FRC with the permanent Federal Communications Commission (FCC) and extending its oversight to telecommunications, as well as broadcasting. In the years leading up to and following the 1934 act, the FCC, broadcasters, Congress, the federal courts, and citizen groups continually debated what "public interest" actually means and what role the administrative agency should play in assuring that it is met.

The award of a broadcast license, and thus the ability to use what Congress had deemed a scarce public resource (the airwaves), ostensibly has obligated licensees to serve the public interest, as defined by U.S. regulatory agencies, in exchange for this privilege. Although broadcast licenses must be renewed by the FCC, the commission has only infrequently denied license renewal. Accordingly, the decisions made by the FCC when first allocating radio and then television licenses, and the subsequent awarding of licenses when new frequencies had become available, have set precedents that structure the medium. Though a broadcast license technically does not award a licensee property rights to a particular frequency, in practice it often has operated in this manner. The FCC historically has not only been reluctant to revoke a license once granted; it has privileged incumbents over challengers when faced with competing applications at renewal time for a broadcast license.

Although the regulation of the airwaves was rationalized as serving the public interest, it quickly became apparent that they also served commercial interests and tended to privilege those with the greatest resources. The FRC and FCC in the 1920s and 1930s in their licensing decisions initially prioritized commercial broadcasters, especially those affiliated with national networks, as well as applicants with the most extensive financial resources to build and operate a broadcast station. These considerations also would play a determinative role in the allocation of television licenses in the 1940s and 1950s.

The political and economic power of broadcasters has thus served as a profound barrier to movements for social change, which in turn made media policy and debates about the extent of the "public interest" in broadcasting important to many of the major social movements in the twentieth century. Furthermore, government licensing decisions were made in eras of institutionalized discrimination against women and people of color—people who not only were the targets of social bigotry but also were subject to myriad forms of economic inequality, from employment discrimination to substantially restricted access to bank loans and other forms of capital. It is thus perhaps unsurprising, given the preferences afforded incumbents and the environment in which licenses had been granted, that in 1978 less than 1 percent of broadcast stations in the United States were owned by women or people of color.[7] Though Russwurm and Cornish could plead their own cause, Baraka seems to recognize—a recognition implicit in the words *if* and *give* of his statement—that to access the most powerful form of communication of the second half of the twentieth century would require some transformation in media policy and in the structure of the broadcasting industry that policy decisions had enabled. Pleading one's cause over the airwaves would require media advocacy.

Thus what historically has distinguished broadcasting in the United States from other forms of cultural expression has been the role of the state both in constituting the broadcasting sector through the creation and awarding of broadcast licenses and in shaping broadcasters' obligations to their publics through the interpretation of the "public interest" clause. Broadcast policy making furthermore has functioned not only to allocate resources (in the form of broadcast licenses) or to place parameters on acceptable and desirable forms of content but has relied on often unspoken articulations of who composes the public. In other words, broadcast policy and law not only instantiate and legitimate institutional formations; they instantiate and legitimate conceptions of the public itself.

As *Public Interests* illustrates, it is, in part, for this reason that struggles over broadcasting policy have been so important to various social movements. While television reform campaigns continually have been efforts to alter what kind of programming appears on air or whose stories and perspectives are represented onscreen, they also have been campaigns to alter how regulators and broadcasters conceive of the "public," as well as broadcasters obligations to it.

Broadcast Policy Makers and the Public Interest

The particular structure of U.S. regulatory agencies has had a profound effect on contests over whether and to what extent broadcasters can and should serve a "public interest." The possibilities for media advocacy have been enabled and constrained by media policy, but they also have been enabled and constrained by the particular way it has been enacted by the FCC, understood by Congress, and interpreted by the federal courts. Though federal administrative agencies are part of the executive branch, Congress oversees them and has myriad avenues to weigh in on their rule-making, from passing legislation to shore up or reverse an agency decision to using its power of budget appropriation to pressure the FCC to act. Congress additionally holds hearings on administrative agency performance, broadly, and specifically on the political and social implications of broadcast regulation. Congress has not had a stable relationship with the FCC, broadcasters, or broadcasters' publics. At times Congress has acted as watchdog, pushing back against the perception of the FCC as lapdog to the industry it is charged with regulating. At other times Congress has obstructed the FCC to protect the interests of broadcasters. Members of Congress also routinely have weighed in, both informally and formally, on pending commission actions, from revision of the FCC's indecency policy to revision of its media ownership policies.[8] Federal courts also engage in policy making, through their judicial review over FCC decisions. They can determine whether FCC decisions are constitutional, adhere to statutory requirements, and conform to the strictures of the Administrative Procedures Act (APA), legislation passed in 1946 to address concerns over the performance of administrative agencies like the FCC.

The origin of federal broadcasting policy lies within progressive and New Deal–era legislation that promoted the need of government to regulate U.S. capitalism. While administrative agencies, bureaus, and departments had been a feature of American governance since the early years of the republic, the number of administrative agencies and regulatory commissions grew substantially after the creation of the Interstate Commerce Commission in 1887. During the New Deal, not only did the scale of the administrative state expand, but so did many citizens' experience of government as interactions with administrative agencies. As Joanna Grisinger has persuasively argued, the APA of 1946 redirected complaints over the constitutionality and legitimacy of administrative agencies to questions over the most effective and efficient way for agencies to make and enforce rules. The law strengthened the power of judicial review, provided for public participation in agency rule-making, and lent a framework—especially in its prohibition against the making of "arbitrary" and "capricious" rules—to courts to assess the process by which rule-making had been conducted.[9] Since the passage of the APA, federal courts have varied both in their understanding of the "public interest" and the degree to which they have been willing to sanction the FCC's vision of administrative efficiency and efficacy.

With the growth of federal regulatory agencies, organized groups emerged to pressure those agencies and identify themselves as stakeholders in the regulatory process. As part of this process, therefore, television reform has often been in the crosshairs of the different political agendas and power struggles among the various branches of the federal government, and reformers have had to navigate competing governments', politicians', and courts' understandings of the legitimate role of the state in not just regulating television but in regulating capitalism. Conceptions of the public interest varied accordingly across time, meaning different things to different actors depending on their various institutional positions.

Thus *Public Interests* underlines how this very concept of the public interest has been a site of contestation, conflict, and struggle for policy makers and reformers alike. To study these media reform movements, and to examine the "public interest" through the lens of broadcast policy advocacy, is to see the "public interest" as a discursive construction, something that is produced through social conflict over control of the airwaves rather than something that exists independent of power struggles. The public interest is not a singular, knowable thing. It is a device that reflects the interests of the person or community who invokes it, from the policy makers who historically have conflated it with the interests of corporations to the many media reformers imagining a public interest in line with their own political commitments. Indeed, a central goal of broadcast reformers has been to make their definitions legible and credible and to persuade that they should have purchase on policy makers' own. In addition, a consistent objective of media advocacy has been to puncture the veneer of neutrality within broadcast policy making and to demonstrate how seemingly neutral decisions are imbricated within existing forms of inequality and injustice. Accordingly, as *Public Interests* demonstrates, broadcasting policy battles simultaneously have been fights over cultural resources and for political recognition.

So *Public Interests* takes as a given one of the central insights of critical policy studies: policy making is not a series of technocratic or administrative decisions, in which policy makers, governed by expert knowledge, deploy rational scientific methods in order to regulate existing media technologies.[10] Rather, media policy making constitutes an "arena in which different political preferences are celebrated, contested, or compromised."[11] That is, policy making is political, not neutral. It is the result of a clash of interests, not of dispassionate reasoning. As the following chapters make clear, television reformers have continually tried to redefine how policy-making actors define the "public," conceive of the "public interest," and understand how the object of its regulation, television, matters within the U.S. economy and American society.

Narrating Histories of Media Advocacy

Public Interests joins a burgeoning subfield in media history focused on media reform. These works reimagine the history of radio and television as not only the history of institutions or of textual practices but of political struggles over broadcasting itself, frequently played out in the terrain of media regulation. To write these histories has been to demonstrate how the broadcasting system that developed in the United States was neither natural nor inevitable but the result of a clash of interests. These works are recuperative stories that bring forth narratives of resistance long invisible in histories of American broadcasting. Yet they also are often declension narratives that chart how alternative visions of what broadcasting could do, and of what the public interest should mean, were upended by powerful media corporations that had the ear of the policy-making community and were successfully persuaded of the continued synergies between the public interest and the corporate interest.[12]

In addition, histories of media reform have sought to provide "usable pasts," narratives of previous fights that can inform contemporary struggles over media policy. Accordingly, media historians frequently have chosen to study reform campaigns whose objectives line up with their own political commitments. Their works both honor the goals and labors of their subjects, while also flagging errors in tactics in order to draw lessons from the past for the present. As a result, our picture of what media reform was has been somewhat selective, focused on battles over structural reforms to diminish the power of corporations, and the dominance of commercialism, over the most powerful form of communication in the twentieth century. In addition, to read histories of media advocacy is primarily to grapple with struggles over radio in the years leading up to and immediately following World War II. A significant exception to this general trend would be the important scholarship on the relationship between media advocacy and the civil rights struggles of the 1960s and 1970s.[13]

And yet, as *Public Interests* demonstrates, media advocacy battles continued throughout the twentieth century and coexisted with the medium of television as well. These fights, furthermore, encompassed a range of concerns over television's role in a democratic society, including but not exclusively its dominance by commercial networks. Both liberal and conservative groups saw in television an obstacle to their realization of a better society, and both saw in media regulation an important arena in which to address their concerns. Their struggles often hinged not on a public interest/corporate interest binary but rather on a reconfiguration of the public interest that took stock of the diversity of the nation and the role of broadcasting, and broadcast regulation, in sustaining prevailing forms of inequality or injury. In this, both entertainment and news and public-affairs programming have been imagined to bear on television's function as a public sphere, as the site where, as FCC commissioner

Nicholas Johnson asserted, social and political reality is constituted. As Johnson put it in his 1970 call-to-arms *How to Talk Back to Your Television Set*, "We are living in an age in which television has become confused in a crazy way with reality. If an event is not on television it hasn't happened. And if you—or those with whom you can identify—are not on television you don't exist."[14] Television advocacy operated as a way to reimagine the civic body, both who gets represented onscreen and who is envisioned to be a member of the broadcasting public.

In foregrounding a continuous history of media advocacy, *Public Interests* thus avoids the notion of the "critical juncture" or "constitutive moment" to its history of reform.[15] Robert McChesney's useful model for periodizing the history of media reform, rooted in the notion of a critical juncture, outlines key moments of opportunity when meaningful change to the performance and structure of our media systems are actionable, moments that require the coordinated efforts of reformers.[16] While the critical juncture model has explanatory power, it also implicitly sanctions hierarchies of value—of which policy decisions have meaning, of what counts as a crisis or turning point, and of what kind of media texts are critical to democratic self-governance—that naturalize a particular vision of what media policy does and how the public and its interest ought to be imagined. Additionally, the notion of a critical juncture identifies when structural change is possible but does not indicate when media reform activity has taken place.

But if we broaden our definition of what media advocacy looks like to include struggles not wedded to a corporate interest/public interest binary, then we can see how broadcasting continually has been a site of conflict and resistance. And as a result we can see the participation in media reform struggles of people long absented from our understanding of who has engaged in fights over broadcasting, its regulation, and its sociopolitical role. *Public Interests* focuses on communities often relegated to the margins of histories of media advocacy; thus, it expands what media reform has meant, which political projects it has served, and who has fought for a more inclusive, democratic media.

Public Interests: Case Studies in Media Advocacy

The communities discussed in the following chapters were reformist, not revolutionary. In seeking reform, they implicitly believed in the possibility of transforming existing institutions to be more compatible with their vision of a better society. Excluded from my discussion are the important radical communities who sought a broader overhaul of what they saw as corrosively corrupted institutions and who often disagreed with the more tempered and often accommodationist approach of reformers. In focusing on reformers, this book is by definition selective and incomplete in how it discusses second-wave feminism, for example, or Latino rights advocacy. Its focus on struggles over media policy requires that it examine communities who have believed not only that television is a pivotal site of public culture, but that law and policy are credible instruments for meaningful political reform. Accordingly, the focus here is on media *advocacy*, efforts to reform the media through official channels (such as legislation, administrative action, and legal challenges) rather than media *activism*, actions that exert external pressure on the media industries (such as sponsor boycotts and public protests). While many of the communities I examine participated in both forms of protest, my emphasis is on their engagement with law and policy, seen as central to their goals of expanding who is visible and what is thinkable in the public sphere.

These reformers were actors able to secure the financial and human resources to mount credible reform campaigns. As the chapters across *Public Interests* make clear, media reform is a labor-intensive enterprise, one that relies on myriad forms of capital: financial, cultural/reputational, and political/institutional. Accordingly, meaningful public participation in media policy debates frequently has been limited to the communities and organizations with the economic, informational, and experiential means to contribute. In addition, *Public Interests* stresses the work of media advocacy. It specifically flags how media reformers routinely have engaged in two forms of labor: the practical work required to identify, prepare for, and execute a reform campaign and the political work of demonstrating how the assumptions that drive policy decisions have operated to privilege certain speakers, to erase or ignore members of the polity, and to reinforce the very hierarchies that these social movements have aimed to topple.

Public Interests begins with the fight in the 1950s to secure television licenses for educational purposes. The proven importance of incumbency to licensing decisions was a prime motivation to educators in the early 1950s to request reserved frequencies for noncommercial television. Without securing access to the airwaves early, educators arguably rightfully assumed, it would be very difficult to get a toehold in this medium. This battle for educational television, led by the Joint Committee on Educational Television (JCET), was a coordinated campaign to persuade the FCC that a television sector dominated exclusively by commercial interests would be contrary to the public interest and the needs of the polity given the exigencies of postwar American life. In its efforts the JCET secured a range of allies from across the political spectrum who shared its commitment to educational television, even as they disagreed over the contours and uses of educational broadcasting. The JCET's successes, as this chapter underlines, hinged on its catholic approach to educational television, one that made space for myriad uses of noncommercial stations. What its coalition shared was a commitment to a noncommercial television sector, as well as the belief that television could inculcate good citizenship, though the terms by which this was understood varied. In the process, the JCET broadly imagined television as a tool to help U.S. citizens prepare for the exigencies and stresses of cold war life. The JCET fights marked the first significant television advocacy effort, and its tactics would provide a template for subsequent reform campaigns.

The next two chapters examine the role of media policy and media advocacy during the ferment of the social movements of the 1960s and 1970s. Chapter 2 explores how the Black Freedom Movement fundamentally redefined the terms of debate about the "public interest" within television regulation. As civil rights activists successfully challenged the licenses of two broadcasters on racial discrimination grounds, they destabilized the notion of a singular public and enfolded media advocacy within broader fights for racial justice. In this the presumed unitary public of the "public interest" was shattered by social movement advocacy that compelled local stations, the FCC, and the courts to see the existence of multiple publics and to respect their interests in regulatory decisions. As a result a wide range of communities posited a relationship between the discrimination they faced in multiple spheres of American life and the way they appeared on the small screen, as well as the way they were treated by broadcasters and their federal regulators. Chapter 3 thus turns to the National Organization for Women (NOW), for whom media advocacy became a means to challenge derogatory images of women onscreen but also to demonstrate to broadcasters and policy makers how seemingly gender-neutral policy decisions were implicated in women's past denial of, and current struggles for, equality. NOW's media campaigns led to material concessions from broadcasters and regulators and instructed them in how to locate sexism within policy decisions and media texts.

The following three chapters examine media advocacy in an era of deregulation. They address how three different communities responded to a neoliberal shift in broadcast policy making—one that defined broadcasters not as stewards of a public resource but as competitors in a marketplace and one that imagined viewers not as citizens in a democracy but as consumers of products. The dismantling of regulatory oversight of broadcasters from the 1980s onward had made the kind of media advocacy that NOW took part in during the 1970s very difficult. As chapters 4 through 6 illustrate, however, media advocacy persisted: a range of groups pushed back against the definition of television, and the understanding of the public interest, at the center of what FCC chairman Mark Fowler dubbed the "marketplace approach to regulation."[17] In each case they did so by invoking a particular group of people—African Americans, children, and non-English-speakers—as deserving protection from deregulated capitalism.

Chapter 4 focuses on the work of the NAACP in the 1980s and 1990s to conserve the policies adopted in the 1960s and 1970s to advance minority interests in broadcasting. At stake in its media reform actions were both the preservation of measures to address structural inequalities borne from past policy decisions and a frontal attack on revisionist histories of both broad-casting and the civil rights movement that were working to the disadvantage of people of color. The NAACP's media advocacy in this era, which involved myriad campaigns to protect broadcast diversity, reasserted the continued import of historic inequalities on the citizenship rights of people of color, leg-acies that free-market enthusiasms and faith in an already realized color-blind society could not eradicate.

Chapter 5 turns to the Parents Television Council (PTC), a socially conser-vative media advocacy group formed at the height of the culture wars. While conservative politicians played a key role in promoting the deregulation of television broadcasting, social conservative groups like the PTC criticized the deregulated media environment as a market failure when it came to program-ming for American families. The PTC's media advocacy, which centered on a campaign to restore a "family hour" in prime time, asserted a definition of the public that conflated families with children, presented television not as a "toaster with pictures" but as a dinner guest within families' homes. The media advocacy of groups like the PTC flagged another arena of resistance to the shift to deregulation of the 1980s.

Chapter 6 examines the long-standing struggles of Latino media advocacy groups over Spanish-language broadcasting. These fights exposed the limita-tions in how the FCC had defined minority media rights in the 1960s and 1970s and the resistance posed by Latino groups from the 1980s onward to the FCC's continued devaluation of Spanish-language broadcasting in its regulatory decisions. The chapter specifically traces the shifting policy battles between the National Hispanic Media Coalition (NHMC) and its shifting relationship with Univision, the largest Spanish-language television network in the United States. In so doing, it analyzes how Latino advocacy groups have sought to promote a vibrant Spanish-language public sphere in the face of a regulatory apparatus that was both insensitive to the intersections between media policy and ethnoracial inequality and dismissive of Spanish-language broadcasting as a civil rights issue.

Public Interests traces the evolution of the "public interest" from a unitary definition in the 1950s, which broadly imagined television as a tool to help citizens prepare for the exigencies and stresses of cold war life, to the multiple publics brought into visibility in the 1960s and 1970s, to the myriad resis-tances from the 1980s onward to a neoliberal understanding of the public that conflated consumerism and citizenship. It thus charts how the public inter-est, and broadcast policy advocacy itself, has evolved alongside broader socio-political change. Across this wide range of reform activity has been a shared understanding of the centrality of television as a site of public culture and a belief that its reform would be necessary to bring about important political and social change.

1

The Battle for
Educational Television

///

Broadcasting and Citizenship
in the Postwar Era

Television "can be a blessing such as rarely comes to mankind," *New York Times* critic Jack Gould opined in 1946, or it "can be a veritable menace of frightening proportions."[1] For the majority of Americans in 1946, however, television was more of a promise than a part of their everyday lives. Few stations were on the air, and programming was an erratic mix of sporting events (boxing, roller derby, wrestling), cooking shows (*I Love to Eat*), and game shows featuring charades (*Play the Game*) and grocery stores (*Cash and Carry*).[2] Yet utopian visions of television circulated widely—from hopes that television would be a technology of domestic bliss to expectations that television programming could bring about mutual understanding and world peace.[3] For Gould television was a neutral technology, and its blessings or menaces would accrue based on its use. If television were to go the way of radio, as Gould suspected it would, it would become an even more insipid mechanism to advertise goods to potential consumers: "Mr. Heatter will not talk of that hair tonic; he will rub it into his scalp so that we can see how it's done night after night."[4] But television also presented a "golden opportunity for the educational institution," which, if seized, could become a valued part of the nation's cultural and civic life.[5] For that to happen, educators would have to embrace the aesthetics and logics of television in a more forceful manner than they had done with radio. The past should not be prologue, in other words, but a cautionary tale.

Gould's framing of television as having two possibilities—one commercial and private, one educational and public—was not specific to him. Rather, it was a discourse embraced by educational organizations of his time. This chapter uses the history of advocacy on behalf of educational television to explain how advocates created a space for noncommercial television. First, they drew on the history of radio's commercialization to emphasize the need for dedicated educational television stations, to be secured through reserved channels. Second, they created an advocacy group—the Joint Committee on Educational Television (JCET)—to persuade the government to set aside parts of the airwaves for educational broadcasters and then to consolidate and expand on this victory. The JCET connected existing educational broadcasters, and mentored new ones, not by directly challenging corporate broadcasters but by presenting noncommercial television as a solution to various postwar social problems.

In its advocacy battles the JCET argued that, as an antidote to the depredations of commercial mass culture, educational television could inculcate respect for high culture. It would also offer an economical and efficient way to address a perceived "education crisis" and help win the Cold War by addressing the "education gap" between American and Soviet students. And educational television could equalize educational materials across black and white schools in segregated areas or provide continued educational materials in the face of public school closures by segregationists engaged in "massive resistance." The JCET's advocacy strategies thus united middlebrow cultural guardians, professional educators, and southern segregationists in a common struggle, bound by a shared goal of shoring up the noncommercial sector and a discourse of equality and uplift that framed the cause of educational television as politically and morally essential.

Prologue: Radio and the Perils of Commercialism

The campaign to create educational television in the late 1940s and 1950s began as a campaign to resist the dominance of commercial stations in the emerging medium. That campaign was based on the perceived failures of radio broadcasting policy but conditioned by the limits placed on criticism of private industry at the beginning of the Cold War. The decline of educational radio stations, and the ascent of commercial radio networks, had resulted from a series of legislative and regulatory decisions that favored the latter and hamstrung the former. Broadcasting policy had been critical to constituting how radio would operate in the United States, especially in who would have access to the airwaves. And by the 1940s the escalation of commercialism in radio raised concerns among, and provoked resistance within many communities, whose discontent the promoters of educational television sought to exploit.

The use of the airwaves for educational purposes had a long history in the United States that predated the ascent of commercial broadcasting. Universities, especially physics and engineering departments, operated some of the earliest radio stations. Land-grant midwestern universities especially experimented with radio technology and used the airwaves to extend the educational mission of their institutions. These stations frequently combined the skills and priorities of radio amateurs, public agencies like the U.S. Department of Agriculture (USDA), and university departments in a shared effort to distribute useful information to citizens.[6] University stations programmed a wide array of materials—agricultural reports, "schools of the air," lectures, music, correspondence-course curricula, athletic events, and so on—and imagined their value in opposition to that of competing commercial broadcasters. As Richard Hull, president of the National Association of Educational Broadcasters (NAEB) and manager of educational broadcasting at Iowa State, remembered, the goals of the stations were multifaceted but also were a corrective to commercial fare: "We talked about giving the mature adult choices and about having programs for out-of-school children. We felt that radio should have values. It should be more than a penny arcade."[7] Thus, although educational radio had multiple functions, one was to present an alternative to commercial stations, one premised on a dyad that imagined educational radio as having "values" and commercial radio as a "penny arcade" of amusements lacking substance.

As the number of broadcasting stations proliferated in the 1920s, problems of interference and "chaos" over the airwaves provoked Secretary of Commerce Herbert Hoover to hold four national radio conferences to discuss the future of radio regulation. The Radio Act of 1912 had placed the power to issue radio licenses in the Commerce Department. It had not, however, granted the department authority to deny licenses to qualified applicants. The "broadcast boom" of the 1920s rendered this system seemingly untenable, and Hoover's radio conferences would provide the backbone of what would become the Radio Act of 1927. In this act Congress retained public ownership over the airwaves but authorized a newly created, temporary agency—the Federal Radio Commission (FRC)—to allocate radio frequencies and charged it with assuring the "public interest, convenience, and necessity." The 1927 Radio Act coincided with the creation of the National Broadcasting Corporation (NBC), formed in 1926, and the Columbia Broadcasting System (CBS), formed in 1927 originally as United Independent Broadcasters, and would help facilitate their growth.

Understood as a solution to a technical problem, the Radio Act was also an expression of an ideology—one that privileged the national over the local, the commercial over the noncommercial, in its definition of the "public interest." The FRC initially conflated the public interest with broadcasts of a high technical quality that well-resourced commercial stations were in the best position to provide. In 1929 the FRC further articulated its definition of the "public interest" as "general interest" stations or commercial stations. The commission's logic was as follows: since commercial stations tried to attract the largest possible audience to sell to advertisers, they were best able to serve the greatest number of listeners and thus provide the best service to the broadest public. Expressing a strong hesitance to "balkanize the dial" by granting licenses to "special interest" broadcasters—educators, labor unions, churches, and so on—the FRC viewed noncommercial broadcasters as "propaganda" stations invested in advancing a particular view or set of interests.[8] Unsurprisingly, the number of educational stations dropped substantially. In 1928 ninety-four educational institutions had broadcasting licenses; by 1931 that number had dwindled to forty-nine.[9] The FRC reassigned educational broadcasters to less-desirable frequencies, reserving the more powerful ones for commercial broadcasters. Educational broadcasters often were required to share time on a new frequency with a commercial station, which consigned their programming to the least-listened-to hours of the broadcast day. Furthermore, the costs of expensive equipment requirements and of litigation to preserve frequencies against commercial challenges pushed many educational broadcasters to give up their licenses.[10]

As Robert McChesney has illustrated, a broad-based broadcast reform movement emerged after the 1927 act to challenge what was becoming a broadcast system dominated by commercial interests. The educators, public intellectuals, labor unions, civil liberties organizations, and religious groups who composed this movement sought a series or reforms, and they engaged in a range of tactics, from filing petitions to and testifying before the FRC to lobbying for legislation and filing challenges in the federal courts. Their advocacy gained most traction in Congress, which considered but ultimately did not pass a bill that would have voided all existing broadcast licenses and implemented a new system in which 25 percent of desirable frequencies would be reserved for educational, religious, or nonprofit groups. The 1934 Federal Communications Act reaffirmed the 1927 act, but it replaced the temporary FRC with the permanent Federal Communications Commission (FCC), which would oversee both broadcasting and telecommunications. In this act Congress instructed the FCC to investigate the need for dedicated educational stations, for which the commission held hearings and determined in 1935 that there was no such need. With the failure to secure robust government support for noncommercial broadcasting, the broadcast reform battle ended in defeat.[11] Although not all was lost, as Hugh Slotten and Josh Shepperd have illustrated through their studies of post-1934 educational broadcasters, what followed was an era, as Gould's admonitions so clearly express, when the educational potential of radio was seen to have dissipated.[12]

Throughout the 1930s and 1940s, resistance to the escalating hegemony of commercialism in broadcasting persisted in two ways. First, intellectuals leveled biting critiques of commercial radio. Critics of mass culture decried the quality of radio broadcasts, asserting that the pursuit of a broadly popular audience yielded programming that was banal and insipid and sacrificed aesthetic excellence for widespread appeal.[13] Others considered the implications of radio's control by large-scale, for-profit corporations and expressed concern that it would function as a ministry of propaganda for business interests and would silence dissenting perspectives. If advertisers determined what was permissible to speak about on air, they could play a tremendous role in shaping listeners' values and ideas and could naturalize a worldview consonant with consumer capitalist values.[14] Free-speech advocates feared that concentration of ownership within centralized, national networks threatened the marketplace of ideas and hindered the circulation of diverse perspectives.[15]

Second, as Elizabeth Fones-Wolf and Victor Pickard have documented, throughout the 1940s a media reform movement worked to address what it saw as the corrosive effect of commercialism both on radio and in the public sphere it instantiated. This movement—which included intellectuals, labor unions, and civil rights organizations—fought for "listeners' rights" to hear a diversity of perspectives over the air. According to these reformers, diversification of ownership coupled with more stringent regulations on broadcast licensees would be necessary to redress commercial network radio's failures to inculcate a robust marketplace of ideas. The reformers—many of them supporters of President Franklin D. Roosevelt and New Deal Democrats—had allies on the FCC, notably Chairman James Fly and Commissioner Clifford Durr. Under Fly's leadership the FCC imposed restrictions on broadcast station ownership and adopted regulations regarding the relationship between networks and their affiliated stations. These rules were intended to promote diversity on the air and to enable stations to dedicate more time to local programming. In addition, the FCC in 1946 issued its *Public Service Responsibilities of Broadcasters*, or its "Blue Book," so called because of its blue cover. The Blue Book articulated a vision of the public interest consonant with the concerns of the media reform movement of the era, one that emphasized the importance of local programs, robust discussions of public affairs, and sustaining (unsponsored) programming, as well as one that cautioned against the excesses of advertising.[16]

Directly challenging the hegemony of commercial broadcasters became highly difficult with the onset of the Cold War. Both the Blue Book and the reform movement that had called for more aggressive regulation of radio were quickly tarred as "anti-American," an assault on "free radio" and the American free enterprise system of which it was a part. The Blue Book itself was never enforced. Indeed, as Fones-Wolf and Pickard have argued, the reform efforts of the 1940s were politically neutralized by broadcasting industry attacks that took advantage of the anticommunist fervor of this early Cold War period. Broadcasters conflated any criticism of commercialism with the destruction of "the American system of broadcasting" and conflated support for public regulation with communism. By the end of the 1940s, as Pickard has demonstrated, the fight for a more responsible and responsive media had devolved, in this early Cold War context, into a regulatory paradigm of "corporate libertarianism," which nodded to public interest concerns while allowing media companies, imagined to be capable of self-regulation, to best determine how they would be met.[17]

It was in this context that educational interests, led by the JCET, leveled a battle against the dominance of commercialism in the emerging television sector. Significantly, especially given the political climate of their fight, this campaign against the hegemony of commercial broadcast interests would win.

The Formation of the JCET

If one was watching television in the years immediately after World War II, one was most likely living in a major city and viewing a channel owned by or affiliated with NBC or CBS. Stations would have broadcast only in the VHF (Very High Frequency) band, composed of channels 2 through 13. Educational institutions were welcome to apply for television licenses, though in so doing they would have had to compete with better-resourced commercial applicants. In the mid-1940s the FCC had considered, and rejected, the idea of setting aside television channels for education. Television thus seemed poised to be a predominantly commercial medium that, like radio, would be dominated by national networks. And the emergence of the Cold War had made it difficult to challenge this likely dominance.

Yet, remarkably, advocates of educational broadcasting found a language and formed a coalition capable of securing new licenses to put television to educational, and not just commercial, uses. The FCC began a television-licensing freeze in September of 1948 that lasted nearly four years. Of the many issues the commission weighed during the freeze was whether to reserve television channels for educational uses, a matter pursued by the JCET. As the JCET worked to secure educational television reservations, the group, like Gould, hitched its arguments to the powerful prospective potential of television, on the one hand, and the record of commercial radio, on the other. The JCET and its allies inserted a construction of the public interest into the television hearings in which, contra to FCC policy to that point, the public could not be served in a broadcasting system dominated only by commercial stations. In 1952, when the FCC ended the freeze and reserved 242 channels for noncommercial educational television, it delivered a tremendous victory for the JCET and future educational telecasters, one that had eluded educational radio broadcasters in decades prior.

The licensing freeze began for technical rather than public interest reasons, but it opened the door for media reformers to organize. During this period the commission was to make decisions about the technical specifications of television broadcasting. It would assess the viability of the Ultra High Frequency (UHF) band, channels 14 and higher, and determine how, if at all, to allocate VHF and UHF channels in communities across the country. It would evaluate the respective color television systems developed by CBS and RCA, and it would decide how best to interconnect local stations into national networks.[18] But beginning in the fall of 1950, it also began to discuss whether to reserve a portion of television channels for noncommercial, educational uses.

This key opening for educational television resulted largely from the formation and labors of the JCET. Of critical import to the educational television movement were two gatherings in 1949 and 1950 at Allerton House, the conference center of the University of Illinois, organized by communications researcher Wilbur Schramm. Providing a forum for extended face-to-face conversations to parse out the failings and successes, as well as past goals and future ambitions, of education and broadcasting, Allerton galvanized educators and enabled a shared sense of mission, purpose, and belonging within a like-minded community.[19] Though organizations like the NAEB long predated the Allerton seminars, it was during these weeks in Illinois that many participants in educational broadcasting felt for the first time as though they were part of a larger movement. This spirit of cooperation and unity led to discussion of the promise of television and the need for educators to ensure that this new medium had a place for them.

When educators first met at Allerton in 1949, the FCC was one year into its television licensing freeze. Prior to the freeze, even though the FCC had determined that there was insufficient evidence to merit establishing an educational TV band, it had opened the door to future considerations of dedicated educational television channels by announcing that should interest in educational television develop further, it would revisit the issue.[20] At the start of the freeze the most visible educational television station was WOI in Ames, Iowa. Though run by Iowa State University, WOI was a commercial station affiliated with the then four major national networks, though it would run network programs in ways that ran counter to commercial practices, for example putting religious programs on during prime time.[21] WOI thus occupied the odd position of being an educational commercial station.[22] WOI's fusion of educational and commercial programming would loom over the JCET as it debated how best to advocate for educational television.

So, too, would recent developments in FM radio. For years the history of FM (frequency modulation) radio had been intertwined with the growth of television. In comparison to AM (amplitude modulation) radio, which had been the dominant mode of broadcasting since the 1920s, FM carried little to no static and produced a far clearer sound. However, FM posed a challenge to

AM radio—in which major broadcasting companies like RCA had substantial interest—and threatened to utilize valuable frequencies that companies like RCA wanted to use for television broadcasting. In 1940 the FCC assigned FM to the 42 to 50 MHz band; then in 1945 it reassigned it to a much higher band, 88 to 108 MHz. This new assignment, justified on dubious technical grounds, posed a substantial obstacle to the growth of FM, as it rendered existing FM receivers obsolete.[23] Edwin Armstrong, inventor of FM, saw the FCC's attitude toward FM as informed by pressure from RCA, which was intent on protecting its investment in AM and its interests in television. However, while the reassignment of FM damaged its commercial prospects, it provided an opportunity for educational radio.[24]

When in the mid-1940s the commission worked on an allocation plan for FM, it considered a U.S. Office of Education request to set aside channels for educational purposes, one enthusiastically supported by Commissioner Durr. Commercial interests, which evinced little excitement over FM, did not oppose the reservations. Even so, the FCC required a showing of support from the educational community for dedicated FM channels for education. Belmont Farley of the National Educational Association (NEA), who would subsequently be a member of the JCET, along with the Office of Education, recruited educators to testify on behalf of the FM reservations.[25] In 1945 the commission reserved twenty FM channels for noncommercial, educational uses.

The setting aside of FM reservations for educational use helped mobilize supporters of educational television in two ways, even though the NAEB, the leading professional organization for educational broadcasting, did not participate in the FM hearings, and educational institutions expressed only modest interest in the potential of FM.[26] First, it established an important legal and cultural precedent, on which the JCET would draw, for reserving channels for educational purposes and presenting education as a legitimate basis for government regulation of airwaves in the public interest. In addition, the FCC designated the reserved channels as "noncommercial, educational" stations. In so doing, the FCC tethered the mission of the service to its mode of financing, eliminating for eligibility nonprofit educational stations that either broadcast commercial programs or sold airtime to finance their programming. The noncommercial designation was to guarantee the "purity of motive and the earnestness of intention" of the broadcasters and to free them from having to compete with commercial broadcasters.[27] The conflation of educational radio with noncommercial radio was thus a regulatory classification; for many educators there was no necessary conflict between selling airtime and providing educational content. As the educators considered strategies for advocating for educational television reservations, the "noncommercial" designation of the FM precedent would weigh on their deliberations.

The JCET was founded as an outgrowth of the second Allerton meeting of educational broadcasters and their allies. Hull, president of the NAEB, and Frank Dunham of the U.S. Office of Education convened a meeting in October 1950 of representatives of educational organizations to discuss the FCC freeze and the need to agitate for channel reservations for educational television. Although educational groups had filed petitions the previous year with the FCC, they had presented the commission with competing requests regarding educational television.[28] The purpose of the October meeting was to bring together educational leaders so that they could present a unified front to the FCC in their advocacy for educational television. It was at this meeting that the JCET formed as an ad hoc committee to represent seven educational organizations: the American Council on Education, the Association for Education by Radio, the Association of Land-Grant Colleges and Universities, the National Council of Chief State School Officers, the National Association of Educational Broadcasters, the National Association of State Universities, and the National Education Association.[29] Each constituent organization contributed a representative to the JCET board, and the organization was led by a chairman and executive director. In 1951, after receiving a $90,000 grant from the Ford Foundation, the JCET transitioned from ad hoc committee to permanent organization.[30]

The JCET's leadership and membership drew on educational broadcasting stalwarts and on people who bore the battle scars of previous fights over educational radio. I. Keith Tyler, the JCET's first chairman, had helmed the Institute for Education by Radio at Ohio State University, where he also was a researcher in its Bureau of Educational Research. The Institute annually brought together educators, broadcasters, and researchers to discuss the pedagogical possibilities of radio. Tyler also conducted assessments on the effectiveness of educational radio, broadly defined to include broadcasters on commercial and educational stations, and led workshops on educating by radio.[31] Edgar Fuller, its next chairperson, also acted as the executive secretary of the National Council of Chief State School Officers, one of the JCET's original constituent partners. Richard Hull, president of the NAEB and an educational broadcaster, was the JCET's first executive director. He returned to Iowa in 1951 to develop educational programs under a grant from the Ford Foundation's Fund for Adult Education and was replaced by Ralph Steetle, who had been director of broadcasting at Louisiana State University. In the fall of 1950 the JCET recruited Telford Taylor to be its lead attorney. Taylor had been an attorney for the FCC and most recently had acted as chief counsel during the Nuremberg trials. In addition to Taylor, Seymour Krieger would act as counsel for the JCET.[32]

The JCET went to work immediately to advocate for educational television. In so doing, it had to unite educational interests in a common fight, persuade policy makers of the public interest benefits of educational television reservations, and convince local communities of the educational potential of a medium identified strongly with entertainment and commercialism in the public mind. And, as part of this work, the JCET would take seriously the lessons from previous battles against the hegemony of commercial interests in radio to assure a similar fate did not await television.

Advocating for Educational Television Licenses

As the JCET planned its advocacy for educational television reservations, it had to settle two questions about the particulars of the plan it would ask the FCC to codify as policy. The first centered on the issue of bandwidth allocations. In 1945 the FCC had authorized television only in the VHF band. One of the crucial questions during the licensing freeze was whether and how to distribute both VHF and UHF stations geographically. To license stations in the UHF band would greatly increase the number of television stations on air and would ideally lead to more diversity and competition within the television sector. However, most television sets on the market in the early 1950s were not equipped to receive a UHF signal, so to operate using a UHF license was automatically to struggle for audiences who could actually view the programming. Other concerns over UHF included the fact that proper transmitters and receivers of UHF signals still had not been produced and that, because UHF signals were located at higher frequencies, there would be more "shadows," or areas of weak or nonexistent signals, in areas of obstructions like hills or high buildings. In addition, VHF signals traveled farther and were clearer than UHF; to equalize coverage with a VHF transmitter, a UHF station would have to transmit with much more power than VHF and thus spend a good deal more on electricity costs. While some educational organizations saw in UHF their best hope for participation in television, others argued that it would be desirable, when possible, to advocate for VHF stations.[33] It was this latter course that the JCET pursued, asking for a mixture of VHF and UHF reservations.

Another question that the JCET had to confront was what kind of classification the group would request: "noncommercial" or "nonprofit"? A noncommercial classification would place a far more rigid constraint on how stations could operate financially and what kind of programming could be part of their broadcast schedule. Nonprofit classification would provide flexibility to air sponsored programs and to fill parts of the broadcast day with shows acquired from commercial stations or networks. Ultimately, the JCET went with the noncommercial designation. Intending to draw on the FM allocations as a template, the JCET believed this classification would make the strongest case in front of the FCC.[34] The nonprofit designation, according to Taylor, also could lead to far more intrusive FCC oversight of the educational stations. The group also determined that educational institutions that preferred to operate as commercial stations could apply for commercial licenses but that it would ask that the *reserved* channels be for noncommercial entities.[35]

The JCET first made the case for reservations from November 1950 through January 1951 during FCC hearings. Its petition requested that the commission reserve one VHF station in each metropolitan area and major educational center and that 20 percent of all UHF channels be reserved for education; in "closed cities," places like New York and Los Angeles, where all VHF channels had already been assigned, the JCET asked that the commission require licensees to devote time to educational programs. To support the petition, the JCET very speedily enlisted seventy-five witnesses to testify.[36] In addition to educational broadcasting stalwarts, the JCET's witnesses included senators and congressmen from both major political parties, school superintendents, professors, university presidents and chancellors, and representatives from labor unions and from the Parent-Teacher Association.

The roster of the JCET's witnesses is important, as it speaks to how well-positioned the JCET was to solicit support from high-profile and powerful people. The history of advocacy for public media in the United States often has been told as a David-and-Goliath struggle, in which highly resourced media companies exert their will within a regulatory process already sympathetic to their vision of the public interest. Although financially the JCET did not have anywhere near the resources of commercial interests, the organization did have a good deal of reputational capital to draw on. Comprising many of the leading educational groups in the nation, the JCET could marshal support—on short notice—from well-positioned allies like university presidents and elected representatives, which both lent gravitas to their cause and legitimized their campaign, as well as the premises on which it rested.

The JCET's case, as offered by its witnesses, discussed reserving channels for educational purposes in four ways. First, they pointed to the history of radio, and the diminished role of education over broadcast stations, as justification for dedicated educational television channels. Cooperative relationships with commercial broadcasters, which had animated the approach adopted toward educational radio in the 1930s, sold broadcasting short, as commercial stations were erratic in their scheduling of educational programs and consigned them to the least consumed hours of the broadcasting day. If the history of radio was predictive, therefore, educational uses of television would require dedicated channels rather than relying on commercial telecasters to include educational programming as part of their schedules.[37]

Second, the witnesses cited the history of public provision for education in the United States as precedent for the reservations. Just as the 1862 Morrill Act had set aside public lands for schools, the witnesses encouraged the commission to set aside public airwaves for education. In so doing, they reasserted that the spectrum was a public resource—like public lands—and accordingly could be regulated to promote a form of public education rather than be designated solely for private, commercial ends.[38]

Third, the witnesses also gestured to the important role the FCC had played, and could play in the future, in determining the fate of educational broadcasting. Specifically, they identified the history of FCC decisions themselves as partially culpable for the state of educational radio in the United States. Referring, for example, to the FCC's decision not to set aside educational AM channels in 1935, Harold McCarty, director of Wisconsin radio station WHA and the Wisconsin School of the Air, opined that after holding hearings on the necessity of educational radio, the FCC did not "take the courageous stand which the testimony indicated was necessary for solving the problem."[39]

And, finally, while arguments on behalf of the reservations relied on the stories of the past—of failed relationships with commercial broadcasters, the fallout of previous regulatory decisions, earlier instances of reserving public resources for education—they also were directed to prospective visions of the role of educational television during the postwar period. It was imagined to engender access to an education to people who, because of income or disability, were unable to attend formal classes. Television was to be the "strong right arm" of education, one that would enable the United States to thrive and be victorious in a global struggle to promote its "democratic philosophy."[40]

Undergirding the JCET's testimony was a classic appeal to the power of social science to justify government regulation in the public interest. Along with the testimony and a public relations campaign to drum up support for educational television, the NAEB and JCET, under the auspices of Dallas Smythe and Donald Horton, conducted a monitoring study of one week of programming on all the television stations currently operating in New York City. Fifteen women were the primary monitors, who conducted their study from the Waldorf-Astoria hotel on eight television monitors from January 4 through January 10, 1951. Aided by "three gallons of coffee, nearly half a jar of aspirin tablets and enough cigarettes for a political convention," the monitors watched twelve hours of programming per day.[41] While watching, they filled out cards with the name, length, and time of the program; whether it was live or filmed; the running time of commercials; and the classification of the program.[42] Among the findings were that entertainment shows made up 49 percent of telecast time, advertising 10 percent, news 5 percent, public issues 2 percent, and religion 1 percent. And it was worse than it sounded. Smythe explained to the commission that one-third of the news programming was accounted for by a WOR program in which facts are flashed onscreen accompanied by "completely unrelated music."[43] In his testimony before the FCC, Horton indicated that there had been only a half hour of educational information during the week and asserted that the study revealed "only a hodgepodge of relatively superficial information scattered through a lot of other material."[44]

The monitoring study would become a central component of media advocacy efforts in decades to follow. In 1951 it was a "pioneering project" that surveyed the material offered on commercial stations.[45] It provided reformers with concrete rather than anecdotal evidence that their claims about media content were credible and deserved either regulatory or legislative action. As reformers would learn, it would be the kind of evidence that a monitoring study could yield—especially statistical, quantitative data—that would be considered legitimate by the policy-making community. To complete a monitoring study required a good deal of labor, as the reports of the women who participated in Smythe and Horton's work underscored, as well as expertise and money. As it became a mainstay of media advocacy campaigns, it both limited who could participate in policy battles to communities with the time and labor force to conduct a study and defined what counted as meaningful evidence as things that could be counted and classified.

The warm reception that the JCET testimony received was not just attributable to its cultural capital or use of social science. Frieda Hennock, a commissioner on the FCC, was a strong advocate of educational television. Hennock had been alerted to the issue of educational television by Morris Novik,[46] who had run WNYC in New York, worked as secretary for the NAEB, and in the years after the freeze would arbitrate labor disputes between educational stations and the broadcasting unions. At Novik's invitation Hennock visited Tyler's Institute for Education by Radio at Ohio State in 1949, where she encountered a diverse range of people committed to broadcasting for educational purposes.[47] Hennock quickly became an advocate of educational television, insisting as early as 1949—before the formation of the JCET—that the FCC set aside channels for education. The cause of educational television lined up with Hennock's political comments as well as her personal biography. As Susan Brinson has demonstrated, Hennock understood that, as a daughter of immigrants, her rise to become the first woman appointed to a federal agency owed a great deal to her own educational opportunities. In addition, educational television, with its promise to use the public airwaves as an instrument of edification, not only meshed well with her political commitments but was an apt issue through which a female politician, and the first female FCC commissioner, could gain credibility in the 1950s.[48]

In addition to having Hennock as their very vocal and well-situated champion, educators also benefited from the fact that commercial broadcasters initially took little interest in their testimony. Presuming that the FCC would not take the educators seriously, the commercial networks and their trade association, the National Association of Broadcasters (NAB),[49] at first allowed the testimony of the educators to go uncontested. In this they perhaps underestimated the coordinated efforts of the JCET. Past commercial broadcasters had successfully warded off attempts by educational interests to redirect resources to educational AM radio. In addition, RCA and CBS were embroiled in the early part of the freeze in a heated battle over color broadcasting systems. In the fall of 1950, when educators began to make their case in front of the FCC,

RCA was in the midst of filing suit against the FCC's decision to adopt CBS's color standards. The cause of educational television may have seemed an irritant of less import to the two dominant networks than the battle over color standards.[50] In January of 1951 commercial interests requested time to present counter-testimony, but by then they were on the defensive.

A final advantage to educators was bipartisan support of educational television. In addition to receiving an endorsement by the White House Conference on Youth and Children in 1950, the educational reservations were backed by prominent leaders in the House and Senate, including Sen. Edwin Johnson (D-Colo.), Sen. Leverett Saltonstall (R-Mass.), Sen. Clinton Anderson (D.-N. Mex.), and Rep. John M. Vorys (R-Ohio).[51] One of the earliest and most vocal advocates for educational television was Sen. John Bricker (R-Ohio).[52] Bricker had been attorney general in Ohio in the 1930s and, in that capacity, had routinely protected Ohio State University's educational channels against challenges by commercial broadcasters. It was then that he developed a commitment to educational broadcasting, one that animated his support of the JCET's plan.[53] Bricker was and would remain a steadfast advocate of educational television, testifying in support of the reservations and introducing a resolution in Congress to require the commission to investigate the need for dedicated educational channels.[54]

Bricker's support was politically important. Not only was he a member of the Senate Interstate and Foreign Commerce Committee, which oversaw the FCC, but he was one of the most conservative members of the Senate in the 1950s. Bricker had opposed the broadening of the federal government under the New Deal and the 1935 Wagner Act's expansion of the power of organized labor, believing them to be steps toward a dangerous collectivism and authoritarianism. A supporter and friend of Joseph McCarthy and an isolationist in regard to foreign policy, he believed the best way to win the Cold War was to assure American economic strength through its free enterprise system. Bricker is perhaps best known for his sponsorship of the Bricker Amendment, which would have amended the Constitution to limit the executive branch's ability to enter into international treaties.[55] Yet, despite his staunch commitment to limited government and free-market capitalism, Bricker both advocated for educational reservations during the freeze and supported the noncommercial sector in the face of challenges by commercial interests in the decade following the freeze. In this he found himself on the same side as educational institutions and the labor movement.

The very public approval of Bricker and other political allies made it difficult for broadcasting corporations to simply dismiss noncommercial television as somehow un-American or socialist. Instead, when commercial broadcasters lobbied against educational television, they did so by arguing that to reserve stations for educators would waste a precious public resource. Frank Stanton (president of CBS), Justin Miller (president of the NAB), Kenneth

Baker (research director of the NAB), and Charles F. Church Jr. (director of education and research at KMBC in Kansas City) testified in front of the FCC to contest the JCET's petition in January of 1951. In their testimony they claimed that educational programming had been "a dismal failure" in the past because of its inability to attract audiences or to understand the aesthetics and mechanics of the medium and that educators would not be able to afford the operation and maintenance of stations; thus, the reservations would waste a precious public resource on them. Baker emphasized that the history of radio "indicates that [educators] neither understand the medium nor are willing to use it when they do."[56] Stanton similarly stressed the "reasonable doubts" regarding the commitment of educators to broadcasting that the history of radio raises, while also insisting on the need for a "general television service" and the construction of a mass audience for television before any considerations of specialized services, like educational television, could be countenanced.[57] In so doing, Stanton drew on the very definition of the "public interest" deployed by regulators in the 1930s that privileged commercial stations as "general interest stations" and portrayed educational stations as serving niche audiences. The commercial broadcasters' witnesses concluded that the best path was to encourage cooperative relationships between commercial stations and educational institutions and for the commission to consider license applications on a case-by-case basis.[58]

The FCC's *Third Report and Order*, issued in March 1951, presented a tentative allocation scheme for television and signaled the inroads the JCET had made in making the public interest case for the reservations. The most controversial part of the plan was its setting aside of 209 channels, approximately 10 percent of all stations, for educational television. Though 127 of these reservations were on UHF channels, and 82 in VHF, education received the sole remaining VHF channel in a number of major cities. Commissioners were not unanimous in their recommendations, and the allocations were tentative—contingent on demonstrated interest by educators that these reservations actually would be utilized in the near future.[59] But the order marked a substantial victory for reform advocates.

The commercial industry, meanwhile, was not unified in its opposition to the reservations, as the set-asides for education worked to the imagined benefit of some networks and the detriment of others. Some opponents filed opposition comments with the FCC that lamented the "waste" of television licenses and argued that educational radio's history signaled that educators were not equipped to enter into television broadcasting. The FCC Bar Association, in its opposition filing, took the position that the commission's entire allocation scheme was unlawful and had exceeded the authority of the FCC, while the NAB insisted that the reservations were not smart and invalid. Of the commercial networks, only CBS and DuMont filed opposition comments. DuMont requested an entirely new allocation plan, asking for more channels

in larger markets and more VHF allocations and suggesting that UHF channels were sufficient for educational television's purposes. CBS's comments,
though more narrow in scope than those of other petitioners, according to
Taylor, were the most threatening to the JCET. CBS specifically opposed the
educational television VHF allocations in Boston, Chicago, and San Francisco, where the network had hoped to secure its own VHF stations. The
theory at the core of its opposition was that UHF would be good enough for
educators, especially since neither educators nor UHF were currently at an
operable stage; hence, their need—and solution to that need—would coin-
cide in time. Importantly, NBC and ABC did not take a similar position, most
likely because they saw in the educational television reservations a protection
against CBS competition.[60]

Steetle, who assumed the directorship of the JCET after the issuance of
the *Third Report* was issued, remembered that the job of the JCET "was to
take the Third Report and change it from 'tentative' to 'actual.'"[61] The FCC
initially planned on holding city-by-city hearings to hear public comments
on the *Third Report*'s allocation plan. So the JCET first worked to enlist as
many educators, public officials, and citizen groups as possible to secure the
opportunity to participate in the hearings. In so doing, the JCET received
help at the grassroots level from its constituent organizations, as well as from
the American Association of University Women, the American Library
Association, the National Musical Educators' Conference, and the American Federation of Arts.[62] In July 1951 the FCC abandoned the city-by-city
hearings in favor of another round of written comments.[63] In the following
months the commission received more than fourteen hundred filings on its
allocation plan. In addition to filing its own nearly three-hundred-page brief
in support of the reservations, the JCET enlisted 838 schools, colleges, state
departments of education, superintendents, and so on to file 349 comments
with the FCC.[64] In places where a reservation had been made, but where
the educational establishment failed to file an official statement with the
commission, the JCET filed on behalf of the reservation, often submitting
supportive letters or documents from educators indicating their enthusiasm
over the channel.

The JCET's brief provided its most elaborate case for the public interest
rationale behind the educational television reservations, in many ways extending the case for educational television it had presented in earlier testimony.
The eight-part brief to the commission offered a condensed overview of the
filings in support of the education reservations, reviewing 355 statements on
behalf of reserved channels in all of the states and Puerto Rico. It offered,
on the one hand, a national argument for educational television, and, on the
other, a multifaceted and heterogeneous picture of past, present, and future
visions of broadcasting's potential rooted in the particular needs and experiences of particular communities.

In addition to restating arguments its advocates had made in its hearing testimony, the JCET's brief also offered an extensive definition of television. Television was imagined as an instrument of education and democracy, as a means through which the problems facing the nation could be remedied, and as a tool to ameliorate social divisions and inequalities. The potential of television, as "one of mankind's most powerful and compelling media of instruction, education, exchange of information and culture," was tremendous and could function as a technology to redress social problems.[65] For example, the statement of the New Mexico State Department of Education asserted that television could address the uneven distribution of educational resources in the state: "New Mexico is a rural state with unevenly distributed population. Educational television broadcasting would bring many of the resources available to urban centers to people in the rural areas."[66] Television was positioned as enabling a bridge between rural and urban populations, one that could help address the social problems of individual states through strategic informational and educational programming.

The democratic potential of television, as envisioned by educators, involved a number of interpretations of citizenship and participation. While some made the case that television could equalize access to education and correct for structural inequalities, others tied the promise of television to republican conceptions of civic virtue, defining television as an instrument that would enlighten the citizenry. Through educational television, according to the Atlanta Board of Education, it would be "conceivable [to] raise the cultural and educational level of the masses of the American people to an unprecedented degree within a generation."[67] The plan of the Hillsborough County public school system in Florida would be to telecast programs of a "highly cultural nature" to "help raise the level of general enlightenment," and the Philadelphia Board of Public Education similarly imagined programming in the evening "hours designed to cultivate proper use of leisure time."[68] Educators thus argued for a definition of the public interest tethered to middlebrow notions of uplift and enlightenment, ones that posited that equal rights and civic participation were contingent on access to equal educational opportunities and exposure to ennobling forms of culture. Significantly, across the testimony and statements provided for educational television there was no unified understanding of what it would do or what kind of audience it would serve. Rather, myriad hopes and ambitions for educational television were proffered and presumed unlikely if commercial interests completely controlled the sector.

Key to the JCET's advocacy was how it couched its criticism of commercial broadcasting. Though the JCET described commercialism as inconsistent with the ambitions of educational television, the JCET and its allies never advocated for a television system in which commercial interests were subordinate. Instead, educational television was to be an alternative and a supplement but not the primary use of television. This conception of television was clear in the JCET's request at the end of the brief for a special dispensation for channels reserved in major educational centers in which the educational channel would be the only VHF station in operation. In these situations the JCET asked that the FCC relax the "noncommercial" designation temporarily so that the station could "render a full television service," to include commercial programs.[69] Presenting this request as a temporary fix, rather than a departure from the basic philosophy of noncommercial educational reservations, the JCET perhaps signaled its own recognition of the limited appeal of educational stations or the already entrenched expectations of what television *is*, even in communities that, under the freeze, had yet to access it firsthand. Indeed, though the fight for the reservations was a challenge to the *hegemony* of commercial stations, it was not a fight against the legitimacy or centrality of commercialism in the television sector.

The culmination of the JCET's efforts was the FCC's *Sixth Report and Order*, issued in April 1952, which the JCET and its constituent organizations experienced as a tremendous victory for educational television. Not only did the FCC expand the number of reserved channels to 242, but its report affirmed the arguments made by the JCET and its allies over the compatibility of educational television reservations to the public interest. The FCC posited that the benefits of both in-school and adult education programs via educational telecasts, and the record of quality radio programming that educators had established, indicated that educational television "would provide a valuable complement to commercial programming."[70] The commission also dismissed the claims of commercial broadcasters that the reservations would be wasting precious spectrum space through nonuse. In justifying its reservations—which were premised on the very idea that there would be temporary nonuse, requiring channels to be *reserved* for future use—the FCC underscored that its purpose was "to forestall a haphazard, inefficient or inequitable distribution of television service in the United States throughout the many years to come."[71] The allocation plan was to avoid a television system that was dominated, by virtue of their comparative access to capital, by commercial broadcasters. To solely consider applicants immediately able to activate a station was to trade the future benefits of a diverse television system for the ostensible urgency of getting stations on the air.

Furthermore, the FCC dismissed arguments that the comparatively smaller audience for educational television signaled that it would not serve the public interest. The commission retorted that "the justification for an educational television station should not, in our view, turn simply on account of audience size. The public interest will clearly be served if these stations are used to contribute significantly to the educational process of the nation."[72] The *Sixth Report* fundamentally rejected the conflation of the public interest with general interest stations. The diversity that educational television would bring with "programming of an entirely different character from that available on most commercial stations" legitimated the reservations.[73] In sum, the arguments and rhetorical strategies that commercial broadcasters had used in the past to derail the efforts of educators for favorable policies failed here, the FCC instead articulating a vision of the public interest consonant with that of the educational community.

Though the commission was sympathetic to the JCET's arguments, it rejected its request to finesse the "noncommercial" designation when the sole VHF channel would be educational, and it similarly rejected the requests of educational institutions to extend reservations to nonprofit, rather than noncommercial, stations. According to the FCC, to even allow partial commercial programming by stations run by educational institutions would "tend to vitiate the differences between commercial operation and non-commercial educational operation." For the FCC the very goal of the reservations, "the establishment of a genuinely educational type of service," would be upended if educational institutions operated "in substantially the same manner as commercial applicants though they may choose to call it limited commercial non-profit operation."[74] Much like the case of the FM reservations, it was the commission, more than those advocating for educational television, that insisted that the "noncommercial" designation was as important as the "educational" one.

The educational television reservations were a big deal. They not only signaled a rare crack in the corporate liberal ethos that had governed broadcasting policy making for decades, but they legitimated the alternative uses and spaces for television as imagined by educational reformers. While some scholars celebrate the reservations, emphasizing how they provided for significant diversity in the televisual public sphere,[75] others have interrogated how the rhetorical appeals and justifications for educational television made by groups like the JCET and the NAEB set in motion some of the problems to beset public television later, from its elitism and denigration of the popular to its political timidity and conservatism. From this latter perspective the reservations enabled the growth of public television, but they also structured the limiting way that its public, and its public obligations, would be understood.[76]

In viewing the winning of the educational reservations as primarily the prologue to the public broadcasting system to emerge in the late 1960s—as the necessary first step in the creation of the public television and radio systems familiar to us today—these assessments gloss over the rhetorical and practical labors required to secure the reservations *and* the continuous work necessary after the freeze to assure the existence and expansion of a noncommercial television sector. If we instead situate the campaigns for educational television in their historical moment, rather than reading them with an eye toward the public television system that would supplant educational television, we can see the variety of visions that structured noncommercial television's development, the significance of postwar political culture to its development, and the coalitional politics that facilitated its growth. And importantly, the work of the JCET, which had united educational interests in a common fight for the reservations, would continue after the freeze. Indeed, the reservations were just the beginning of the advocacy work needed for educational television to flourish.

Building and Sustaining an Educational Television Sector: The JCET after the Freeze

The *Sixth Report and Order* was a victory for the JCET and its allies. In the decade to follow, the fear that the reservations would go to "waste," and that building an alternative to commercial television was but a pretty dream, would be quite live. To build an alternative to commercial television required not only protecting the reservations from commercial challenges but routinely asserting the public interest benefits of educational television and the subsequent need for regulatory decisions that nurtured its growth.

There are a number of ways to narrate the history of educational television in the decade after the freeze. It is a history of institution building, facilitated by national, regional, and local organizations dedicated to the development of an educational sector, broadly understood. It is also a history of experimentation, as educational television stations were deployed in a variety of ways for a diversity of uses; during this period there was not a univocal, shared vision of what educational television should be or should do but rather multiple notions of the uses, spaces, and politics of educational television. It is a history of struggle, as educational television faced a number of problems—economic, technological, and legal—that impeded the pace of the sector's development. And it is a history of advocacy, in which educational telecasters and their supporters consistently had to fight to preserve the gains made during the freeze and to ensure that the FCC and Congress attended to the obstacles in the way of educational television's growth. It is also a history of opportunity for educational television, as the mix of pressures facing both local communities and the nation fostered conditions hospitable to advocacy on behalf of educational television.

As the story of the JCET demonstrates, all of these narratives were profoundly intertwined. In the decade after the freeze, advocacy on behalf of educational television was inseparable from institution building within the educational television sector. After securing the reservations during the freeze, the JCET's priority was to protect them, which involved not only warding off commercial challenges to the reservations but also demonstrating to the commission that interest in educational television was translating into action. To make the case for educational television thus required routinely reasserting the philosophy behind the educational television reservations and demonstrating continued progress in the use of the reservations. Consequently, the JCET's activities after the freeze involved continued advocacy in front of regulators and legislators, as well as work on the ground with local communities and other educational broadcasting organizations to get educational television stations up and running.

The first tasks the JCET faced were to provide information to myriad local groups about opportunities to create educational television stations and to defend these opportunities from hostile challenges. The organization routinely filed comments or petitions in defense of reserved channels when under threat by commercial interests. It was clear, indeed, from the period immediately after the freeze that the reservations would be challenged. The FCC had included in its *Sixth Report and Order* a provision that no portion of its allocation plan could be disputed for a year. The ban was to provide a period for the FCC to review applications for television channels without the additional administrative burden of handling a slew of petitions challenging individual assignments. This one-year ban, however, generated confusion over the status of the educational reservations. Misinformation circulated that the reservations would no longer be in effect after the one-year ban ended, that educational institutions had one year to "use or lose" the channels set aside by the commission. Hennock attributed this misperception to the malevolence of commercial interests; it was not accidental, in her view, that although the one-year ban applied to the commission's entire allocation scheme, only the educational reservations were imagined to be up for grabs once it ended. Nonetheless, the ban confused people about the intended duration of the reserved channels for education.[77] Thus one of the early postfreeze goals of the JCET was to clarify that the end of the year ban did not, in fact, mark expiration of the reservations.

As predicted, once the one-year ban expired in June 1953, commercial interests filed petitions with the commission to delete or reassign educational reservations in communities across the nation. The petitions overwhelmingly targeted VHF reservations and asked the FCC to free up VHF for commercial broadcasting and move the reservation for education to a UHF channel. It would be hard to overstate how much of the JCET's activity in the decade after the freeze was oriented toward defending the reservations. In response to these petitions representatives of educational interests in the community would respond with their own filings, in which they would affirm interest in activating the reserved channel and make the case for how preserving the reservation would serve the public interest needs of the community. The JCET typically also would file on behalf of the reserved channel, speaking both to the particular needs of specific communities and also to the philosophy of the reservations on whole. Time and again, the JCET had to continue to argue that the public interest could not be met by a television system wholly dominated by commercial stations.[78] This advocacy was enough, in the early years after the freeze, for the JCET and local communities to capably ward off these challenges to the reservations.

Yet as time passed, the commission became less patient with setting aside channels in the hopes that some entity, someday, may decide to activate them. The philosophy behind the reservations, which implicitly acknowledged the power of incumbency and thus the need for set-aside channels for noncommercial broadcasting, became increasingly less persuasive to the FCC as a justification for denying the benefits of competition and diversity, in the form of an additional television channel, in communities where commercial interests desired to use the unused reserved channel. Whereas in the early years after the freeze, the FCC typically dispensed with commercial petitions for deletion or reassignment of educational reservations, beginning in 1955 the commission was far more likely to initiate a rule-making process to address the question of whether particular reserved channels should be unreserved and opened up to commercial interests. In communities where there was concrete movement toward filing for a construction permit for a reserved channel, and where there was tangible evidence of local interest in building a station, the FCC tended to retain the reservation. Increasingly, though, in communities where there was no such movement, the FCC was more inclined to honor the requests for reassignment or deletion. By 1961 the commission had opened up three reserved channels for commercial uses.[79]

Though the VHF reservations posed a threat to commercial aspirants, by and large educational telecasting actually proved advantageous to commercial broadcasters. Activated educational stations hailed a different, and substantially smaller, audience than commercial stations, and the reservations themselves prevented an additional commercial telecaster from competing with incumbents in local markets. In addition, supporting educational television was a means to demonstrate one's commitment to public-interest goals and community service, an effective way to curry favor with the commission. And though they would deny it in front of Congress, commercial broadcasters also likely saw in a robust noncommercial sector fewer obligations on their own stations to program informational or educational shows.

Thus while the JCET defended the public interest against challenges by commercial broadcasters in the 1950s, it also benefited from the support of commercial broadcasters. Although the JCET and commercial interests battled over especially valuable VHF channels, in the decade after the freeze commercial broadcasters became allies to educational telecasters—lending financial support, providing technical training, donating equipment and studio space, and collaborating on educational programming. Of the forty-six applications filed with the FCC by June 1953 for educational stations, fourteen had been made possible by gifts from commercial broadcasters.[80] In 1954, when the JCET presented demonstrations at the annual American Association of School Administrators (AASA) conference to enable school superintendents to learn about the various types of school television broadcasting, RCA loaned equipment and sent engineers to enable live demonstrations.[81] That same year, RCA, DuMont, NBC, CBS, and General Precision Laboratories provided the meeting places, speakers, and equipment for a workshop for educators to learn about the latest television broadcasting equipment.[82]

Furthermore, throughout the 1950s commercial and noncommercial broadcasters found common cause in trying to find a solution to the problems posed by UHF. The UHF problem was a big one for educational broadcasters and occupied much of the JCET's time. The majority of the reservations were in the UHF band. Not only did UHF require more power to cover an equivalent area as VHF, but most television sets owned by households were not equipped to receive UHF stations. One of the few educational television stations to go on and then off the air was KTHE in Los Angeles, a UHF station that failed in large part because of its frequency. UHF channels, when used, were often for in-school instruction, as the potential viewer base for at-home programming was substantially limited.[83] UHF was a problem for commercial broadcasters as well. Given the vastly smaller audience base for UHF, UHF stations were not able to attract anywhere close to the advertising revenue garnered by VHF stations because there were far smaller audiences for UHF stations to sell to advertisers. Accordingly, both educational and commercial telecasters had a common interest in addressing the UHF problem. But UHF could also exacerbate tensions between commercial and educational telecasters, as the former sought additional VHF channels often at the expense of educational television.

The JCET attacked the UHF problem through an array of tactics—from lobbying senators about the necessity to address the limitations of UHF, and especially to consider legislation to mandate that television sets be manufactured to receive both VHF and UHF signals, to participation in FCC proceedings over the UHF question and concrete strategies to address it. Steetle also served as one of five members of the FCC's Television Allocations Study Organization (TASO), to research solutions to the problems of UHF.[84] Throughout this advocacy work the JCET saw the answer to the UHF problem, for both commercial and noncommercial stations alike, as critical to the growth of educational television. The UHF reservations would only be valuable in communities where households had television sets that received UHF channels and, importantly, that were accustomed to viewing UHF stations. The JCET reasoned that consumers purchased television sets to view commercial television. Accordingly, if commercial broadcasters did not make use of UHF, few people would spend money on receivers or adapters to access UHF channels.[85] Whereas during the freeze the JCET positioned the interests of commercial and educational television as adversarial, in the years after the freeze it often tethered the success of educational television to the success of commercial television, and it presented the two systems' futures as intertwined rather than at odds with one another.

In addition to its partnerships with business, the JCET largely existed because of philanthropic support. In the mid-1950s the Joint *Committee* on Educational Television became the Joint *Council* on Educational Television. The newly named organization would have the same responsibilities as the previous one. What did change along with the name was the source of funding for the organization. Ford's Fund for Adult Education (FAE) had provided the bulk of the JCET's funding. Starting in 1955, the organization would receive support from the Ford Foundation itself, not the FAE. In addition, the Joint Council on Educational Television was to be an even stronger national organization, to be realized through its expanded membership. In addition to the original seven constituent members, the Educational Television and Radio Center (ETRC) and the National Citizens Committee for Educational Television (NCCET), both Ford-supported organizations, would join the JCET in the mid-1950s, as would the National Congress of Parents and Teachers.[86]

This financial and coalitional support allowed the JCET to go beyond policy advocacy and help build the educational television sector faced with the "use or lose" condition placed on the reservations. Thus, the JCET expanded its range of activities in the years following the freeze. Beginning in the summer of 1952, the JCET provided legal and engineering support to communities interested in activating a reserved channel. Dubbed its Field Consultation Service, the JCET assigned a small staff dedicated to provide this support and drew on a network of professionals involved in educational broadcasting, paid on a fee-basis, to consult and explore the most feasible organizational and financial models for educational TV for particular communities and regions.[87] As James Day, general manager of San Francisco station KQED and later head of National Educational Television (NET), remembered, most educational stations in the 1950s owed their development in part to this JCET service.[88]

In addition, the JCET saw as its mission to persuade local communities of the benefits of educational television. In making the case to communities across the country of the utility and power of educational television, it had to counter what it saw as prevailing assumptions about television itself, views perhaps best summed up by architect Frank Lloyd Wright's quip that television was "chewing gum for the eyes." As Steetle put it, television in the early 1950s was perceived as "Uncle Milty and dancing cigarettes," and intellectuals suspected that "pablum was about to become the living room's basic meal. So that in talking to groups, whether university or school or citizens or whatever, I occasionally thought of myself as someone speaking of the economic uses of electricity when the only known use was the electric chair."[89] The JCET, along with other national educational broadcasting organizations, had to challenge this cynical narrative and reframe television as a neutral technology that could improve the educational and cultural life of the citizenry. Such a shift in perspective was necessary to convince a range of stakeholders—state legislatures, school districts, higher educational institutions, community groups, and the public at large—of the benefits of educational television and thus of the benefits of activating the reserved channel in their community. This project involved not only the labor of meeting with citizen groups, community organizations, and educational institutions about their prospective participation in educational television but the rhetorical work of convincing educators and citizens that television could be an instructional, cultural, and community medium.

The JCET codified its public outreach and information activities in June 1952 with the inauguration of its first monthly publication, *The JCET Reports*. The newsletter circulated updates on progress in the construction and operation of educational television stations and provided information about the status of challenges to the reservations. The JCET also would subsequently publish an *Educational Television: Factsheet and Box Score* that similarly provided information about developments in educational television and especially informed readers about the battles and issues taking place in the policy-making arena that would have an impact on educational broadcasting. The purpose of these publications, Steetle explained, was "to show each of the communities what the other was doing, who was involved, what were their problems, what were their achievements."[90]

In addition, the JCET periodically assembled comprehensive reports on the developments of educational telecasters, primarily for the commission and Congress, to concretize, and also to celebrate, the growth of the sector. These JCET reports were informative and pedagogical documents. They culled together pertinent information about the development of educational television, such as the number and location of stations on the air, sources of financing for educational television, and range of programming provided by the stations. But they also both affirmed the justification for dedicated, educational channels and instructed the commission and Congress in how to read the pace of development of the educational television sector. The JCET tacitly asked for the progress of educational television to be seen beyond the mere number of activated channels. So it also flagged the enthusiasm for educational TV via the numerous conferences hosted by an array of national organizations; the outpouring of financial support it has received from legislatures, educational institutions, philanthropic foundations, business interests, and individual donations; and glowing press coverage that assessed its potential.[91]

In making the case for educational television's progress, the JCET also celebrated the diversity of stations on the air, as well as the divergent uses to which educational television was being put. As the educational television sector developed in the decade after the freeze, its communities of service ranged from local viewers, statewide publics, and regional audiences to the nation at-large (or at least the parts of it that could access an educational television station). In addition, stations were run by state educational television commissions (frequently created by state legislatures), universities, school districts, state boards of education, and nonprofit organizations constituting a consortium of interests, including educational institutions—both public and private—cultural institutions, and civic organizations. The functions of the stations also varied. Some saw their raison d'être as providing instruction in the schools or courses for credit to be completed at home. Others emphasized adult education more broadly conceived or sought to provide cultural and public-affairs programming distinct from that which would have been available on commercial stations.

The variety of the JCET's activities thus was mirrored by the diversity of stations its advocacy sought to support. Critical to the expansion of educational television in the 1950s was a coalitional politics that united various visions of what educational programming was for and who it should serve. In its advocacy the JCET tended to and celebrated these multiple understandings of the functions, spaces, and politics of educational television. In addition, the JCET's big-tent approach to educational television enabled the organization to position the service as a solution to postwar problems, as critical to the public interest not only for the alternative that it provided to commercial stations but for its capacity to tackle some of the exigent crises of the 1950s.

Educational Television, the Education Crisis, and the Jim Crow South

These myriad partnerships served as a basis for the JCET to present educational television as a resource for responding to an escalating concern—the so-called education crisis of the 1950s. As one 1953 newspaper article noted, concern about public schools had reached such a fever pitch that "attacking the schools is assuming the proportion of cross-word puzzles, bridge, and golf as a favorite sport, inside and out."[92] The 1950s saw the publication of multiple screeds—both books and articles—that lamented the state of education in the United States with titles like *Quackery in the Public Schools*, *Educational Wastelands*, *The Diminished Mind*, *Why Johnny Can't Read*, "The Educational Malaise," and "Are High Schools for Morons?"[93] Of the many complaints that animated the education crisis—which included critiques of progressive education, anxieties over the quality of teachers and teaching, and fears that Soviet children were better educated than American ones—was the concern that there were insufficient teachers and classrooms to address the growing enrollments resulting from the baby boom and that students in different communities had starkly divergent access to a good education.[94]

The JCET responded to this moral and political panic by offering television as a solution that could enable a singular teacher to teach hundreds, if not thousands, of students at the same time and allow students in underserved schools to get a comparable education to those in better-resourced schools.

Educational television, according to the JCET, could level unequal playing fields and produce "an informed citizenry and a healthy democracy."[95] Many of the most celebrated educational television systems of the era, such as the Midwest Program on Airborne Television Instruction, were premised on television's ability to equalize access to quality educational materials.[96]

The use of television as a technology to solve the education crisis exemplified a long-standing tendency, as Larry Cuban has demonstrated, to see communication technologies as "solutions to school problems in swift technological advances" implemented without consideration of or consultation with actual classroom teachers.[97] As Cuban argues, and as the work and vision of the JCET illustrated, education reformers were often foundation executives and educational administrators who enthusiastically embraced communication technologies as innovative, exciting, effective, and efficient learning tools. Their techno-utopianism frequently relied not just on a lack of consideration of the views of the teachers asked to implement these technologies in their classroom but on a devaluation of actual teachers' instructional capabilities and a dismissal of their own expertise. Democratizing access to educational resources, in other words, hinged on a sometimes implicit, sometimes explicit, denigration of classroom teachers and a corresponding shift of power from workers to managers of education.[98]

And importantly, the "equality" promoted by advocates of educational television became part of southern equalization campaigns to maintain segregated schools in anticipation and in the wake of the *Brown v. Board of Education* (1954) decision that ruled segregated public schools to be unconstitutional. Southern states were some of the most active in building educational television stations and networks in the 1950s. By 1956, one-third of all educational television stations were located in the South. Alabama was the first state to build a statewide educational television network, and the Southern Regional Education Board (SREB) was one of the most active organizations in facilitating regional and local educational television stations. By 1961 twenty-one of the fifty-four educational television stations on air were in the southern United States. Of the many benefits television was imagined to bring, one was its ability to provide identical instruction to white and African American children without requiring them to occupy the same physical space. As Jim Robertson summarized, based on his extensive oral history project on educational television, the South was interested in using television to extend educational opportunities, and some states "even hoped that in this way integration of schools might not be necessary."[99]

Television, like other equalization efforts, sought to bring African American schools on par with white schools, with the expectation that making good on the "equal" part of "separate but equal"—the doctrine established in the 1896 *Plessy v. Ferguson* case that had provided the constitutional scaffolding for segregation—would put their schools on more stable legal ground.

Arkansas, Georgia, Mississippi, North Carolina, and South Carolina all adopted measures in the years before the *Brown* decision was issued to invest more money in the African American schools that, for decades prior, had received a substantially smaller amount of financial support than their white counterparts.[100] Equalization campaigns accelerated after the *Brown* decision, especially in the Deep South states, as legislatures struggled to find resources to improve the facilities and teacher salaries in African American schools in an attempt to preserve the legality of segregated schools.[101] Educational television, which emerged concurrently with these issues, was seen by segregationists as providing another means for equalization.

The statewide educational television network in Alabama, for example, provided both in-school and at-home instructional programming, but part of its mission was to equalize educational materials across its public schools. In this it sought to address racial disparities borne by resources and location but also to obviate the need for school desegregation. As Hull, who was sent by the JCET to consult with Alabamians about educational television in 1952, remembered, "They were looking for ways to offer education in a divided South, I think before the Supreme Court [*Brown v. Board of Education*] decision."[102] Raymond Hurlbert, one of the first commissioners of the Alabama Educational Television Commission (AETC) and its general manager from 1955 until 1973, routinely stressed how experiments like the Alabama Educational Television Network (AETN) would bring new meaning to the term *equal opportunities*. Put another way in a promotional pamphlet, "As a facet of public education, it is making available to all the citizenry, regardless of age, sex, religion, color, or geographic location, the educational opportunities and informational resources of the State. This medium provides the most rapid statewide equalization of educational opportunities."[103] Telecasting quality instructional material to schools, Hurlbert implicitly claimed, was a better means of providing equal educational opportunities than the vision of integrated schools articulated by courts.

The Alabama network served numerous functions. Its programming instructed school children in subjects ranging from French language instruction and music to science and civics; brought cultural works (ballet, opera, theater) to the homes of people who otherwise would be deprived of these experiences; and telecast lectures and lessons on topics like mythology and Zen philosophy, allowing it to become a "space age Chautauqua" for "the discriminating viewer."[104] But its imagined public was a segregated public, and it used television in part to shore up Jim Crow conditions in its state at a time when its legitimacy was coming under growing attack.

This use of educational television was perhaps most baldy expressed in a 1962 *Time* magazine article on educational television in South Carolina. The South Carolina Educational Television system, formed in 1958, initially was intended to provide a "backup mechanism" to educate the state's children should South Carolina decide to close its public schools rather than integrate them.[105] The South Carolina state legislature in 1957 allocated around $8 million for educational television, and in the years to follow ETV would continue to be supported by segregationist state legislators.[106] *Time* reported on a "top-flight white teacher" who "drilled Negro students in a small high school in rural South Carolina." It continued that "white and Negro children were getting the same TV lesson all over segregated South Carolina—the state has the most complete commitment to classroom TV in the US." Accompanying the story were two side-by-side photos of black students watching television and white students watching television, captioned by "Separate But Equal Classroom TV in South Carolina."[107] Although educational television was used in South Carolina to improve the quality of education in a state that was one of the poorest and desperately needed qualified teachers, television also reinforced the state's dual, segregated school system.

The JCET, the NAEB, and the Ford Foundation also were supportive of southern educational television networks and especially of the SREB. The SREB formed in 1948 in the wake of Supreme Court decisions that required states to admit African American students to white professional schools when no in-state African American facility existed.[108] The SREB was to create regionally run professional schools, thereby displacing the need for each state to support its own professional schools but also facilitating regionally segregated schools. Importantly, the SREB's first action was to put Meharry Medical College in Tennessee, the only African American medical school in the South, under regional southern control.[109] The SREB's efforts to coordinate a regional television network emerged in this context.

The JCET routinely celebrated the advances in educational television made in the South and actively supported the SREB's efforts to build a regional network. The big tent that it rhetorically constructed for educational television had a place for these uses of the medium. Indeed, not only did the developments in the South contribute to the picture of a robustly expanding educational television sector that the JCET routinely tried to paint, but they garnered the political support of southern congressmen who, in turn, were some of the most vocal advocates for resources for educational television. Louisiana congressman Hale Boggs and Alabama congressman Kenneth Roberts were leading advocates for federal support for educational television. They also were signatories on the 1956 "Declaration of Southern Principles," also known as the "Southern Manifesto," which decried the *Brown* decision as a substitute of "naked power for established law" that encroached on the rights of southern states and opened the gates to "outside agitators" and "revolutionary changes" in the South.[110] In the 1950s these positions could be seen as complementary.

In the 1950s the racial politics of educational television, and the sector's role in perpetuating a system of segregation, was unremarkable to leaders of national organizations like the JCET, who supported all iterations of educational television as a diverse tapestry serving the public interest in myriad ways. The JCET, as the advocacy face of the educational television sector, was fairly agnostic about the mission, goal, or politics of the diverse stations within it. There also is no indication in the JCET's records that its members objected to uses of educational television in the segregated South or found them in any way inconsistent with the mission of educational television. It was only in the 1960s that the coalitional politics of the 1950s that had built educational television began to fray, especially over the racial politics of the sector.

Educational Television and the Cold War

In 1958, in the wake of the launch of the Soviets' *Sputnik* satellite, Congress passed the National Defense Education Act (NDEA). The act's passage infused public debates over the quality of education in the United States with the urgency of national security and in turn provided resources to those who promoted public education as a weapon for waging the Cold War. The NDEA granted federal money to myriad areas in education including educational loans for higher education; promotion of science, math, and foreign language instruction; funding for college preparation courses and counseling; and money for uses of audiovisual media in education.[111] The NAEB in particular would take advantage of the NDEA, receiving grants to conduct research on educational broadcasting.[112]

By the late 1950s the JCET and its allies responded to the act's passage by promoting educational television as a weapon for winning the Cold War. It was a strategy that further clarified the organization's pragmatism and the constraints placed on the politics of social reform at the time. This argument was most prevalent in the JCET's testimony in support of what would become the 1962 Educational Television Facilities Act (ETFA), which provided one-time federal allocations to support the construction of educational television stations. Sixteen iterations of the ETFA were introduced in both houses of Congress between 1958 and 1962.[113] The ETFA was supposed to build on the NDEA but would provide more targeted support for educational television stations.

Throughout hearings over the ETFA, members of Congress heard from both representatives of national organizations like the JCET and representatives of the stations themselves, both of whom made the case for the necessity to build a more robust educational television sector through federal support of station construction. When, for example, Steetle testified during 1959 senate hearings, he relayed to the senators that when he had visited the Soviet Union in 1958, he learned that the Soviets had not used television for education but rather only for the "same kind of internal propaganda that one finds in every newsstand, in every airplane, in every hotel." Educational television, in his vision, was an area in which the United States could surpass the Soviets, who had "had some fairly negative comments to make about most phases of American education until they came to educational television."[114] Not only could educational television improve the educational resources of the nation, but it could be an arena in which American uses of technology exceeded those of the Soviets.

It was a sentiment that recurred throughout the hearings in both houses of Congress, as witnesses and members of Congress alike saw in television, in the words of Robert Anderson, former head of the SREB, a technology "to help meet the tidal wave of students coming into their classrooms during the years ahead," to educate adults "in the cities, in the farmlands, and in industry and business," and to maintain a "strong economy and a resolute defense" of the nation.[115] A statement of William Harley, president of the NAEB, echoed this position: "Let us hope that Russia does not have to launch the equivalent of a sputnik in the use of television for educational purposes in order to bring the breakthrough which American education so desperately needs if it is again to seize a position of world leadership in education."[116]

The vision of how educational television, with the support of federal dollars, could serve the public thus centered on a construction of a vulnerable public, beset by the pressures of the Cold War and the cracks in the American educational system. Over the course of the hearings senators and representatives were persuaded of the national stakes in growing educational television through federal funds. They were instructed to see that civic participation, national security, and equality of opportunity intersected and perhaps even hinged on the expansion of educational television.

The Educational Television Facilities Act received widespread and bipartisan support. Those less enthused by the proposal objected not to the social and political uses of television imagined within it, or to the shoring up of the educational television sector, but to the use of federal funds to accomplish this goal. This concern centered on dual anxieties over whether there was room in the federal budget to commit $50 million to educational television and whether this issue should be more properly a concern of the states, like education more broadly, than of the federal government. The bill finally passed, aided by the enthusiasm of President John F. Kennedy, and was signed into law in February of 1962.[117] The act would be the most significant display of federal support for educational television since the freeze and until the 1967 Public Broadcasting Act, and it was brought into being in part by the successful conjoining of the benefits of educational television's expansion with concurrent Cold War anxieties over the quality of education within the United States.

The Fraying of the Cold War Consensus in the 1960s and the Legacy of the JCET

The labors of the JCET facilitated the building of an alternative to commercial television in the 1950s. The organization helped write into television regulation the importance of educational stations and the provision of public resources, in the form of reserved channels, to assure the development of a noncommercial sector. In this it brought to fruition a long-standing goal of media reformers: to diminish the hegemony of commercialism in American broadcasting. The JCET leveled a sustained and effective advocacy campaign in which it capably persuaded the FCC and Congress to define the public interest as it defined it—as contingent on the development of broadcast stations seeking to educate rather than entertain for private gain. The JCET's success was a result of its capable translation of the benefits of educational television to address the issues facing local, regional, and national publics in the 1950s. At the center of its vision was a television system that would equalize access to educational, informational, and cultural resources deemed critical to the health of American democracy in the postwar period.

While the campaign for educational television would challenge the hegemony of commercialism, the creation of an alternate television sector also softened the need for content-based regulations on commercial stations for educational programming. And while much of the rhetoric of the JCET echoed mass culture critiques of broadcasting, criticisms that, as Laurie Ouellette has demonstrated, hinged on the denigration of the popular and on unexamined hierarchies of aesthetic value, it did not echo the more trenchant assessments of the politics of commercial broadcasting that had animated previous challenges to commercialism.[118] Educational television in the 1950s offered an alternative use of television, but it did not constitute a counterpublic sphere. Rather, it presented a technological solution to the problem of structural inequality, provided access to ennobling forms of high culture, extended opportunities for adult education, was offered as a domestic weapon in the battle against global communism, and facilitated the equalization of southern schools. Educational television, in other words, was supposed to solve problems. In the 1950s its promoters did not ask regulators, legislators, or its audience to see them through a different lens.

The noncommercial television sector changed substantially in the 1960s. The ETFA was passed the same year as the All Channel Receiver Act, which mandated that all television sets be manufactured to receive UHF and VHF channels. This act, which was championed by FCC chairperson Newton Minow, not only bolstered competition across stations in local markets but also made the educational television sector more robust and more accessible. These laws paved the way for the 1967 Public Broadcasting Act, which would rename *educational* television *public* television and provide for sustained federal support for noncommercial broadcasting.

In the early 1960s the Ford Foundation's priority in the educational television sector was building up the quality and scale of educational programming. It thus redirected its financial support to National Educational Television (NET), which produced and distributed programming for educational television stations, and ceased funding the JCET. In 1961 the Joint Council on Educational Television became the Joint Council on Educational Broadcasting (JCEB). Although this name change seemed to signal an even greater role for the organization, in fact it indicated a substantial restriction of its mandate. The JCEB would continue to be the "forum for the formulation of policy on national issues that affect all aspects of educational broadcasting," and it would provide leadership on policy issues, before the FCC and Congress, of significance to educational broadcasting.[119] Its contribution to the sector would be in its policy advocacy; its role in helping to build the educational television sector would be absorbed by other national organizations, primarily NET. The JCEB operated on a modest budget, predominantly coming from small grants from General Electric and Standard Oil New Jersey, which greatly restricted what its mandate could be. The JCEB's financial situation would continue to diminish in the 1960s, its staff functions increasingly performed by its constituent organizations, leaving its mission and necessity debated by its members.[120]

As NET took over many of the jobs of the JCET, it also rejected the broader, multifaceted vision of what educational television could do that had animated much of the JCET's work throughout the 1950s. The successes of the JCET in the 1950s had resulted from the strategic positioning of television as an answer to postwar problems. But as popular understanding of those problems began to change in the 1960s—and especially as social movements fighting for social, political, and economic equality in the United States flourished—the politics of the noncommercial sector became more frayed, the coalition that had enabled it in the 1950s giving way to a more fractured constellation of interests who disagreed over the role that noncommercial television was to play in this era. Within the sector were conflicting ideas about whether noncommercial television should be a voice for or a bulwark against the social movements of the 1960s. NET, which tacked toward the former, would be met with hostility from many local stations, which saw in the programming that NET provided an abrogation of noncommercial television's purpose rather than its fulfillment.

These tensions within the noncommercial sector were part and parcel of a reevaluation of the politics of U.S. television in the 1960s and a challenge to the unitary notion of the "public interest" that the JCET had helped legitimize during the height of the Cold War. Commercial and noncommercial television alike would become targets of advocacy and activism, broadcasting policy an important battleground in 1960s struggles for a more just and egalitarian society. It is to them that we now turn.

2

The Black
Freedom Struggle
and the Broadcast
Reform Movement

///

By the late 1960s the Alabama Educational Television Commission (AETC),
which operated the state's public television network, received substantial criticism for the near invisibility of African Americans in its programming. Less
than 10 percent of its programming was "integrated," defined as shows in
which at least one African American appeared onscreen; and 71.4 percent of
the network's "integrated" programming was filled by *Sesame Street*, which the
network telecast twice a day.[1] Not a single African American had served on
the AETC since it was created in 1953. Of the state universities with whom the
AETC had contracted to produce programming for the network, not a single
one was an African American university. Very few African Americans were
employed by the AETC, and those who were performed mostly low-status
janitorial work.

In the late 1960s, at the suggestion of Al Kramer, an attorney at public interest law firm Communication Citizens Center, Steven Suitts, a student at the
University of Alabama who had been a visible free-speech advocate on cam-
pus, filed formal challenges to AETC's licenses. In 1975 the FCC revoked the
AETC's licenses on the grounds that its practices had been racially discriminatory and thus contrary to the public interest.[2] The Alabama Educational

Television Network (AETN) joined WLBT-TV, a commercial broadcaster in Jackson, Mississippi, in the unenviable distinction of being the only broadcasters in the history of American television to have their licenses revoked on racial discrimination grounds.[3]

Suitts's participation in the AETC license challenge redirected his work after college toward media advocacy. As part of an Alabama Media Project, he worked in Alabama's Black Belt with civil rights leaders to challenge radio station licenses. As a result of his work, a number of stations were sold to local African American entrepreneurs, while others hired more African Americans and dedicated more airtime to African American music and programming. For Suitts this work mattered because "we were changing the landscape in the South." The Civil Rights Act of 1964 and the Voting Rings Act of 1965 had altered the law to prohibit various forms of racial discrimination. But it was clear to Suitts that to "transform the South into the beloved community that Martin Luther King fought for" required wrestling with what Suitts called the "primary instruments of communication" in society. In this way, what began as a campaign to challenge how segregationists used media to undermine the civil rights movement evolved into a lifelong commitment to treat media reform as central to the struggle for racial justice.[4]

The work of Suitts and others did not simply add media reform as a site of civil rights struggle. Black Freedom Movement campaigns against racism in broadcasting transformed media reform politics in the 1960s and 1970s. The AETC case, along with the myriad interventions in local communities over racially discriminatory broadcasting practices, promoted an alternative conception of the public interest that was attentive to the needs of multiple publics. It paved the way for a flurry of reform activity during the 1960s and 1970s, primarily in the form of license challenges, enabling a broadcast reform movement, or what Robert McChesney has defined as the third critical juncture of communications history in the United States.[5] As the social movements of the era sought, in McChesney's words, to bring "all social institutions under closer examination," they included broadcast media in their critique of how existing institutions perpetuated forms of injustice and inequality.[6] The broadcast reform movement, broadly, not only targeted how broadcast programming was discriminatory; it also questioned the presumed neutrality of broadcast regulation and the construction of the "public" on which it had rested for decades—one broadly premised on an abstracted, undifferentiated public. Indeed, though groups like the JCET in the 1950s argued for educational television to redress forms of inequality, borne by social class and location, its own vision of the "public" was similarly normative: educational television was to bring everyone into the fold of a shared cultural heritage and provide equivalent access to a quality education. In contrast, participants in the broadcast reform movement—especially identity-based groups—sought to shatter the notion of a unitary "public." Their media advocacy was a means to acquire status for those who had been derided or rendered invisible both onscreen and, importantly, in regulatory decisions.

The Black Freedom Movement's media reform advocacy opened the doors to community activists like Suitts, who would play a key role in developing new opportunities for minority employment and leadership at both commercial and public broadcasting stations. By the end of the 1960s and early 1970s, these campaigns shifted the meaning of the "public interest" to something that served the cause of redistributing power to those who had historically been discriminated against. As the case of the AETC indicates, both commercial and noncommercial broadcasters alike were targets of civil rights groups and activists. Their media advocacy asked broadcasters and their federal regulators to confront how broadcasting content and broadcasting policies, as well as their implementations, operated as technologies that reproduced a system of racial hierarchy and privilege. Their goals were both to change conditions on the ground and to assert that any understanding of the "public interest" that did not recognize the existence of multiple, racially diverse publics—or that did not see how broadcasting and broadcast regulation was, and could continue to be, imbricated in racial discrimination—did violence to the very term and the promise of civic obligation at its center.

This chapter analyzes the intersecting histories of the Black Freedom Movement and media advocacy in the 1960s and discusses how the federal government was compelled to apply civil rights law to the regulation of television. It specifically examines three important events: the challenge to WLBT-TV's license in 1966; the scathing criticism of media racism in the Report of the National Advisory Committee on Civil Disorders, or Kerner Report, in 1968; and the successful challenge to AETC's license, initiated in 1969. These were not fights over commercialism or corporate power but over racism and whether the construct of a singular, knowable, general public that had guided broadcasting policy for decades had also provided cover for racist broadcasters to use the power of the media to naturalize racial segregation. The rhetorical, legal, and mobilization strategies pioneered by the Black Freedom Movement would be picked up by other communities and would structure claims of injury and appeals for justice in the realm of media policy for decades to come. But in the 1960s this transformation in media advocacy and media regulation began as a result of, and was structured by, the process and politics of broadcast licensing.

The Black Freedom Struggle
and the Politics of License Renewal

Licensing has been at the center of U.S. broadcasting policy since 1912, when Congress required users of the "ether" to be licensed by the Commerce Department. The broadcast license was the instrument that enabled private entities access to a public resource, the airwaves, with the provision that they use this resource in the public interest. Yet there had been a number of concerns with licensing. Since at least the 1950s, economists have debated the efficacy of the broadcast licensing system and, in the process, have disagreed over the synergies or tensions between economic efficiency and democratic principles.[7] For the public the implementation of the commission's licensing power had been the source of two specific problems. Though license renewal ostensibly was tied to the public interest performance of the licensee, the FCC had been overwhelmingly predisposed to renewal and very rarely revoked a license. In addition, until the late 1960s members of the public did not have "standing," or a legal right to be heard, in license renewal cases.

This began to change when civil rights activists challenged television stations in the South for reinforcing Jim Crow segregation. WLBT-TV, an NBC affiliate and one of two commercial stations in Jackson, Mississippi, had had a long, notorious record among the African American citizens of Jackson, who composed 45 percent of its population. The FCC had received complaints about WLBT since the revival of the Black Freedom Movement in 1955. The station's newscasts on the issue of racial desegregation provided time solely to segregationists, and the station refused time to civil rights leaders to respond. The station would not air national network programming that featured civil rights leaders or that discussed the civil rights movement in a sympathetic way. Medgar Evers, Mississippi field secretary of the NAACP and a resident of Jackson, routinely asked for and was routinely denied airtime to respond to disparaging claims made about him and the NAACP.[8]

As Steven Classen has illustrated, the challenge to WLBT's license was part of a larger struggle against racial discrimination in Jackson. When the Reverend Everett C. Parker of the Office of Communications of the United Church of Christ arrived in Jackson and proposed to challenge WLBT's license, he tapped into a community of local activists who had been resisting the impact of Jim Crow on their lives for about a decade.[9] Parker was able to enlist local civil rights activists Aaron Henry, president of the Mississippi NAACP, and the Reverend Robert L. T. Smith, leader of the Mississippi Freedom Democratic Party, as signatories on the petition to deny WLBT's license. In an interview with Robert Britt Horwitz, Rev. Parker remembered that a lawyer for the NAACP had warned him and Henry not to file, arguing that affixing their signatures on the document made them potential targets for white supremacists and was unlikely to do much good anyway.[10] The lawyer's skepticism was not only tied to the disparate power of white and black citizens in Jackson, and the country overall, but to the restricted definition of *standing* in the renewal process.[11] At the time, standing before the FCC—or the legal right to be heard—was restricted to those entities or individuals who could demonstrate electrical interference or economic injury. Residents of Jackson, under this definition, did not have the legal right to petition against WLBT's license renewal. The commission, in turn, granted the station a temporary one-year renewal and dismissed the petition to deny on the grounds that the petitioners lacked standing.[12]

Yet the petitioners appealed the decision and, remarkably, the U.S. Court of Appeals for the District of Columbia ruled against the FCC in 1966 and extended standing to "representative" and "responsible" members of the broadcasting public for the first time in U.S. history. By encouraging public participation in license renewal hearings, the court's ruling suggested that the FCC itself could not independently ascertain the quality of the service any individual broadcaster had provided to its public.[13] This case, along with a subsequent one in 1969, led to the revocation of WLBT's license and the ultimate assignment of the station to an African American–controlled entity.[14]

The WLBT decision contributed to the development of a new broadcast reform movement in three ways. First, as the case was widely reported in the national press, articles emphasized how the station's racist programming had jeopardized the station's license. These reports connected WLBT's loss of license to its rendering the city's African American community invisible, its ignoring national civil rights activity, and its using slurs and derogatory terms in its address of African Americans.[15] Even though, as Classen has demonstrated, the 1966 court decision itself sanitized the particular charges of discrimination at its center—the ruling essentially redefined a case about the civil rights of African Americans as one about universal consumer rights to participate in administrative proceedings—the case put the relationship between broadcasting practices and racial discrimination in the center of public discourse and provided another lens on how racial prejudice operated in the Jim Crow South.[16]

Second, the case raised the question of broadcast regulation's complicity in the racially discriminatory practices of its licensees. As such, it challenged the FCC's own understanding of the "public interest" as insufficiently attentive to the needs and interests of the diverse publics within broadcast markets. This critique was most baldly expressed in the appellate court's second ruling, which overturned the FCC's renewal of WLBT's license after hearings had been held in Jackson over its public interest performance. In his final ruling on the appellate bench before assuming the position of Supreme Court chief justice, Warren Burger issued a blistering decision, asserting that the "administrative conduct [by the FCC] reflected in this record is beyond repair."[17] The decision excoriated the Administrative Law Judge's (ALJ) dismissive treatment of Jackson's African American residents during the public hearings, as well as the FCC's protectionist stance toward the broadcaster. Burger pointed in particular to the FCC's decision to renew despite substantial evidence that, for example, the station repeatedly had been in violation of the Fairness Doctrine, a rule adopted in 1949 that required broadcasters to air both sides of controversial issues. The decision articulated a concern widespread at that time over regulatory capture—the notion that administrative agencies had become "captured" by those they were charged with regulating and had become lapdogs rather than watchdogs.[18]

Finally, the WLBT case was the launchpad for a flurry of license challenges in the late 1960s and 1970s. From 1969 to 1974 the number of petitions to deny filed with the FCC rose from 2 to 150. In 1972 there were 68 petitions filed against 108 stations.[19] The expanded definition of *standing* thus provided an important opportunity to communities that saw themselves ignored by, or demeaned by, their local broadcasters to fight back and to redefine the public interest in line with their own needs and concerns. As the publication *Broadcasting* summed up in 1970, the WLBT case "did more than establish the right of the public to participate in a station's license-renewal hearing. It did even more than encourage minority groups around the country to assert themselves in broadcast matters at a time when unrest was growing and blacks were becoming more activist. It provided practical lessons in how pressure could be brought, in how the broadcast establishment could be challenged."[20] The WLBT case changed who could participate in media advocacy and modeled how different communities could hold broadcasters to account. And it laid bare that the notion of a unitary public, and a singular public interest, had in practice been used by white supremacists to institutionalize and legitimatize racial segregation.

These shifts weren't just legal. They were cultural. The WLBT case provided a basis for African Americans to reinterpret the public interest, assert their own membership within constructions of the public, and challenge broadcasters who ignored or evinced hostility toward the nonwhite members of their communities. In the process they initiated a much broader "minority rights revolution" in media reform politics.[21]

The Kerner Report: Media Reform as Crisis Management

The second WLBT ruling was issued around a year after the Kerner Report, or the Report of the National Advisory Commission on Civil Disorders, was released. President Lyndon Johnson had assembled the Kerner Commission (named after its chair, Illinois governor Otto Kerner) in 1967 to investigate the urban rebellions of that year. The report, released in 1968, was instantly controversial and famous because it foregrounded "white racism" in its diag-nosis of the causes of urban violence and, as Kevin Mumford has written, "avoided the theory of black rage and culture of poverty, subtly transferring the blame for the tragedy of the riots from black rioters to the problem [of] inequality."[22]

In this the Kerner Report represented a break from the findings of the McCone Commission, which had studied the 1965 Watts uprising in Los Angeles and had concluded, in the words of Robert Fogelson, that the "rioters were marginal people and the riots meaningless outbursts," resulting from the "irresponsible agitation by Negro leaders" and from the fact that the rioters were recent migrants to Los Angeles who had yet to acculturate to urban life.[23] The McCone Report had been critical of the role of television in the Watts riots in its reporting of "inflammatory incidents" and had recommended that the press voluntarily withhold coverage of incendiary events until tensions had died down. According to this report, the press, especially television, had not acted as a responsible steward of the public but as entertainment that pro-vided dramatic and sensational coverage of events that inflamed passions on all sides.[24] As the McCone Report placed some of the blame for the race rebel-lions on television, it anticipated a common discourse of the time. Members of Congress, established journalists, and editors frequently opined that telecasts that featured trenchant criticism of racism in the United States, and not the racism itself, had delegitimized American institutions and fomented the riot-ing and looting that scarred cities across the nation.[25] For these critics, televi-sion was imagined to have sown the seeds of discord, irresponsibly stirring up illegitimate anger in its black viewers and alarm for its white viewers.

The Kerner Report fundamentally challenged this notion that irrespon-sible television broadcasts contributed to urban uprisings. In its analysis of television coverage of the rebellions in 1967—the largest of which took place in Newark and Detroit—the Kerner Commission concluded that television coverage had overcorrected. Newscasts of the rebellions were overly cautious and constrained, focused more on the efforts of law enforcement to quell the violence than on the underlying grievances of the rioters or the underlying causes that accounted for their discontent. Kerner found that television cov-erage greatly favored white interviewees over African Americans and tended to give the impression that the riots were racial confrontations between Afri-can Americans and whites rather than responses to the conditions of African American life in the city.[26] And as a result of its shifting its focus away from the reporting on the riots alone, and onto how the media operated, the Kerner Commission came to the conclusion that television broadcasters functioned as "instruments of the white power structure" (373).

As the Kerner Report summarized in its introduction to its discussion of the media, "The media report and write from the standpoint of a white man's world. The ills of the ghetto, the difficulties of life there, the Negro's burning sense of grievance, are seldom conveyed. Slights and indignities are part of the Negro's daily life, and many of them come from what he now calls 'the white press'—a press that repeatedly, if unconsciously, reflects the biases, the paternalism, the indifference of white America" (366). Kerner's contrast between "a white man's world," in which most institutions were controlled by white people, and "the Negro's daily life" of navigating these institutions was stark and framed the report's analysis of media. Not only was the "world that television and newspapers offer to their black audiences . . . almost totally white, in both appearance and attitude" (383), but the press consistently had imagined its viewership and readership as a white audience. African Americans were presented as subjects of news reports but not as community members who "read the newspapers or watch television, give birth, marry, die, and go to PTA meetings" (383). In its recommendations, the Kerner Report advised that television stations and newspapers hire African American journalists and editors and that they provide greater visibility to African Americans in all television programming, from newscasts and documentaries to advertisements and entertainment (384–386).

The Kerner Report's recommendations intervened in a political climate in which the Black Freedom Struggle was similarly coming to embrace an institutional analysis of racism and refiguring of desegregation as requiring black influence in, and in some cases control of, the institutions that structured their daily lives. The ascent of black power and black nationalism, along with public expressions of rage and outrage, presented a face for the movement on television very different from that of the well-dressed nonviolent protesters of the early 1960s. The primarily favorable national news coverage afforded southern civil rights campaigns did not translate to television's coverage of either the race rebellions, which often circulated what Aniko Bodroghkozy has described as the "angry, violence-prone ghetto black" who became a "familiar folk devil in the American visual and mental landscape," or to images of black power advocacy more broadly, its leaders frequently tarred as extremists and racists themselves for their views.[27] The Kerner Report reshifted the burden back onto the white power structure broadly and unveiled the complicity of the media industries in discarding African Americans as legitimate members of the civic body.

In the wake of the report, similar if not harsher critiques of television circulated, which indicted television as a part of the broader edifice of racial discrimination that rationalized and preserved the second-class status of African Americans. Richard Meyer, for example, evoked the Kerner Report when he chastised educational television for having done nothing to address the War on Poverty or ameliorate domestic social conditions, and he insisted that African Americans would see public broadcasting as part of the problem until its programming addressed their needs.[28] In a scathing article in *The Nation*, television critic John Horn insisted that the indictment of news broadcasts within the Kerner Report was far too narrow. Television operated, as Horn characterized it, as a "fifth column of bringing into Negro homes white nonsense, white violence, white affluence, white materialism, white indifference to fellow Americans of color," making television "a major alienating force" for "all racial minorities."[29]

Though the Kerner Report's recommendations for changes in media were largely directed at media companies and not at government, they unquestionably inspired policy makers to reexamine how media regulation and its implementation abetted or addressed racial discrimination. The Kerner Report not only engendered widespread deliberation over how the media perpetuate a racial caste system, but it contributed to a shift in the political environment that made it possible for the FCC to adopt policies to further ethnoracial diversity on the airwaves. In 1969 the FCC, in response to a United Church of Christ petition, adopted Equal Employment Opportunity (EEO) rules for broadcast licensees. In so doing, the commission stated that federal civil rights law (particularly Title VII of the 1964 Civil Rights Act, which outlawed employment discrimination) had changed the public interest obligations of broadcast licensees. Henceforth, licensees who discriminated in their employment practices would be considered in violation of the public interest. Importantly, the FCC's notice on the EEO rules appealed not just to the rationality of the principle of equal employment but to broadcasters' "conscience." Heavily citing the Kerner Report's findings, the FCC asserted that the nation is "confronted with a serious racial crisis" and that "the media can contribute greatly in many significant respects" to resolving that crisis.[30] The FCC's EEO rules, like early affirmative action plans devised by other branches of the federal government in the late 1960s, were thus presented as a form of crisis management that could forestall the development of black radicalism by integrating African Americans into the body politic, and broadcasters were encouraged to understand that the "nation requires a maximum effort in this vital undertaking."[31] To underscore the relationship between the urban crisis and the need to redefine the public interest obligations of broadcasters, the FCC sent a copy of the Kerner Report to all broadcasters along with a copy of its notice announcing the EEO rules.

Kerner's legacy extended well beyond the late 1960s. In the late 1970s, when the FCC adopted specific rules to enable people of color to own broadcasting stations, it began its statement of policy with reference to the Kerner Report and its role in instigating the commission's EEO rules.[32] The United States Commission on Civil Rights' 1977 important report on the status of women and minorities in television, *Window Dressing on the Set,* cited the Kerner Report as the "first major study" of how television perpetuated racial discrimination.[33] In 1990, when the Supreme Court ruled on the constitutionality of the FCC's minority ownership policies, it, too, cited Kerner and the report's warnings of the media's disregard for African American culture, thought, or history.[34] In the 1960s Kerner's indictment of broadcast media would structure how many stakeholders—audiences, FCC commissioners, broadcasters, critics—reinterpreted the public and the public interest.

Taken together, the courts' rulings in the WLBT case and the Kerner Report provided activists with a powerful basis to challenge the notion that the public interest was somehow divorced from addressing racial inequality or that there was a singular, general public for broadcast licensees. And as the FCC took steps to address these issues, through, for example, its EEO rules, a range of identity-based civil rights organizations began to submit a flurry of petitions to deny that demanded that the FCC hold local broadcasters to account to their diverse publics. What had begun in the early 1960s as a lone and improbable challenge to one of the most racist television stations in the South had evolved within a decade into a new broadcast reform movement that would redefine how government regulated the airwaves. The fate of one celebrated educational television network would attest to this transformation.

The Alabama Educational Television Network and the Broadcast Death Penalty Applied

During the 1960s the coalition politics of the noncommercial sector fractured over how to respond to the civil rights movement, the antiwar movement, and a growing counterculture. In 1958 John White had taken over leadership of the Educational Television and Radio Center (ETRC), a Ford Foundation–supported entity created in 1953 to produce and distribute programming to noncommercial stations. Local broadcasters collectively had been disappointed with the quality of the programming the ETRC circulated, considered by many to be "duller than dishwater."[35] Renamed first the National Educational Television and Radio Center (NETRC), then National Educational Television (NET), the organization was relocated to New York by White, who, with a new grant from the Ford Foundation, embarked on actively producing as well as distributing programming for educational television stations. White explicitly rejected the catch-as-catch-can approach to educational television that had marked the 1950s, and through NET he worked to transform the sector into a unified "fourth network"—one with a shared commitment to quality in programming and with shared philosophical goals regarding the role of noncommercial television in American life. In White's vision noncommercial television was to operate similarly as a commercial national network but would program controversial and compelling shows that commercial television shied away from.[36] Abandoning the instructional mission so central to many local stations, White transformed NET to circulate a wide range of public-affairs and cultural-affairs programs and to address hot-button topics like the Cuban revolution, the war in Vietnam, psychedelic drug use, homo-sexuality, poverty, and African American civil rights.[37]

Many people never saw NET's telecasts. Educational television stations responded to NET's commitment to controversial, exigent programming in a number of ways. First, stations frequently refused to air programming that they found objectionable or contrary to what they perceived to be the interests of their communities. In 1964 NET began to collect evaluations and patterns of use of its programming by affiliated stations. It found that while some stations carried all of its programming, "some southern stations refused civil rights programs and thereby provided the only discernible pattern of nonuse."[38] This pattern would recur throughout the decade. NET routinely surveyed its stations and found that broadcasters in Alabama, Arkansas, Virginia, South Carolina, Georgia, Florida, and elsewhere rejected its programming addressing civil rights.[39] But the South was not the only region where broadcasters refused to air NET programs. Many stations outside the South also rejected a wide range of NET programs, including some of its civil rights offerings, and many of its productions on other topics aside from civil rights were rejected by affiliated stations. For example, some stations refused to air NET programs on Fidel Castro and on North Vietnam.[40] When violence broke out in cities across the nation in the mid to late 1960s, increasing numbers of NET affiliates chose not to air programming addressing racial inequality.[41]

Although national noncommercial programming became increasingly invested in progressive political topics and themes, many local noncommercial stations stayed wedded to a more conservative vision of what television should provide. This fissure widened over the course of the 1960s, as NET programming became more brazen and station resistance more entrenched. In 1966 the South Carolina Educational Television network canceled its affiliation with NET, deeming its public affairs programming, especially in the arena of civil rights, unacceptable. In 1967 broadcasters from fourteen states in the South formed the Southern Educational Communications Association (SECA) both to coordinate regional broadcasters and to "achieve strength through numbers" in advocacy at the national level on behalf of the South.[42] One of SECA's initiatives included an effort to clean up the nationally circulating programming that offended the sensibilities of station managers and, presumably, their audiences.[43]

Tensions between the NET and local stations centered on conflicting understandings of what noncommercial television should do and what kind of citizenship it should promote. White's NET sought to "induce people to think critically about public issues, to provide information to them and instill in them the desire for more information, to provoke in them a new awareness, alertness, and responsibility."[44] Arguably many local stations sought to promote a sense of citizenship that was dutiful rather than questioning, to reinforce patriotism and shore up existing power relations. They used their stations not to challenge authority but to promote a public culture that in practice naturalized white supremacy, traditional conceptions of social mores, and American exceptionalism. Not coincidentally, southern stations that rejected NET programming often operated in communities that had substantial African American populations yet employed virtually no African Americans and offered little to no programming that included African Americans.

The release of the Kerner Report, coupled with the assassination of Martin Luther King in April 1968, functioned for NET and its producing stations as a call-to-arms of sorts to produce more programming focused on the lived experience of racial discrimination in the United States. Although white production teams produced the public affairs programming on racial discrimination circulated by NET in the earlier part of the decade, these later programs frequently were produced by and for African Americans. The public-affairs program *Black Journal*, which premiered in 1968, operated, as Tommy Lee Lott has illustrated, as a "corrective" to the images and ideas about black people, black culture, and black history circulating in the media.[45] *Soul!*, a public television show "dedicated to cultural expressions of the black freedom movement," similarly was produced and circulated in the wake of these events.[46] It would be these very kinds of programs—indeed, these programs themselves— that would be eliminated from the program schedules of stations like those in the Alabama Educational Television Network, which subsequently would lead local citizens to challenge its licenses on public interest grounds.

The challenge to the Alabama Educational Television Network's license became an important reproach to southern broadcasters' resistance to the social movements and cultural changes of the 1960s. Faculty and students at the University of Alabama and Catholic priest Eugene Farrell wrote letters to the FCC accusing the AETC of racial prejudice in its programming decisions. They encouraged the FCC to hold hearings on whether renewal of the AETC's licenses served the public interest. Included in these documents was a petition drafted by Judy Austin, signed by fifty-eight students and two professors at the University of Alabama, protesting that the AETC had censored programs with African American themes and perspectives.[47] In addition, in an inspired move, Father Farrell wrote a letter to Vice President Spiro Agnew, who in 1969 had railed against the mainstream press as a "tiny, enclosed fraternity of privileged men elected by no one."[48] In his letter Farrell brought the AETC's actions to Agnew's attention because of his "well known concern when just a few people control and manage the news and pretty well dictate to the rest of us what we are to see and hear."[49]

General Manager Raymond Hurlbert, who provided the AETC's official response to these charges, initially defended the AETC's programming decisions in two ways. He insisted that the priority of the AETC was local programming, and the abundance of locally produced shows limited the number of national programs the network could handle. In addition, the AETC had the responsibility of selecting shows "of the widest and most general interest" and that "lewd, vulgar, obscene, profane or repulsive material[s] have no place in the crowded AETC schedule."[50] The shows removed from the schedule, according to Hurlbert, fit into this category, and, he reasoned, it was well within the licensee's purview to reject them based on standards of taste and decency. However, Hurlbert only identified offending content contained in single episodes, even though the AETC had refused to air entire series. In addition, the accuracy in labeling some of the content as indecent was dubious. An offending episode of *Soul*, for example, was partly considered unacceptable because of a song critical of Vice President Agnew and Alabama governor George Wallace.[51]

In 1970 the FCC, in a 4–3 decision, voted against holding a hearing and renewed the AETC's eight licenses. The majority decision stated that the FCC was not concerned with matters of "licensee taste or judgment" and affirmed licensee discretion in programming decisions.[52] Commissioners Kenneth Cox and Nicholas Johnson issued strongly worded dissents, both maintaining that a hearing on the AETC had been warranted and expressing skepticism over the AETC's responses to the allegations. In his dissent Johnson warned that the commission had been down "this road before" when it renewed WLBT's license in the face of claims of racial discrimination, and he insisted that the commission needed to heed the warnings of the Kerner Commission.[53] Appalled that his colleagues refused to hold a hearing to learn about the performance of the AETC, Johnson summed up that the "FCC's undistinguished record in the area of race relations has not been improved by today's action."[54]

In July 1970 Farrell, Suitts, and Linda Edwards filed a petition for reconsideration, as did Tony Brown and William Wright. The first set of petitioners had participated in the initial license complaint. Suitts and Edwards both had been students at the University of Alabama and had been signatories on the Austin petition. Neither Brown nor Wright had been involved until they filed a petition for reconsideration, and neither resided in Alabama. Brown was a producer on *Black Journal*, a NET public-affairs program that routinely had been refused broadcast by the AETC, and a representative of the National Association of Black Media Producers. William Wright was a representative of Black Efforts for Soul in Television (BEST), a media advocacy group. BEST had formed in 1969 to advocate for minority media rights and had adopted a multipronged strategy—including filing license challenges, working with local communities on advocacy efforts, campaigning to defeat protectionist legislation for broadcasters, and lobbying for an African American commissioner on the FCC—to address the racism structuring television programming practices.[55] Acknowledging their unlikely ability to achieve standing in this case, Brown and Wright submitted the petition anyway, asserting that as black men they had an interest in the plight of their brethren in Alabama and that they wanted to "bring to the Commission the perspectives of blacks."[56]

Importantly, the petitions for reconsideration invoked civil rights law in addition to broadcast licensing law. Both petitions, for which the Citizens Communication Center acted as legal counsel, were sent to the Office of Civil Rights of the Department of Education in addition to the FCC. Although only the FCC had the power to renew or revoke licenses, the Education Department had been distributing federal monies to educational telecasters since the passage of the Educational Television Facilities Act. Title VI of the 1964 Civil Rights Act prohibited any program or activity that received federal funds to discriminate based on race, color, or national origin. By sending along the petitions for reconsideration, the parties involved hoped to demonstrate that the AETC, a past and prospective recipient of federal funds, may be in violation of this statute. In a similar vein Suitts sent a letter to Attorney General John Mitchell detailing how the AETC discriminated against African Americans, summarizing that "black people hold a nadir position" in the AETC's universe and that the "exclusion from broadcast by preemption or cancellation of programs which contain elementary matters of black power, Afro-American pride and enterprises and cultural experimentation is actuated regularly" by the AETC.[57]

The charges leveled against the AETC boiled down to three interrelated accusations. First, although 30 percent of Alabama's population was African American, the AETC neglected to telecast programs that meaningfully featured African Americans or that addressed African American concerns or perspectives. Not only had the AETC's locally produced programming not included participation or representations of African Americans, but the AETC refused to air national programming (via NET) when it was made available. Second, and a contributing factor to the programming problems, was that the AETC did not employ African Americans. An African American never had served on the commission, and the AETC did not consult with African Americans in Alabama to determine what their programming needs were. Finally, petitioners invoked both AETC's programming and hiring decisions to explain what they considered to be its public interest failure: its negligence in recognizing African Americans as significant members of the community that the Alabama stations were obligated to serve. In his letter to Agnew, echoing the conclusions of the Kerner Report, Farrell defined educational television in Alabama as the "media for White Supremacy."[58] The petitioners to the FCC finessed and expanded on Farrell's claim: "when the licensee of a noncommercial educational station consciously or unconsciously discriminates against blacks and demonstrates by a comprehensive and systematic exclusion of relevant programming a lack of any intention or desire to understand or to satisfy the educational or cultural needs of 30% of its viewing audience, a substantial and material question of fact as to whether renewal would serve the public interest is raised."[59]

Civil rights reformers' invocation of new laws that prohibited racial discrimination fundamentally changed the terms of debate over whether the AETC was meeting its public obligations. The AETC responded on procedural grounds to the petitioners, but the bulk of its response addressed the substance of the complaints and focused on defending the network from accusations that it was racist.[60] It insisted that it had taken all steps to "achieve the maximum educational benefits from television for the children of all races in the state" in both its locally produced and in national programming.[61] Repeating the defenses it had made to the original complaints, the AETC stated that it had "been presenting educational programming for, involving, and including blacks for considerably longer than NET" and that this can be done with "decency and good taste."[62] The AETC bolstered its evaluation of NET programming with evidence that other stations also refused to broadcast its shows on indecency grounds. In part to support the AETC, as well as defend its affiliates from similar complaints, SECA even adopted a resolution in 1970 that claimed that NET programs had offended both FCC and commonsense standards of decency and good taste, and it petitioned the newly formed Public Broadcasting System (PBS) to adopt a code of standards analogous to the National Association of Broadcaster's code for commercial stations.[63] In this the AETC and SECA drew on a long-standing strategy of using charges of indecency as cover for decisions that were, in fact, racially motivated.[64]

The AETC response to the civil rights movement challenge described the network itself as a victim of discrimination. It suggested that long-standing educational stations were being victimized by the pressure placed on them to telecast NET programming that they found objectionable. Identifying the AETC as the target of harassment, the petition also claimed that it was the action of the petitioners, not the broadcasters, that constituted the "true threat of censorship."[65] In addition, the AETC suggested that it was the petitioners, not the AETC, who posed the true obstacles to racial justice—and in the process it implicitly dismissed the perspective of the Kerner Report on race and media in the United States. According to the AETC, the petitioners' "entire presentation is based on the concept that there are two Americas, one white and one black, and that no bridge is to be built between them. The AETC rejects that concept, as must all thinking Americans."[66] In this the AETC evoked, and rejected, the central finding of the Kerner Report—that "our nation is moving toward two societies, one black, one white—separate and unequal."[67] It furthermore labeled some of the material in *Black Journal*, the flagship black public affairs program distributed by NET,[68] as not educational or cultural, but sometimes revolutionary, radical, and "racist in nature," as could be understood if one considered what the reaction would be for a *White Journal* program.[69] The AETC concluded that, as a licensee with an "extraordinary record of achievement," it was the victim of an attack intended to rob licensees of the ability to use "taste and judgment" in programming decisions.[70] If, for the petitioners, this case was about racial discrimination, for the AETC it was about the speech protections to be afforded to broadcast licensees to determine how to serve their communities.

Alabama's white establishment firmly supported the AETC and defended it against its critics by similarly portraying themselves as victims of civil rights law. When in 1972, in response to the petition, the FCC rescinded its renewal of the AETC's licenses and ordered hearings to determine whether the AETC had practiced racial discrimination,[71] Alabama's political and educational leaders reacted by tarring the character of the petitioners. They dismissed the petitioners as "small pressure groups" or subversive elements hell-bent on harassing decent public servants. The AETC and its allies also surmised that outside agitator elements had conspired with local malcontents like Suitts to stir up trouble. As Hurlbert wrote to Governor Albert Brewer in 1970, "the subversive groups involved know no limits in their attempt to persecute the Alabama operation."[72] Representative John Buchanan echoed this sentiment and dismissed the complaints against the AETC as the work of groups in New York and Washington who wanted to take away local discretionary power over programming and impose their own sensibilities on the nation.[73] Similarly, Senator James Allen was "completely convinced that continued harassment is the sole purpose" behind the petition and that "the time is ripe for an investigation to determine whether or not a pattern of harassment has been established and if so, by whom and for what purpose."[74] In addition, rumors circulated that the Nixon White House had pressured the FCC into its decision in order to embarrass Alabama governor George Wallace, perceived at the time as a credible political threat to Nixon.[75]

Yet despite adopting the rhetoric of massive resistance, the AETC changed its practices in response to the legal threat to its licenses. To the consternation of some of its viewers, the AETC telecast NET series including *Black Journal*. The commission previewed individual episodes and, as long as they did not include offensive material, would air them the following week. In 1971 the AETC conducted a survey of five hundred African Americans to get a better sense of their programming needs. In addition, the AETC contracted with Alabama A&M, a historically black college, as one of its programming centers. It also developed minority-oriented programming that, for example, presented highlights from the state's historically black colleges or demonstrated "harmony and cooperation between races in all phases of community life."[76] In addition, the AETC hired African Americans to its staff, and when Leslie Wright's position on the AETC opened, Governor Wallace appointed Dr. Harold N. Stinson, an African American professor at Stillman University, as the first black AETC commissioner.[77] As was clear from the press coverage at the time, the pending decision on the AETC's licenses, coupled with the accusations of racial discrimination, played an important role in Wallace's decision.[78]

But these reform efforts were too little too late. The FCC concluded that the underrepresentation of African Americans onscreen and as participants in the decision-making process "constitutes persuasive evidence that racially discriminatory policies permeated AETC's programming practices."[79] While the FCC conceded that the needs of minorities could be met with a wide range of programming, it determined that only serving the "general interest" was not good enough. It stated that "a licensee cannot with impunity ignore the problems of significant minorities in its service area."[80] The decision tied the programming omissions to the AETC's practices in the 1960s, a period in which there were no black commissioners on the AETC, the production centers were located at predominantly white institutions, and no African Americans served on the State Department of Education's curriculum committee, which coordinated the AETC's in-school instruction materials.

While, as Suitts presumed, the commission's decision may have stemmed from its outrage at the AETC's past performance, many others interpreted the ruling as a northern assault on southern stations, as a discriminatory action by a federal agency holding southern states to standards different from those of the rest of the nation. If conservative southerners responded to the coverage of civil rights activism on national newscasts in the 1960s as evidence of a "liberal media" bias,[81] one that misrepresented the actualities of race relations in their communities, the AETC license revocation inspired similar critiques of the FCC, tarred as a "small group of men in Washington" going to "absurd and harmful extremes" to protect the civil rights of minorities,[82] its actions an "example of unbelievably vast bureaucratic stupidity and misuse of power."[83] Senator Allen attacked the FCC as arrogant "non-elected Federal bureaucrats," the petitioners themselves a "small vengeful group" acting out of "malicious intent."[84]

The *Montgomery Advertiser* perhaps summed up this perspective best when it issued an editorial entitled "Carpetbagger Justice," which asked, "If discrimination is as intolerable as our brothers north of the line would have us believe, why, then was Alabama's public television network discriminated against?" Conceding that the "racial 'balance,' if you will, at AETV was tilted towards whites in its early years," the editorial asserted that the imbalance had been corrected. Given the improvements, the editors surmised that to continue "this ridiculous suit ... smacks of harassment and malice."[85] In defending the AETC against racial discrimination, Alabamians deployed a framework that long had been utilized by segregationists, which deflected attention off of the misdeeds of the state and onto the ostensible overreach of the federal government. They inverted who constituted the injured party, essentially dismissing complaints of racial discrimination and instead asserting that it was the AETC and its viewers, not the state's African Americans, who had been harmed.

In practice the AETC's fall was short-lived. While, under ordinary circumstances, an "ordinary person" that had licenses revoked would have to wait to apply for a license to broadcast, the commission deemed the AETC, as an agency of the state of Alabama, not ordinary; in addition, the commission determined that the strides the AETC had made after the petitions had been filed demonstrated that "it has the capacity to change its ways" and thus held the "requisite character qualifications" to be a licensee.[86] The AETC reapplied for, and was granted, licenses to operate the stations of the Alabama Educational Television Network. In order to ward off a competing application for the licenses, the AETC had negotiated an agreement with Suitts and other civil rights activists, in which the AETC committed to programming and hiring goals in exchange for a commitment that another entity would not compete for the licenses.[87]

Yet in its 1975 decision the FCC did not just revoke the AETC's license. In response to public pressure it redefined the standards through which all broadcasters might be held accountable to the audiences they are supposed to serve. When the petitioners challenged, and the FCC revoked, the AETC's broadcasting licenses, they upended the racial logics of the AETC's governance and the subordinated position of African Americans in its construction of the Alabama citizenry. No longer could the "public" be plausibly conceived as singular and undifferentiated. After WLBT, Kerner, and the AETC, broadcasters would have to contend with a diversity of both publics and their interests.

From Techno-utopianism to Demands for Power

Television, in both media scholarship and histories of the civil rights movement, has long been positioned as a liberatory technology, one that focuses its "glaring light," in the words of Martin Luther King Jr., on southern racism. Civil rights leaders quickly appreciated the power of television and planned their campaigns around sites and individuals that would yield good televisual stories. As audiences witnessed mob violence to prevent the desegregation of the University of Mississippi, police attacks on nonviolent marchers on the Edmund Pettus Bridge, and fire hoses and police dogs assaulting African American protestors in Birmingham, they witnessed the spectacular violence of southern racism and the horrific uses of local power to maintain Jim Crow conditions.

When scholars have turned to noncommercial television's relationship with the Black Freedom Struggle, they similarly have positioned it in celebratory terms. Focusing on African American public affairs programs that circulated locally and nationally in the late 1960s and 1970s, media scholars have emphasized how these programs often put creative control in the hands of African

American producers and enabled a momentary construction of a black counterpublic sphere on TV, one that challenged prevailing representations of African Americans on commercial networks.[88]

But while television coverage unquestionably did shape the Black Freedom Movement, it would be a mistake to simply treat its effect as supportive. As Aniko Bodroghkozy has shown, national television coverage of the southern campaigns constructed morality tales out of local circumstances by presenting narratives that reflected the ideological assumptions of the journalist class reporting on them and, in essence, fitting the black freedom struggle within frames that would make it less intimidating for white audiences.[89] In addition, as is visible in the media advocacy of civil rights activists of the time, the Black Freedom Movement came to critique both commercial and noncommercial television as technologies of white supremacy.

Both the Black Freedom Movement and broadcast policy makers changed through their engagement with each other. Policy makers came to see changes in media regulation and in the implementation of existing policies were needed to rectify how television operated, who had access to it, and how its publics would be imagined. And Black Freedom Movement activists came to see media ownership and regulation as essential to challenging white supremacy. Other social movements, in turn, would see their own struggles intertwined with broadcast policy making as well.

3

Feminists in the
Wasteland Fight Back

///

The National Organization for
Women and Media Reform

Since its founding in 1966, the National Organization for Women (NOW) has identified changing the "image of women in the mass media" as one of its primary goals. NOW reasoned that gender equality would be unrealizable if demeaning images of women continued to circulate on television and movie screens, in song lyrics and advertising copy. How could women be seen as fully capable members of the body politic if the dominant archetypes of them in the media were, in the words of NOW's New York chapter president Jean Faust, of "Helpless Helen," "Flossie the Floozie," "Betty Coed," "Evil Eve," or "Safari Sally"?[1] Throughout the 1960s and 1970s NOW's national office and local chapters fought what they saw as dangerous images of women in popular media, using multiple strategies, including consumer boycotts, letter-writing campaigns, nascent forms of culture jamming, and public conferences on women in the media. NOW's members, for example, held an action day at public broadcasting stations to protest sexist stereotypes on *Sesame Street*;[2] ran feminist public service announcement ads that upended conventional advertising frameworks;[3] gave out "Barefoot and Pregnant" awards to ad agencies and media companies that perpetuated arcane images of women;[4] and participated in a letter-writing campaign to get *3's a Crowd*, a game show that pitted wives against secretaries in a competition of who knew "her" man best, off the air.[5] Gender equality, for NOW, hinged on reconceptualizing how women were imagined in popular media.

Changing the content of programming also hinged on media advocacy. And in this regard NOW's media reform advocacy played a key role in the broadcast reform movement. Throughout the 1970s, NOW chapters filed petitions to deny license renewal to local broadcast stations it accused of discriminating against women in program content and station employment. These license challenges required presenting a new analysis of what constituted the public interest of media regulation. NOW sought to reveal how seemingly gender neutral regulatory policies were imbricated with the maintenance of gender inequality. To do so required policy makers to see women as a distinct class of rights-bearing citizens who, in the past, had been sidelined or ignored in how broadcasters and regulators had defined the "public." At stake in NOW's media advocacy work, in other words, was not just whether *Sesame Street*'s Big Bird disavowed traditional gender roles but a reconceptualization of the "public interest" attentive to the existence of a diversity of publics, especially women.

NOW's fight against discrimination in broadcasting, and its promotion of a distinctly feminist perspective of media regulation, drew heavily from both the legal and cultural innovations of the Black Freedom Struggle in the 1960s and 1970s. NOW's media advocacy was one of many arenas in which the organization, in Serena Mayeri's phrase, "reasoned from race," or drew analogies—and often equivalences—between sexism and racism.[6] As the role of the media in perpetuating racism became part of public dialogue and informed regulatory decisions, and because claims of gender discrimination and sexist stereotyping were often dismissed or ridiculed as trivial, NOW reasoned from race in its media advocacy to make claims of sexism legible to people who took racism seriously but doubted the existence of sexism. In the process the organization sought to elevate the stature of women's civil rights claims—legally, politically, and culturally—to those made by African Americans.

NOW's rhetoric of contrasting the discrimination faced by women with the discrimination faced by African Americans was a common political tactic during what John Skrentny has labeled the "minority rights revolution" of the late 1960s and early 1970s. During this era, he argues, the provision of both antidiscrimination protections and affirmative laws to promote equality of opportunity to, in the parlance of the day, "disadvantaged groups"—defined by identity, not by income or education—hinged on the ability of policy makers and legislators to see them, or their claims of injury, as analogous to those of African Americans.[7]

If NOW's media advocacy drew questionable but strategic comparisons between the experiences of women and African Americans, it also increasingly provided a means through which NOW put itself in solidarity with civil rights organizations as part of a broader fight for a more democratic media. Both feminists and civil rights activists had to gain literacy in the vagaries of American broadcast regulation and in critical analysis of broadcast programming. And both had to push back against conservative forces, both in the FCC and in Congress, that sought to protect broadcasters from the broadcast reform movement and the reconstitution of the licensees' public interest obligations at its center.

Scholars have long identified the import of television to second-wave feminism. They have noted the derision and ridicule through which news anchors discussed the women's movement, as well as how leaders of second-wave organizations, in order to gain more favorable coverage, increasingly contained the ambitions of feminism to mainstream and palatable issues like equal employment and equal pay, eliding the movement's more trenchant critiques of patriarchy and gender roles. They also have interrogated how individual television shows reflected and popularized, while also sanitizing and domesticating, feminism and have investigated how the sexual culture of the 1970s permeated prime-time programming, often fusing sexual liberation with sexual objectification.[8] While, to be sure, NOW's media activism frequently targeted individual shows—from its attacks on *3's a Crowd* to its determined support of the 1972 episode of *Maude* in which the titular character decides to terminate a pregnancy—its media advocacy focused on television as an institution and routinely drew attention to the cumulative impact of the programming day on social perceptions of gender.[9]

This chapter's study of NOW's media advocacy in the 1970s thus reconfigures the relationship between feminism and television in two ways. First, it expands our understanding of the repertoires and strategies that women used to reform broadcasting practices. To be sure, women and women's organizations had been involved in media reform well before and after NOW filed its first petition to deny in 1972. As Kathy Newman has demonstrated, for example, female radio listeners in the 1930s and 1940s were "radio active," engaged in shaping the kinds of programming on the airwaves by exerting consumer pressure on sponsors and stations.[10] Women also had participated in listener councils to monitor early radio programming.[11] This activism was consistent with how women had been configured in relationship to broadcasting—primarily as consumers of its programming and of the goods that its sponsors peddled. Women's capacities to effect change thus have been seen as tied to their close identification with consumerism and their strategic use of their economic power. NOW's advocacy departed from these strategies by invoking the law to position women as citizens, not consumers; as members of the public, not as audiences to sell to advertisers; as a group whose rights against discrimination had to be incorporated into a new civic vision for media regulation and democracy.

Second, the history of NOW's advocacy enables us to see the relationship between television and second-wave feminism as focused on the business and technology of media. Image problems were structural problems—ones that could not be addressed by individual prime-time series or a scattering of "special reports" on the women's movement. For NOW, to bring television in line with feminist goals was to illuminate for broadcasters and regulators how their current practices impeded them. Challenging local broadcasters' licenses became a crucial means to do this.

Race, Gender, and License Renewal Challenges

Before television could be seen as a tool of sexism, it had to be recognized as a technology of white supremacy. NOW's media advocacy, much like that of other social movement organizations at the time, was facilitated by the struggles of civil rights activists to address racism in broadcasting practices and in broadcast regulation. For liberal feminist groups like NOW, license renewal challenges pioneered by the Black Freedom Movement were critical to its broader campaign for women's equality and empowerment. And the legitimacy conferred on African American claims of discrimination would provide the inspiration and roadmap for NOW's advocacy, as well as the wellspring of oft-troubling comparisons between the experience of women and the experience of African Americans.

NOW formed in 1966 as an "NAACP for women."[12] It sought legal and legislative reform to engender women's full equality as citizens. Most directly, NOW was formed by professional women, many of whom were serving on state commissions on the status of women, who were frustrated by the Equal Employment Opportunity Commission's (EEOC) lack of interest in investigating sex discrimination claims that it received. At a June 1966 meeting of the state commissions, delegates tried to pass a resolution to demand that the EEOC act, but leaders of the conference, insisting that its purpose was to share information rather than pursue action, would not allow the motion to come to the floor and be voted on. Furious and embattled, women met in Betty Friedan's hotel room with the idea to start a women's civil rights organization.[13]

Friedan, who was at the time perhaps the most prominent member of a burgeoning women's movement after the publication of her 1963 *The Feminine Mystique*, would become NOW's first president and would pen its Statement of Purpose, adopted at NOW's first meeting in October 1966. By 1967 NOW had ten local chapters; by 1971 it had more than 150 chapters and had achieved prominence as the preeminent mainstream feminist organization in the United States.[14] Though NOW would continue to evolve and adapt, both to the political commitments of its members and to the broader sociopolitical context in which it operated, at its core was a liberal vision of gender equality that was predicated on the assumption that American institutions could work if reformed to be more inclusive of women and responsive to women's needs.

By calling itself an "NAACP for women," NOW signaled its complex and evolving relationship with civil rights organizations, as well as its reliance on an analogy between racism and sexism to make its claims of discrimination legible and credible. If, as Patricia Bradley has argued, this analogy did little to ingratiate NOW to women of color, as its comparison often was premised on a presumed *white* woman and an African American *man*, it also, as Mayeri has argued, was often an expression of how racial and gender inequality were intertwined.[15] The analogy was pioneered by NOW cofounders Pauli Murray, an African American woman, and Mary Eastwood, a white woman, in an article that publicly made the case for the race-sex analogy. They argued that comparing women's rights to civil rights would both make gender discrimination comprehensible and foreground the *intersectionality*, though the term would not come into usage until much later, between race and gender.[16]

Feminist legal strategies by groups like NOW, as Mayeri has uncovered, often intended to address the double burden of women of color, who faced gender and racial discrimination, though federal courts routinely insisted on uncoupling race discrimination from sex discrimination. In addition, Mayeri illustrates that the analogy often enabled important coalitions across feminist and civil rights organizations, and women of color frequently found common cause with, and participated in, feminist organizations like NOW, themselves drawing connections between the racism and the sexism that they experienced. African American congresswoman Shirley Chisholm, testifying in 1970 in support of extending antidiscrimination law in higher education to women, exemplified how women of color themselves drew analogies between racism and sexism: "Blacks and women have both been taught from childhood, because our society is run by and for white males, that they are inherently inferior." Both, according to Chisholm, had been assigned the same characteristics: "that they are more childish, emotional, and irresponsible" than white men, and of "lower intelligence, that they need protection, and they are happiest in routine, undemanding jobs, and that they lack ambition and executive ability."[17] Thus the politics of the analogy was contextual, hinging on whether the person making it sought to underline or erase the intersections between gender and race in the distribution of power and resources to citizens.

The race-sex analogy, furthermore, was key to how women's liberation often was framed within the mainstream press. As Bonnie Dow has illustrated, comparisons between feminism and the Black Freedom Struggle structured a good deal of print and television coverage of the women's liberation movement. The analogy was used either to render the positions of feminists as trivial in contrast to the more substantive claims of civil rights activists or to legitimate especially liberal feminists' fights for equality of opportunity through an analogy to similar battles fought by African Americans. Importantly, as Dow stresses, as network newscasts drew parallels between sexism and racism, they also routinely erased the visibility of women of color who participated in second-wave feminist activism, presenting white women overwhelmingly as the face of the movement.[18]

In the realm of broadcasting policy, much like with NOW's efforts in combating employment discrimination, the race-sex analogy operated as a strategic tactic to draw on existing precedent, to make sexism legible to the FCC, and, importantly, to persuade the commission that women constituted a distinct class that had been injured historically by discrimination and whose treatment at the hands of broadcasters had contributed to their denial of full citizenship rights. But this argument could also downplay the continued discrimination faced by African Americans. That is, as NOW drew comparisons between racism and sexism, it also at times presumed racism in broadcasting was of the past, while sexism was of urgent concern in the present. Thus it not only drew equivalences but sometimes suggested that sexism was as pressing a social justice issue, if not more so, than racism.

NOW's New York chapter's petition to deny against WABC-TV and its D.C. area chapters' petition to deny against WRC-TV marked the organization's first attempts to connect redefining the public interest in broadcasting regulation to challenging sexism in television. Both NOW chapters had been active in media reform activity since their founding. But because of its geographic proximity to corporate offices and advertising agencies, the New York chapter was the locus of NOW's initial challenges to degrading images of women circulating in the culture industries. In February 1967 the New York chapter formed the "Image of Women" task force under the leadership of Pat Trainor to challenge negative depictions of women. Its principal goals were to identify campaigns for immediate action and to conduct research on the history and current status and sociological effects of popular representations of women. Many of the initial members of this task force were women who worked in advertising and journalism or were academics in fields like sociology interested in sex-role stereotyping.[19]

In addition to conducting extensive monitoring campaigns of advertisements and television channels, the New York chapter's Image of Women Committee participated in a wide range of campaigns. These included filing petitions to local newspapers to desegregate their job ads along gender lines, hosting conferences on women's representation in popular media, making presentations to and attending meetings with advertising agency executives on sexism in advertising, and challenging local newspapers' coverage of the women's movement.[20] This committee also participated with other NOW chapters in a protest against National Airlines' infamous "Fly Me" print ad campaign—which had featured photos of National flight attendants, above which was copy that read "I'm [name]. Fly Me"—and orchestrated a protest against the promotion of feminine hygiene sprays.[21] While their methods of protest were diverse, their ultimate goal, according to a 1967 mission statement, was to improve women's image "by all the forms of protest and pressure on networks, advertisers and editors which have been effective in abolishing the stereotyped images of Negroes and Jews."[22] Although both Jews and African Americans likely would have disagreed that derogatory images of them had been abolished by 1967, the framing of the committee's mission spoke to how NOW's New York chapter sought to establish equivalencies between sex discrimination and already-acknowledged forms of oppression, how they attached those equivalencies to progress narratives for U.S. history, and how the work of race and ethnic civil rights groups served as their model for their media advocacy.

The New York chapter selected WABC, an ABC network flagship station, for a license renewal challenge at the end of 1970 for a number of reasons. By choosing a network-owned and -operated station, the organization took aim at one of the most powerful stations in the country. Though NOW sought to transform the television industry, it was constrained by the doctrine of localism that undergirds broadcast regulation and judiciously chose stations like WABC, against which challenges could make the greatest impact.[23] In addition, as Deborah Biele, the head of the New York chapter's Image Committee, remarked, all of the committee members were unanimously in favor of challenging WABC's license because Roger Grimsby, the anchor of *WABC News*, "infuriated every woman on the committee." Grimsby had made a habit of making dismissive and offensive comments about the women's movement. He referred to the nationwide Women Strike for Equality day as an "item of trivia," focused his report on the march in New York on images of women's legs and miniskirts, and featured interviews with women who, by a four-to-one margin, disapproved of the ambitions of the women's movement.[24]

Like the members of the New York chapter, feminists in D.C.-area NOW chapters targeted images of women in the media early on as a site of local activism.[25] Although they engaged in myriad forms of protest, from petitioning newspapers to end sex-segregated job advertisements to participating in feminist film festivals, the primary focus of their media efforts was monitoring the programming of local TV stations. Beginning in 1971, under the leadership of Whitney Adams, the D.C.-area chapters started monitoring the programming and advertisements on local stations to accrue data on gender roles onscreen. In November 1971 Adams drew on these studies in her testimony before the Federal Trade Commission when arguing about the destructive impact of television ads on women's well-being. In addition, the findings of the monitoring studies became starting points for discussions with local broadcasters. On August 31, 1972, NOW filed a petition to deny against WRC, an NBC station chosen because it was deemed the most sexist of all the stations in the D.C. area.[26] The WRC petition was filed on behalf of four NOW chapters, four political caucus groups, the local Women's Equity Action League (WEAL) chapter, and the D.C. chapter of Federally Employed Women (FEW).

In assembling their petitions to deny, the NOW chapters drew on a model proposed by feminist attorney Nancy Stanley in her 1971 law review article

"Federal Communications Law and Women's Rights: Women in the Waste-land Fight Back."[27] Her title, though drawing on Newton Minow's famous admonishment of television as a "vast wasteland," offered an alternative under-standing of television to Minow's address.[28] Minow had been concerned, while serving as chair of the FCC under President Kennedy, that television program-ming was escapist rather than engaged with the events of the world, that it was formulaic and dull rather than of high aesthetic quality, and that it appealed to its audiences' frivolous tastes rather than provoking them toward greater knowledge and insight. But Stanley and other feminist media advocates of the 1970s were concerned with television's myopia regarding its depiction of women in its entertainment programming and its disregard for the goals and achievements of the women's movement in its news and public affairs. Stan-ley and NOW's emphasis was not on the corrupting influence of commer-cialism but of an unchecked sexism. In her article Stanley provided practical guidance to feminists seeking to reform television station practices and set the rhetorical terms by which NOW chapters would make the case that "televi-sion discriminates against women" and that this discrimination was "at least as damaging to women as discrimination in employment."[29] She suggested that feminists could claim that broadcasters had not met their public inter-est obligations by demonstrating their failures to adhere to the equal employ-ment opportunity (EEO) rules, ascertainment requirements, and the Fairness Doctrine. The New York and D.C. NOW chapters hewed to this model, mak-ing the case that WABC and WRC had discriminated against women in all three areas. In addition, Stanley consistently "reasoned from race" and, accord-ingly, instructed potential feminist media reformers to see analogies between the treatment of racial minorities and women and to use these comparisons to make the moral and legal case for women's media rights.

Changes to the FCC's EEO rules, originally created in response to civil rights movement pressure, marked the first substantial broadcast reform vic-tory for NOW. In 1971 NOW successfully petitioned the FCC to include "sex" in its equal employment antidiscrimination rules and "women" as tar-gets for affirmative employment programs; beginning in February 1972, all licensees would have to devise affirmative programs to hire, train, and promote women.[30] As Stanley suggested, however, enforcing its prohibition against sex discrimination likely would not be a high priority for the FCC, and it would be up to feminists to push for compliance and to demonstrate the relationship between women's employment in the broadcast industry and women's fight for equality. "Women, like blacks and other minorities, are crippled by their lack of influence at the policy-making levels of society," noted Stanley. "Reduc-ing discrimination in the broadcast industry will lead to better programming, to greater understanding of the historical traditions which have oppressed women, and hopefully, to the end of invidious sex discrimination in American life in general."[31] The EEO rules were thus critical not only for material but also symbolic reasons. They would guarantee not only women's access to jobs but also their ability to redress the representational practices that had legitimated discrimination against women in the first place.

Ascertainment, adopted in 1960, required broadcasters to consult with their communities of service to determine the key issues of public concern within their broadcast area. Broadcasters were to conduct a general survey of their public and to meet with community leaders to learn about the pressing interests of their audience. The ascertainment process was then to inform the station's prospective programming and was to shape how it understood the public interest in relation to its programming priorities. Feminist groups, according to Stanley, needed to assert that women constitute a discrete group whose interests could be ascertained, because "discriminatory treatment has given them interests and problems in common."[32] The identification of women as a class, and of their unitary set of interests, went hand in glove. But from Stanley's perspective, for the purposes of ascertainment, not all female leaders were equally capable of speaking to the needs of women as a class. Stations, Stanley argued, must seek out women who are involved in feminist organizations and could thus speak to *women's interests* and address areas in "which women are asserting their legal, economic or moral rights as a class."[33] Similarly, she argued, they should avoid what she called "Aunt Toms"—a term used at this time not only by Stanley but by Betty Friedan to describe a woman who by refusing to acknowledge and fight for women's issues is seen as abetting and contributing to her own subordination rather than working to dismantle it.[34]

Perhaps Stanley's most creative recommendation that NOW drew from was her expansive definition of the Fairness Doctrine. FCC precedent had affirmed that on-air attacks of particular groups or discussions of civil rights issues raised issues of public import and thus were subject to Fairness Doctrine requirements. According to Stanley, if the FCC had decided that "an unbalanced presentation of opinion about black or Jewish members of the community is unacceptable, so too is an unbalanced expression of opinion about women." In this Stanley's interpretation of the Fairness Doctrine was consistent with how the FCC had interpreted it, yet she sought to expand the scope of Fairness Doctrine complaints to include discussions of the women's movement. Prohibited practices might include "editorializing against the admission of women to an all-male state university, distorting national news about the Equal Rights Amendment, or trying to discredit the women's movement by calling the participants lesbians or bra-burners."[35] While newscasters may have seen the women's movement as frivolous or wrongheaded, it was in fact a legitimate issue of concern, according to Stanley, and one that should afford its advocates a right to defend themselves and their actions in the face of the dismissive comments made against them on air.

Stanley innovated in expanding on FCC decisions that had applied the Fairness Doctrine to programming other than news or public affairs discussions.

The commission had conceded in the 1960s that smoking advertisements promoted one side of a controversial issue—that smoking was harmless—and thus stations that aired them had to make time for opposing viewpoints. When environmentalists tried to level a similar Fairness Doctrine charge against car and gasoline commercials, the FCC denied their petition, fearful that it would set a precedent in which broadcasters would be deluged with airtime requests to counter claims made by the sponsors on their stations. In 1971 a federal appellate court remanded the FCC's decision, scolding the commission for its protectionist stance toward the industry it regulates and highlighting the congruities between antismoking activists and environmentalists in their interpretation of the Fairness Doctrine. Building on these recent decisions, Stanley encouraged feminists to define women's role in society as a controversial issue and to argue that a station's overall programming—inclusive of its entertainment shows and advertisements—constituted one position in this controversy. Consistent representational practices that offered a particular, and particularly offensive, depiction of women and their capabilities, for Stanley, constituted a discussion to which stations owed feminists time to respond.[36]

In the WABC and WRC petitions to deny, NOW's chapters put Stanley's ideas into practice. Doing so required the practical work of monitoring station programming to make credible claims about Fairness Doctrine violations and reviewing station public files to assess their ascertainment and employment records. After consulting with Carol Jennings, who had worked with the United Church of Christ on a monitoring study to document racial discrimination, and with Whitney Adams, the chair of NOW's National FCC Task Force, the New York chapter began its monitoring of WABC's programming. For two weeks in 1971, more than one hundred volunteers monitored WABC's programming. During those two weeks the apartment of Sandee Cohen became a "communications headquarters" of sorts, as volunteers came in for their shifts and took copious notes on color-coded monitoring forms about representations of men and women on all forms of programming and advertisements. Deborah Biele and two other members of the Image Committee then compiled and analyzed the results, after which they consulted with three attorneys at the Center for Constitutional Rights in New York, who agreed to take on the case for free. In addition to the monitoring study, the New York NOW chapter and its lawyers inspected the station's public files and renewal application in preparation for its license challenge.[37]

The WRC monitoring study in D.C., conducted under the guidance of sociologist Muriel Cantor, was far more extensive than that for WABC. It was divided into two parts—one on a wide range of programming (news, advertisements, talk shows, children's programs, dramatic programs, variety shows, quiz shows) and one specifically focused on news and public-affairs programming. Based on this study, the petitioners made claims of Fairness Doctrine violations based on specific instances when the station failed to cover newsworthy events, and they provided hard statistics on how women and their interests fared in both entertainment and news programming. For example, out of 4,179 minutes of monitored news programming, 12.5 minutes of the station's coverage, or three-tenths of 1 percent, pertained to women's rights or the issues of concern to women as a group. In addition, stories that composed those 12.5 minutes "were treated in ridiculing fashion and usually appeared as a humorous anecdote at the end of a program."[38]

Highlighting their debt to Stanley's law review article, the NOW National Capital Area Chapters published the monitoring study with the title *Women in the Wasteland Fight Back*. Its epigraph was from John Lennon and Yoko Ono's song "Woman Is the Nigger of the World," released only a few months before the completion of the monitoring study and to much controversy.[39] The epigraph read:

> Woman is the nigger of the world . . .
> We insult her every day on T.V.
> And wonder why she has no guts or confidence
> When she's young we kill her will to be free . . .
> Woman is the nigger of the world

Very few radio stations were willing to air the song, as station managers worried that their listeners would find the title and the lyrics offensive. Lennon and Ono performed the song on the *Dick Cavett Show* in the summer of 1972, with Lennon offering an introduction in which he justified both his use of the racial epithet and the sentiment expressed in the song itself. Cavett himself provided, in his words, a "mealy-mouthed" disclaimer to his ABC audience before airing the segment of the show in which the song was performed. The song, whose title and sentiment came from a 1969 interview that Ono had given to *Nova* magazine, made the case that women were the most oppressed group in the world and that within oppressed groups themselves women were the most mistreated and relegated to the lowest status rung.[40] NOW, a big advocate of the song, had given it an award in August of 1972.[41] And while the inclusion of the epigraph in *Women in the Wasteland Fight Back* underlined its support of the song, it also was one of the more bald instances of NOW's elevation of sexism over racism. Its reasoning from race in this case not only served a means to express an equivalence between racism and sexism; it also suggested that women had had it harder than African Americans and entirely glossed over the experiences of women for whom the application of this pernicious racial epithet was not merely metaphorical.

Both petitions to deny charted NOW's accusations regarding the stations' compliance with policies on ascertainment, equal employment, and the Fairness Doctrine. The WRC petition had the advantage of being filed on the heels of a formal complaint submitted to the EEOC by twenty-seven female employees against NBC/WRC-TV. In November 1971, a little less than a year before the license challenge was filed, the EEOC issued a finding of fact on the case that corroborated the reasonability of its discrimination claims. The EEOC's finding was based on large discrepancies in earnings between male and female employees at the station and the restriction of upper division and managerial jobs to men.[42] The EEOC also was investigating accusations that the station had intentionally blocked women's access to sales jobs, which often functioned as entry into management positions, and had made retaliatory threats against female employees involved in a women's rights committee. The WRC petition supplemented the EEOC complaint with claims that the station's maternity policy was discriminatory; that it had maneuvered to restrict high-status positions for men; and that the station's affirmative action policy was overly vague, did not meet the commission's requirements, and was not tailored to its local community but rather was to encompass all network stations. The New York chapter's petition against WABC made similar claims about that station's affirmative action policy and offered evidence of stark underemployment of women broadly, especially in professional, managerial, or technical positions—if a woman was employed by WABC, she was overwhelmingly likely to be employed in a clerical position.

Not unexpectedly, the petitions also repeatedly drew on comparisons between sex and race, often evincing the assumption that the commission already had found racially discriminatory practices outside the pale of the public interest. In a case that would provide an important precedent for NOW's ascertainment arguments, the FCC in 1970 had ruled against a station that claimed that its African American community had been ascertained because it had conducted an interview with a black farm agent. According to the commission, this individual was addressed in his capacity not as a member of the community's African American population but as a farm agent and therefore could not be listed by the station as a leader of their black community.[43] NOW made a similar claim that women interviewees were not necessarily, by virtue of their gender, capable of speaking to the interests of women in the community. Both the WABC and the WRC petitions claimed ascertainment violations for the stations' failures to speak to women's rights groups and their inclusion of very few women in community luncheons that served ascertainment purposes. To make plain why this was a violation, the petition against WABC pointed out that the station "did interview such members of the Black and Puerto Rican communities, and should have treated the community of women with equal concern and with respect."[44]

The race/sex analogy was perhaps most vividly presented in the petitions' discussions of the stations' programming. Citing numerous television shows and commercials accumulated through the WABC monitoring program, the petitioners illustrated that women were presented overwhelmingly as wives, mothers, and homemakers. Furthermore, if one watched WABC, one would see an image of women as "flighty, frivolous, simple-minded persons, physically attractive but totally incapable of filling positions of independence and authority outside of home."[45] Significantly, the petitioners concluded their discussion with this statement: "They [viewers] will believe women are emotional, childlike, sexy, and irresponsible—although generalizations about women as a class are no more valid than similar generalizations about Blacks."[46]

New York NOW continually drew these comparisons between women's struggles and the civil rights gains of African Americans. For example, according to the petition, one of WABC-TV's most disturbing broadcasts of 1972 involved the Olympics. That year, seven of the eight American gold medalists were female athletes. WABC's newscast dedicated less than a minute to their accomplishments and did not mention the names of the medalists on air, though the station did broadcast a two-minute, fifteen-second segment on a pancake-eating contest. To members of NOW's New York chapter this slight was emblematic of the way television stations denigrated the accomplishments of women. To underscore the severity of the slight, the petitioners wrote, "No doubt, we would have been shocked if, while Jesse Owens was walking away with the 1936 Olympic prizes, the news coverage was devoted to a watermelon eating contest for Blacks."[47] The NOW petition most clearly underlined this comparison when it stated, "WABC-TV, like other stations, has abandoned the 'Amos 'n' Andy' image. It would never call Black leaders 'boy' or snicker about the civil rights movement. Nor would it portray Black men exclusively as porters, waiters, and song-and-dance men. Women should be accorded similar unbiased treatment."[48] NOW's claims hinged on the questionable premise that because racially discriminatory practices had supposedly been stopped, sexist depictions constituting an analogous harm should also be abandoned.

If the race/sex analogy rigidly presented race and gender as separate categories of identity, it also overlooked how African Americans were fighting simultaneously against racism on the air and in station practices. That is, New York NOW presumed a more racially egalitarian present at the same moment that African American organizations were filing their own petitions that outlined how local station practices were discriminatory. The same year as that of the petition against WABC, for example, the Paterson Coalition for Media Change filed a petition with the FCC against stations in New Jersey that ignored African American and Hispanic members of the community.[49] In May 1972 Black Citizens for the Media signed agreements with WNBC and WABC, both in New York, in which the stations agreed to hire more African Americans and to program more black-oriented shows. It also filed a petition to deny against WCBS, with whom the activists could not reach an agreement.[50] A little over a year before the WRC petition, African Americans in D.C. had filed a petition against WMAL-TV, arguing, among other things, that the station's programming largely ignored the African American residents who composed 70 percent of the city's population.[51] Indeed, numerous organizations formed in the 1970s specifically to combat racism on television, and their advocacy stood as a retort to the presumption of the pastness of racial discrimination presented by NOW petitions.

The race/sex analogy, however, was deployed as part of the pedagogical project of NOW's petitions to deny. The petitions not only made cases against the public interest performance of the stations but modeled how to view broadcaster practices and programming through a feminist lens. This latter objective hinged on persuading the commission and broadcasters to see sexism as an important obstacle to equality and justice, much as NOW imagined they understood racism. In addition, it turned on convincing the FCC and broadcasters not only to recognize women as a distinct class but to reimagine the sociopolitical impact of television programming. In other words NOW's petitions to deny were at once efforts to bring broadcasters in line with feminist understandings of the public interest and documents seeking to redefine the very terms by which women, television, and the public were understood within the regulatory arena.

Indeed, the very lines of disagreement between NOW and the respective stations were over what conclusions to draw from the stations' past performance and how to assess their compliance with existing regulations. Take ascertainment. In their responses to the petitions, WABC and WRC emphasized their extensive ascertainment procedures, noting that they yielded no substantial evidence that men and women differed in their views on important issues or that women's rights and the problem of sexism ranked high on the list of problems facing their areas of service. If issues of concern to groups like NOW were not evident in the results of their ascertainment process, it was not because their process had been flawed, or because it had been overwhelmingly conducted by men, but because NOW's own sense of pressing public issues did not line up with those of the community at large.[52] In their petitions, in contrast, NOW tried to demonstrate how the very assumptions on which the stations' ascertainment was conducted—over who qualified as an important community leader, or what kind of issue is a credible community concern, or what were appropriate or germane ascertainment questions—were not neutral at all. If women's issues did not surface as important to the community, it was because the ascertainment process was imbricated in the sexism of the station and the disregard it afforded to the women within their communities.

Similarly, NOW and the stations disagreed over what television programming did. NOW's petitions insisted that entertainment programming was political, that it shaped ideas about women's roles and their capabilities. The petitions also emphasized the cumulative impact of television programming, eschewing the notion that an individual broadcast or series could undo the overwhelming depiction of (white) women on television as inferior to men, as incapably equipped to participate in the public sphere, and as valued only or primarily for their sexual desirability. In addition, NOW demonstrated that what was considered "newsworthy" by stations was informed by the same sexist logics of their entertainment programming, logics that justified the often dismissive or insulting assessments of the women's movement within their news and public-affairs programming. The problem with programming was not just that women's movement representatives had not received adequate airtime but that the very premises on which stations made decisions about their entertainment and news programming were themselves sexist. That the stations employed male hosts who evinced contempt or condescension toward women, or news anchors who mocked or ignored the women's movement, was part and parcel of a set of standards that held women in low regard, imagined as consumers of programming and purchasers of advertised goods but not a class of citizens fighting for social, political, and economic equality whose struggles should be visible in the televisual public sphere and whose critique of gender roles should inform representational practices.

WABC and WRC, in response, asserted that judgments over the quality of programming fell within licensees' discretion and that it was not in the FCC's power to intervene in how they assembled, in particular, their entertainment programming. They also cast suspicion on the monitoring studies that informed NOW's assessment of their programming, asserting that the monitors were not neutral but pursuing an agenda in their review of station programming, and offered evidence of programs that had aired attentive to women's issues. They rejected NOW's assertion that entertainment programming meaningfully raised Fairness Doctrine concerns, and they dismissed the notion that the cumulative impact of broadcast representational practices bore any impact on the discussion of women's rights or the role of women in society. Such discussions happened in news and public-affairs programming, an arena in which the stations defended their coverage against allegations of sexism and identified instances over the course of their license terms that covered the ambitions of the women's movement.[53]

The FCC Responds: TV, Sexism, and Petitions to Deny

NOW's petitions were filed in 1972. The FCC did not rule on them until 1975, when it issued its Memoranda Opinion and Orders (MO&O) denying them both. Throughout, the FCC eschewed the role of "national arbiter of the truth in broadcast journalism,"[54] affirmed broad discretion to licensees, and characterized NOW's assessments of programming as subjective to the organization, as evidence that NOW disagreed with the stations' programming practices but not actionable charges about the public interest performance of the stations. Whereas NOW asked the FCC to make qualitative assessments of broadcaster practices, both of individual broadcasts and of the cumulative impact of the station's programming, the FCC refused and instead focused on quantitative data—such as whether and how many times the stations had telecast programs about the women's movement—without tending to the impact, time of day, or orientation of such programming. The FCC found that the number of female employees at WABC, both overall and in management positions, fell within a "zone of reasonableness," and it deferred the employment discrimination question in the WRC case to the EEOC.[55]

In these decisions the FCC was somewhat ambivalent in its recognition of the interconnections between sexism and broadcasting practices. While it affirmed sex as a "suspect classification" protected by law and policy from discriminatory hiring practices, reasserted stations' obligations toward recruiting and training female employees, and recognized women as a distinct class that—as part of a diverse public—needs to be interviewed during the ascertainment process, it dismissed all allegations about sexist programming, myopic representations of women, and demeaning coverage of the women's movement. The FCC evinced far more willingness to honor structural than content-based regulations and implied through its orders that it would be through the integration of women into the broadcasting workforce, and via ascertainment interviews, that the needs and grievances of women toward their image in the media would be most capably addressed.

NOW and the FCC fundamentally disagreed over what television is and what television does. For NOW, television programming—all of it—contributes to social perceptions of gender roles. Indeed, for NOW, media images of women were a substantial issue of public import, the impact of how women were imagined on the small screen imagined to play a determinative role in the ideas that structured women's opportunities in the public sphere. Television did not merely cover or discuss issues of import to women; television, along with its images of women, *was* an issue of import to women. This was the very point made by three women interviewed by WABC but that the station left out of its discussion of its ascertainment process.[56] According to the station, and affirmed by the FCC, the goal of ascertainment was not to critique the performance of the station but to learn about community issues.[57] It was a view that presumed that the performance of the media could not be a community concern, that the media reflected and commented on issues, that it gave visibility to social struggles but did not constitute a site of struggle itself.

All members of the commission concurred with the outcome of these cases, though three offered differing perspectives. Commissioner Charlotte Reid announced that she agreed to the principles outlined by the NOW petitions but did not think the petition to deny was the right vehicle to address feminist concerns over broadcast practices.[58] Commissioner James Quello attacked the uptick in citizen challenges to license renewals, casting them as exalting the "private rights of the few at the expense of the needs and interests of the many," and asserted, after quoting Jawaharlal Nehru, that freedom and democracy hinge on the stability of the nation's broadcasting service.[59]

Commissioner Benjamin Hooks, the first African American to serve on the FCC, agreed with his fellow commissioners that the petition to deny was not the way to address sexism in television, especially given that the "grievances transcend the particular station and that the faults are regarded as endemic of television institutionally."[60] Rather than multiple case-by-case proceedings, Hooks recommended an overall inquiry into television and gender. He ended with an admonition to broadcasters that they must "adjust to the shifting mores and conventions of the public they are licensed to serve."[61] Significantly, in his statement, Hooks did not reason from race but rather drew comparisons between the advocacy of feminists and that on behalf of children. In this he drew on the FCC's willingness to see particular audiences within its imagined general audience for broadcasters. If more liberated sexual mores were to be reflected in broadcasting, and if the FCC was to require broadcasters to consider the interests of children as a result, then the commission could consider how the challenges of the women's movement, whose members like many other social justice groups saw broadcasting as a "compact microcosm of our society," should similarly alter how broadcasters—and regulators—imagine their obligations toward their female audiences.[62]

Hooks was consistently one of the more sympathetic commissioners to citizens' media advocacy. In this he followed in the footsteps of Nicholas Johnson, who as an FCC commissioner had penned *How to Talk Back to Your Television Set*, a call-to-arms for citizens to challenge the hegemony of broadcasters to determine what appeared onscreen. Johnson had understood media advocacy as a critical form of civil engagement. "The right to petition one's government, guaranteed in the First Amendment to the Constitution, has become the need to petition one's media—usually television. That is how a citizen helps to change things."[63] Johnson frequently dissented from his colleagues' decisions on petitions (as in his dissent in the AETC case), finding merit in them for hearings on station performance where other commissioners found none. Both he and Hooks underlined what broadcasters and other members of the FCC were more resistant to embrace: television's role as the public sphere of contemporary life and, with it, its attending obligation to represent the diversity of that public. Media advocacy *was* civic participation, efforts to bring about a more just society, understood to be inseparable from transformations in the content of television programming. It was a sentiment that animated the broadcast reform movement, yet it was one not often condoned by the FCC majority, which more often deferred to the discretion of broadcasters and evinced a hesitation to reconceptualize broadcasters' public interest performance in light of the social and political transformations against which they operated.

Accordingly, one way to see NOW's first two major petitions to deny is as defeats. Neither station lost its license; and, perhaps as important, the premises of NOW's complaints, especially regarding the stations' programming, were dismissed out of hand, the FCC majority supporting the editorial discretion of broadcasters and discharging NOW's claims of sexism as subjective opinions. NOW appealed and lost once more, the federal appellate court in essence affirming what it had ruled in an earlier case: that broadcasters were to be afforded substantial discretion in programming, ascertainment, and employment.[64] Even so, the petitions pushed the stations to change their practices, even as they resisted NOW's claims about them. WABC, for example, in the wake of the NOW petition to deny, established a women's advisory council and increased its number of female employees.[65] In addition, the petitions established NOW as a credible media reform group; through these actions against network-owned and -operated stations NOW gained reputational capital as a media advocacy group that had a record of taking action in response to station practices deemed sexist and therefore contrary to the public interest. As NOW's chapters across the country assessed the performance of their local stations, and considered filing petitions of their own, the WABC and WRC petitions were demonstrable proof that the feminist organization was serious about holding broadcasters to account. These petitions were just the start.

The Politics and Pragmatics of Petitions to Deny

In 1972, shortly after the WABC and WRC petitions, NOW resolved at its national conference to expand the NOW National FCC Task Force, then under the leadership of Whitney Adams, to provide help to local chapters in preparing for and pursuing license challenges. In 1974 the National FCC Task Force and the National Image of Women Task Force would reorganize into one National Media Reform Task Force under the leadership of Kathy Bonk and Joyce Snyder. In 1977 the task force was reconstituted as a National Media Reform Committee to be led solely by Bonk.[66] In all of its iterations the committee informed and instructed local chapters of their rights, provided guidance and legal support for local license challenges and station negotiations, sent members of NOW to testify in regulatory and congressional hearings on media policy, participated in coalitions with organizations of shared political commitments, and enlisted the support of the membership in national actions to challenge sexist representations and practices.

NOW's national task forces distributed newsletters and broadcast reform kits to educate its local chapters in how to file a petition to deny and to inform them of the achievements of one another. This tactic had been a key part of the advocacy labor of the JCET throughout the 1950s as well, and it operated as a critical means both to acquire the literacies needed to engage in media advocacy and the hope—bolstered by the experiences of others—of the efficacy of such work. NOW's kits, action alerts newsletters, for example, outlined the trifecta of media policies central to feminist license challenges (ascertainment,

Fairness Doctrine, and equal employment policies) and offered timelines and guidelines for local chapters interested in dedicating resources to media reform.[67] They thus equipped local feminists with the legal frameworks to challenge sexist images, instructed them about their rights as members of the public, and informed on how seemingly neutral policy initiatives were imbricated with feminist goals and women's rights. In addition, the national task force operated as an epistemic community that publicized important policy initiatives and framed their implications for women and feminist media objectives.[68] In other words the national task forces not only provided local feminists with the tools to level media reform campaigns but also instructed them to see how media policies—practiced by regulators and stations alike—were of utmost concern to women and their fight for social and political equality. The educative role of the national task force was thus twofold, providing both actionable tactics for media reform *and* feminist frameworks through which to view media content and media regulation.

While NOW's national task forces would amass a number of important victories throughout the 1970s, many of the tangible and immediate benefits of its media reform campaign went to its local chapters. Chapters set up local media task forces and pursued potential petitions to deny against local stations. Frequently, though, the threat of a license challenge, which could be costly to defend and always carried the threat of revocation, would encourage local broadcasters to negotiate with members of NOW and to strike agreements in which, in exchange for a promise to retract or not to file a petition to deny, the station would make concessions regarding its programming and hiring practices. In this NOW again built on the precedents of African American civil rights activists, who in 1969 reached the first such agreement with KTAL-TV, a station that served Texarkana, Texas, and Shreveport, Louisiana. KTAL, notorious for its racist programming practices, agreed to programming and employment concessions and to consult with local civil rights groups regarding scheduling decisions in exchange for the rescinding of a license challenge.[69] The NOW agreements featured similar promises from local stations, which agreed to transform their practices to be more inclusive of women and women's interests. The national task force, furthermore, encouraged local chapters to seek out partnerships with other women's and civil rights organizations and provided specific instructions about how to maximize the impact and efficacy of coalitional reform efforts.

The preparatory work to mount local media reform battles required a good deal of time and labor. In addition to examining public files—renewal applications, programming logs, employment records, and audience complaints sent to the station—a crucial part of the preparatory work in these campaigns was monitoring studies. To be sure, the monitoring study had been, and would continue to be, a consistent step in media advocacy work—from the Smythe and Horton study commissioned by the JCET and NAEB in 1951 (to make the case for noncommercial television) to the petitioners in the WLBT case, who monitored for evidence of racial discrimination on the air. Specifically building on the work of the New York and D.C. chapters, local volunteers would pay attention to *how* women and women's issues were represented and discussed and to *how much* time stations dedicated to women's issues. Specifically, monitors would record the characteristics (gender, race, approximate age, occupation) of television characters and personalities. They would register how much time each news story was granted and account for stories that were underreported or neglected. They also were to examine the implied gender and race of voice-over voices and figures of authority both in commercials and in nonnarrative programming and analyze the conclusion of narratives to determine the characteristics of the individual(s) who resolved the conflicts.[70] And while NOW's monitoring studies yielded compelling evidence on which to base a license challenge, they also functioned as training in feminist media literacy, as they provided NOW's members with a critical feminist framework through which to view media representations and narratives. They also were structured around a definition of television that decentered the individual show in favor of the flow of the entire broadcasting day as the text of television.

Many of NOW's local chapters initiated media reform campaigns that led to concessions from local broadcasters. One of the earliest local victories for NOW was in Pittsburgh in the summer of 1972, in which the local chapter scored "the first significant settlements for women with broadcasters." After the New York chapter had filed its petition against WABC, the national FCC Task Force contacted the Pittsburgh chapter about possible license challenges since the stations in its area were up for renewal that August. The threat of a petition encouraged three local stations to reach agreements with the local NOW chapter. According to Adams, two things worked in the Pittsburgh chapter's favor: the WABC petition lent credibility to the Pittsburgh chapter's threat of filing license challenges and the competence of the Pittsburgh chapter's members, under the local guidance of Kathy Bonk, in approaching and negotiating with the stations. KDKA-TV, WTAE-TV, and WIIC-TV each reached agreements with Pittsburgh NOW, and although the specifics of each agreement differed slightly, they all featured concessions in three areas that would be common in feminist negotiations with broadcasters. The stations committed to a minimum number of programs dedicated to women's issues, to send top-level staff to meet with a women's advisory council who would provide feedback on the station's past and future programming, and to recruit and train female employees to ensure women's representative employment and avoid the "women's ghetto" composed primarily of clerical and secretarial jobs.[71] Over the next couple of years NOW chapters reached analogous agreements with broadcasters in cities such as Charlotte, New Orleans, Detroit, Houston, Syracuse, San Diego, Tampa, Los Angeles, Shreveport, and Denver.[72]

For many local chapters, filing or threatening to file petitions to deny resulted in improved relations between NOW and local broadcasters. The Columbia, South Carolina, chapter, along with the local Women's Equity Action League (WEAL) chapter, filed petitions to deny against ten local television and radio stations, after which most stations offered to negotiate with the feminist organizations. Subsequently, according to chapter president Tootsie Holland, broadcasters routinely consulted with the NOW chapter on programming, and the chapter was able to get news coverage whenever it wished. Similarly, in New Orleans the local chapter created a coalition, Citizens United for Responsive Broadcasting (CURB), composed of feminist, minority, environmental, and other public-interest groups, which prepared to mount license renewal challenges.[73] CURB negotiated agreements with three stations, similar in terms to the Pittsburgh agreements; in addition, as Sue Westbrook of the New Orleans chapter reported to Adams, the NOW chapter got "100%" news coverage on the local ABC station, the NBC station gave NOW the opportunity to talk about the ERA on air regularly, and all the stations working with NOW agreed to monitor ads for sexist content. Other chapters—in places like Eau Claire, Knoxville, Tippecanoe County (Indiana), and Chicago—were able to get station commitments to air public service announcements (PSAs) by NOW that explained the goals of the women's movement, while other stations scheduled programs produced by local NOW chapters on a regular basis.[74]

Strategic coalitions became a part of NOW's media reform efforts throughout the decade. Though NOW's primary interest had been in images and representations of women, the organization frequently found common cause with other social justice groups. The most obvious coalition partners were other women's groups. The Los Angeles chapter, for example, spearheaded the L.A. Women's Coalition for Better Broadcasting, a coalition of seven women's organizations that filed four petitions to deny and negotiated agreements with KABC and KNBC, two network-owned and -operated stations.[75] Local chapters were also encouraged at this time to pay attention, in their monitoring of stations' programming, to how women and people of color were depicted, with an eye to forming coalitions with other local groups in a potential license challenge.[76]

In addition to modeling their advocacy work on civil rights precedents and continually drawing analogies between racism and sexism, some local chapters actively worked with civil rights groups and increasingly saw the ambitions of the two movements as intertwined. The Detroit NOW chapter, for example, participated in a coalition of forty civil rights, feminist, religious, educational, and social organizations in its license renewal challenge against WJBK-TV, which charged that the station had "violated the provisions of the Fairness Doctrine and the personal attack rules with respect to issues concerning racial minorities and women. Its programming policies also reflect this insensitivity, inadequately and unfairly portraying persons of minority racial background and women"; the petition also charged that in its ascertainment and employment policies the station did not follow FCC guidelines, especially regarding its treatment of minorities and women.[77] Similarly, the Denver NOW chapter participated in the Colorado Coalition of Women and Minority Persons, which filed two petitions to deny that alleged discrimination against women, African Americans, and "Spanish-surnamed Americans" in programming and employment.[78] Strategically, these local relationships paved the way for feminist participation in national coalitions of public interest groups united to fight regulatory and legislative changes that would greatly impede the public's ability to hold broadcasters responsible for the content of their shows, their hiring decisions, and their assessment of who constitutes their public. The coalitions, along with NOW's advocacy work throughout the 1970s, also argued for the need for analogous, if not identical, affirmative policies at the federal level to bring women alongside people of color into the business of broadcasting.

NOW's license challenges, along with the agreements struck in lieu of a challenge, established women as distinct members of the broadcasting public with not only claims for equal employment opportunities but for programming that addressed their needs. The local media advocacy garnered concessions from broadcasters, but it also functioned as an important form of training for NOW's members. They not only learned about the license renewal process, and the public interest requirements of broadcasters, but gained a form of critical media literacy that trained them to read television shows for explicit and, importantly, implicit claims about gender roles. In addition, as NOW's task forces and its chapters familiarized themselves with the impact, and potential, of broadcasting policy, NOW increasingly was learning to demonstrate how seemingly gender-neutral policy initiatives could help or hinder the ambitions of feminists to transform the media to be more responsive to the needs of women. So as Congress was poised to deregulate the license renewal process in the 1970s, NOW members went to Washington to persuade them that deregulation was, in fact, a feminist issue.

Deregulation Is a Feminist Issue

Throughout the 1970s members of Congress introduced bills to deregulate broadcasting and, in the process, decrease or dismantle the tools that organizations like NOW had used in their media reform efforts. Many of the proposals would have insulated broadcasters from license renewal challenges and formally protected incumbent licensees from competition for their license at renewal time. The members of NOW who testified in opposition to the bills and who worked with coalitions to defeat them marshaled their experiences in challenging broadcast licenses to impress upon legislators how seemingly gender-neutral policy changes would have direct consequences for women in their fight for equality and justice; the license challenge had been the primary way that feminists had persuaded broadcasters to recognize women as members of their publics. Feminist testimony in these hearings additionally provided a platform to NOW's members, in the parlance of the day, to raise the consciousness of legislators and to explain the interrelationships between broadcasters' programming and policies and the forms of discrimination that feminists sought to eradicate.

For example, in 1974 NOW's members testified at hearings in both houses of Congress on the Broadcast License Renewal Act. This proposed law would have extended the term of a broadcast license from three to five years and would have insulated incumbents from competing applicants by requiring the FCC to renew—and not to consider other applications—if the licensee had performed a "good faith effort" to serve the needs of its community and had not "demonstrated a callous disregard for law or the Commission's regulations."[79] One impetus for the bill was an anxiety elicited by a 1969 FCC decision that had awarded the license of WHDH-TV (Boston) to a competing applicant rather than renew the incumbent's license. This decision generated alarm across the broadcast industry that the commission was embarking on a new approach to license renewal that put their own licenses in jeopardy. Though the FCC clarified that the WHDH decision was a special case, and that the station had a long record of subpar performance, the broadcast industry and its allies in Congress feared that it would serve as a precedent to render incumbent licensees vulnerable at renewal time.[80]

In addition, Congress was responding to concerns expressed by the broadcasting industry that, in the wake of the *United Church of Christ* case, stations had been subjected to cumbersome and often illegitimate pressures from community groups, based on questionable claims, that used license challenges as a cudgel to exert excessive influence on stations. The proposals to revise the license renewal process were justified as means to assure stability in the broadcast sector and to relieve the administrative burdens augured by escalating license challenges. However, the public interest and civil rights groups that had availed themselves of the petition to deny process— who constituted the loose constellation of interests dubbed the broadcast reform movement—understood the proposals as protectionist legislation for broadcasters that would take away the one tool in their arsenal to hold local stations accountable to their publics.[81] As Judith Hennessee of New York NOW summed up before the Senate subcommittee, the bills read as though they "were designed by [broadcasters] to enable them to slide out of their obligations to the public" and would mark a "huge backward step" for the "revolution going on among women, blacks, youths, consumers, and ecologists, all of them working for human rights and against the great concentrations of power."[82]

At issue in hearings over the Broadcast License Renewal Act was, in essence, the legitimacy of the broadcast reform movement. Were license challenges necessary actions to hold broadcasters accountable to their publics, or were they frivolous and malevolent acts that placed an undue administrative burden on the commission and fostered an unconscionable instability within the broadcast sector? Did petitions to deny, and the agreements struck in lieu of filing a license challenge, promote or violate speech rights? Was the petition to deny the correct tool to induce broadcasters to respond to shifting social conditions, especially in regard to the status of people of color and women? Was there a meaningful relationship between television programming and practices and societal discrimination, and, if so, was broadcast regulation the proper site to address it?

As representatives of NOW's local chapters and national task forces testified before Congress, they drew on their experiences with license challenges to argue against the legislation. As they responded to skeptical questions from members of Congress over television's role in perpetuating sexism, they made the case that television was both an agent of and itself imbricated within a system of gender discrimination. The problem, and thus the public interest breach, was in representational practices in which, in the words of Jan Crawford, "there is an enormous gap between the reality of women's lives and broadcasting's image of women," in which women on television were depicted in "traditional stereotyped roles of housewife-mother, secretary, nurse, or assistant, leaving the distinct impression in our culture that women can't do anything else." Not only did such practices provide a distorted image of women, but no employer would be wise to hire the "kind of brainless incompetent woman who is ubiquitous on the airwaves."[83] In addition, the derogatory constructions of women and of feminists, as Ann Lang of a Pennsylvania NOW chapter testified, had also affected broadcasters' willingness to take groups like NOW seriously. As she noted, "The broadcasters' belief in the image of the bra-burning radical feminist, an image that they themselves created, combined with a belief in the societal stereotype of women as stupid, ineffective, and immature was hardly conducive to productive discussion."[84] The petition to deny had been the most effective means not only to challenge these representational practices but to bring broadcasters to the table to discuss them. NOW's members emphasized that the petition was a last resort, one undertaken only when direct negotiations with broadcasters failed. They were neither frivolous nor impetuous but the result of hours of volunteer labor and, in some cases, broadcaster intransigence.

In addition, NOW's members sought to invert the presumptions of injury that underlined the proposed bill in the first place. Congress seemingly was responding to a situation in which broadcasters were unfairly beleaguered by license challenges, the FCC overly burdened by the uptick in petitions to deny. The Broadcast License Renewal Act was intended to address this situation and to restore stability to a sector presumably destabilized by the challenges of public interest and civil rights groups. It also was to protect the speech rights of broadcasters, who had felt manipulated into changing their programming in order to fend off license challenges. NOW's witnesses asked members of Congress to see things differently. How much, for example, asked NOW FCC Task Force chair Whitney Adams, had the broadcast industry been destabilized when "less then 4 percent of the stations were challenged during fiscal year 1972 and when only one station [WHDH] has lost its license in a competitive proceeding in all the years of television broadcasting."[85] Not only were a small fraction of broadcasters affected by petitions to deny, but, as Lang underlined, despite claims of a perilous environment, broadcasters had done quite well financially, rendering comprehensible "why the nonprofit, underfunded citizens' groups resent the industry's cry for greater security of license renewals to maintain financial stability."[86]

Perhaps most trenchant, NOW's Bonk and Lang suggested that the broadcast reform movement had tested the FCC's administrative capabilities as guardian of the public interest. This legislation was a means to elide the commission's inadequacies in revising how it regulates in light of the political and social transformations of the era. The Broadcast License Renewal Act thus was to serve broadcasters and their regulators, but it would deny rights to the public at the very moment when they not only see how media rights and civil rights are intertwined but had the tools—within the current regulatory framework—to pursue them.[87] This critique of the FCC, which had surfaced in the WLBT court rulings, also was part and parcel of a larger assessment of administrative agencies in this period. As Cass Sunstein has argued, the 1960s and 1970s were a period of escalating skepticism over the performance of administrative agencies, many of which were suspected of being "captured" by the industries they were charged to regulate.[88] Many of the communities who leveled these criticisms, like NOW, were committed to liberal or progressive visions of reform and hoped to push administrative agencies to adopt more robust public interest commitments; as Robert Horwitz has argued, their critique of the inefficacy of the agencies would be picked up by conservative groups that, in turn, pushed for the kind of deregulation considered by Congress in these bills.[89] The battle over legislation to deregulate broadcasting in the 1970s was part of this reassessment of the performance of regulatory agencies and the proper scope of government action to respond to the political upheavals of the era.

In 1974, when the Broadcast License Renewal Act was defeated, NOW's media reform task force counted its downfall as a victory.[90] Yet throughout the 1970s the policy-making arena would continue to be a crucial site of NOW's media advocacy. Congress considered additional bills that would dramatically deregulate broadcasting. In both House and Senate rewrites of the 1934 Communications Act in 1978 and 1979, a number of substantial changes were proposed to broadcast regulation, including disbanding the FCC and creating a new Communications Regulatory Commission, creating indefinite license terms for radio broadcasters, imposing five-year terms for television broadcasters that would become indefinite ten years after enactment of the act, removing the FCC's EEO and ascertainment rules, eliminating the Fairness Doctrine for radio licensees, and removing the public interest standard for licensing.[91]

The rewrite of the Communications Act panicked public interest and citizens' groups. The bills would all but do away with the petition to deny, as well as with the policies that had provided the base for citizen complaints: ascertainment, EEO rules, and the Fairness Doctrine. To defeat the bills, NOW joined forces with other public interest and citizens' groups who saw in their provisions the death knell of citizen influence within the realm of broadcasting programming and policies. NOW participated in a number of coalitions, including the Telecommunications Consumer Coalition and the Coalition for Public Rights in Broadcasting, to stop the bills and to educate the public on the consequences should they pass.[92] Feminists found common cause with a wide range of consumer and citizen groups, who feared that these bills would, in the words of consumer advocate Ralph Nader, "amount to a virtual expropriation of the public airwaves."[93]

For feminists deregulation was almost tantamount to a denial of women's civil rights. As Karen Boehning of Chicago NOW stated in her testimony before the House, deregulation posed a "threat to women's progress," asserting that the "Equal Rights Amendment and the Communications Act of 1934 essentially address the same question. Will the people, all the people of this nation[,] have full and fair opportunity to avail themselves of the resources so proudly held."[94] It was fairly unimaginable, in other words, that women's rights, both as members of the broadcasting public and as citizens whose rights in other realms were intimately tied to the images of them circulating in the media, would be supported by the deregulation of broadcasting. Bonk's testimony, which primarily focused on the need for EEO rules, also underscored how deregulating the media would enshrine the discriminatory practices of the past, which had placed broadcasting in "the hands of white men."[95] Deregulation would not only dismantle the policies that had been so central to feminist media advocacy but would propel and make inviolate the very conditions that had required NOW's actions in the first place, a media system that had excluded women and people of color from positions of influence and control.

For the time being NOW and its coalition partners had helped stave off deregulation—neither rewrite of the Communications Act became law—and put into the congressional record claims that they had made through their petitions to the FCC. They reiterated the relationship between media representations and societal discrimination, while also underlining how broadcasters had been unresponsive to the diversity of their publics until facing a license challenge. In addition, by the end of the 1970s, NOW also could count shifts in FCC policies as success stories, enabled by its media advocacy, in which the commission recognized how women had been sidelined or omitted from participation in broadcasting. The FCC's 1976 rewrite of its ascertainment policies, for example, specified that "organizations of and for women" be included in the list of communities to be interviewed.[96] And when in 1978 the FCC adopted a series of rules to facilitate more entities controlled by people of color to own broadcasting stations (discussed more thoroughly in the following chapter), the commission decided to include women, in similar but not identical ways, within these rules to diversify the ownership of broadcast stations. As the FCC suggested, "The basic policy considerations are the same. Women are a general population group which has suffered from a discriminatory attitude in various fields of activity, and one which, partly as a consequence, has certain needs and interests with respect to which the inclusion of women in broadcast ownership and operation can be of value."[97] The need to address sex discrimination in broadcasting arose in part from the labor of feminist media advocacy; NOW had demonstrated for nearly a decade how the fight for women's full integration into the civic body hinged on a reimagining of the application of broadcasting policy and the composition of the broadcasting public.

Thus, in the 1970s, at both the local and federal levels, NOW could count victories from its media advocacy work. NOW's petitions to deny only nominally aimed to revoke broadcasting licenses but rather were opportunities for the organization and its members to assert the enmeshed relationship between media representations and women's oppression and, importantly, to lay claim to women's civic membership. Through amassing evidence of discriminatory practices, through engaging with local broadcasters, and through participating in the policy-making arena, NOW made visible sexism both on and off the air. Along with the concessions gained by NOW's chapters throughout the 1970s, this had been one of the important outcomes of feminist media advocacy, to remind how the "public" of the public interest is not a gender-neutral category and how assertions of a singular, stable public can mask historic inequalities.

Feminist Media Advocacy beyond Licensing

The media advocacy of the broadcast reform movement was not limited to commercial stations, as the fate of the AETC indicated. NOW, for its part, not only had an action day to protest sexist stereotyping on *Sesame Street* but participated in the Corporation for Public Broadcasting's Advisory Committee of National Organizations (ACNO). For NOW noncommercial broadcasting had not proven to be a panacea that portended more diverse and responsible forms of programming. In its role in ACNO, NOW sought to address low levels of employment of women and people of color at public broadcasting stations, improve images of women in public broadcasting programming, and secure greater accountability from stations and the national

CPB to women and communities of color.[98] As Bonk noted in 1975, the entire structure of public broadcasting was controlled by "white men who make decisions," a facet reflected in its poor record in employment and programming.[99] Noncommercial television, for NOW, had not proven to disrupt the power dynamics that structured commercial broadcasting or the devaluing of women and people of color within the media more broadly.

NOW's media advocacy throughout the 1970s had not been oriented toward widespread structural change. NOW had not sought to destabilize or threaten the commercial underpinnings of broadcasting, the dominance of national networks, or the reliance on corporations as private stewards of a public resource. In part this resulted from NOW's broadly reformist agenda. But NOW's media reform strategies also resulted perhaps from the performance of public broadcasting in the 1970s and the perception that a more robust public broadcasting sector would not necessarily, or even be likely to, address the problems of discrimination that were at the center of NOW's media advocacy. By the 1970s, noncommercialism had not delivered a more egalitarian television system. If NOW privileged a fight for inclusion, and if it prioritized how conceptions of the "public"—both as imagined on television screens and as conceived in policy making—had to take account of multiple publics, it did so not only because of its own liberal agenda but because of its view that, in the 1970s, both commercial and noncommercial broadcasting alike were agents of sex discrimination.

NOW's media advocacy, much like the broader broadcast reform movement of which it was a part, was premised on twin notions: (1) that media regulation had been a technology of inequality in the United States, and thus its basic tenets—most centrally its understanding of the "public"—had to be reformed to reflect the nation's diversity, and (2) that television itself was critically important to the realization of a more just, equitable society. Unlike the JCET in the 1950s, this vision of reform hinged not on using television to erase distinctions across peoples but rather on understanding the necessity of television to make visible and knowable the differences across communities. It also asked broadcasters and their regulators to see how seemingly neutral concepts and their application in fact were structured by the very same discriminatory habits of mind that the reformers sought to dismantle. For NOW in particular, media advocacy throughout the 1970s would be a means to see, and to instruct others to see, broadcasting policy through a feminist lens, as well as to pressure local stations to be more responsive to their feminist audience and to persuade policy makers at the federal level to recognize the intersections between media regulation and the ambitions of the women's movement. To do so was both to draw on the visibility and gains of the African American civil rights movement and to find solidarity with other communities similarly fighting for a responsive media.

In the 1980s the ability of public interest groups to reform broadcasting was substantially undermined. When conservative policy makers gained power in the 1980s, many of the accomplishments of the 1970s were soon undone, casualties of a neoliberal approach to regulation and a belief that the market would be the best mechanism to tend to the diversity of the public. NOW's own media advocacy would persist after the 1970s, though the petition to deny would not assume the same central place it had in the 1970s and the rate of activity of the early part of the decade would diminish. By the end of the 1970s, NOW's chapters oriented much of their work toward passage of the Equal Rights Amendment (ERA), an issue that overtook the other feminist goals that had structured NOW activism.

Yet throughout the 1970s and 1980s NOW continued its media reform work, most notably defending women who lost their jobs in television because of sexual discrimination or had suffered sexual harassment.[100] As the policies adopted in the late 1960s and 1970s to support greater inclusion of women and people of color came under attack in the following decades, NOW frequently lent its support to fights to retain them. NOW itself would continue to see television and broadcast regulation as important sites of feminist advocacy that affect women's broader fight for gender equality. The struggle would continue, even as the tactics and strategies available to feminist media reformers would have to adapt to a shifting regulatory environment.

In addition, while the ascent of deregulation stymied the activity of the broadcast reform movement, the changes in the regulatory environment would galvanize public interest groups to resist the material changes in the media landscape, as well as the understandings of diversity at their center. In the 1980s and 1990s, however, they would face not only an FCC intent on dismantling existing regulations but an executive branch similarly committed to positioning government as the "problem," rather than the "solution," to the nation's ills, an increasingly conservative federal judiciary poised to support deregulation, and a cultural environment in which "diversity" was increasingly cast with suspicion. Yet, as the next chapter discusses, these conditions did not tamp out media advocacy efforts; rather, they made them all the more important.

4

Diversity and Deregulation

The NAACP and Minority Media
Rights during the Culture Wars

In 1983 members of civil rights organizations appeared before the House of Representatives to discuss the relationship between media representations and the struggle for racial equality. Of concern was not only the paucity of people of color on television but that existing characters seemed to perpetuate worn-out stereotypes, Nell on *Gimme a Break* a latter-day *Beulah*, Mr. T on *The A-Team* an amalgam of minstrel types. Significantly, these conversations took place during hearings over media deregulation. Representatives from the National Association for the Advancement of Colored People (NAACP), League of United Latin American Citizens (LULAC), National Council of La Raza, and Black Citizens for a Fair Media expressed concerns that should the FCC further diminish media regulations, it would hamper opportunities for people of color in the media and worsen an already inadequate system of representation.[1] As representatives of these organizations underlined, there was a profound connection between (1) who controlled the media and who had access to decision-making positions within it and (2) the politics of representation of what appeared on television screens.[2]

The following year, *The Cosby Show* debuted on NBC and became, in Janet Staiger's phrase, a "blockbuster TV show."[3] The tremendous popularity of the show, as well as its focus on an affluent African American family, seemingly marked a new era in the representations of African Americans on the small screen and a rebuke to the stereotypes outlined the previous year by civil rights groups. And while many enthusiastically embraced the show as a welcome depiction of a successful black family, others saw in *Cosby* a narrative of reassurance, one that instructed viewers to see racism as a thing of the past, the post–civil rights era of the 1980s an era of racial egalitarianism. The Huxtable family emblematized what Herman Gray has labeled the "civil rights subject," the beneficiaries of the struggles of the civil rights era who are deserving subjects of full integration into American life.[4] For critics and fans alike *The Cosby Show* seemed to hail the arrival of a color-blind society, the opportunities for success in the United States contingent on one's work ethic and talents, not one's race. The overwhelming ratings success of the show, and its popularity with white audiences, only seemed to reinforce the presumption that the problems of racial discrimination were solved.[5]

Media policy in the 1980s and 1990s was similarly informed by this view of American race relations, which, to some degree, *The Cosby Show* was codifying. Broadcast deregulation was profoundly intertwined with a neoconservative understanding of race, one that presumed racial discrimination to be of the past—solved by previous court decisions and legislation—and that conflated race consciousness with racism itself.[6] As the FCC and the federal courts increasingly reinterpreted the public interest goal of diversity, they gutted a number of policies that had facilitated greater participation of people of color in broadcasting. The NAACP, along with other civil rights groups, fought back against both the concrete changes to media policy taking place and the understandings of the history of broadcasting and the history of race relations on which they were premised. As this chapter demonstrates, the NAACP's media reform efforts exposed how deregulation was not race-neutral but was a process by which civil rights gains were being rescinded.

If in the 1960s and 1970s the broadcast reform movement had worked for a more inclusive understanding of the public interest, these later battles in the 1980s and 1990s were fights over a different form of inclusion. They were premised not on making heretofore invisible communities visible but on pushing back against a set of political and intellectual forces that sought to whitewash both past and continuing forms of discrimination through appeals to a liberal individualism. As the NAACP engaged in media advocacy—which took the form of license challenges, formal petitions, congressional testimony, and participation in legal cases—it performed myriad acts of intervention and preservation. While seeking tangible ends in its campaigns, the NAACP sought to reassert the continued significance of racial discrimination in the face of an increasingly powerful discourse that denied its existence. In this the NAACP's media campaigns insisted on media policy as an arena where battles over "identity politics" and the meaning of racial difference in the culture wars were fought.

Prologue I: Diversity and Broadcast Regulation

By the time of the NAACP's media advocacy campaigns in the 1980s, the meaning of *diversity* had undergone substantial revision. Diversity had been one of three prongs—along with competition and localism—that had defined the "public interest" for policy makers since at least the 1940s. Diversity initially was understood in line with a marketplace-of-ideas metaphor, the promotion of diverse perspectives over the airwaves a key public interest objective. The FCC had pursued diversity primarily through structural regulations, most directly restrictions on the ownership of broadcasting stations. Presuming a nexus between ownership and viewpoint—that diversity of owners would maximize diversity of perspectives—the FCC adopted local and national ownership limits, as well as cross-ownership limits. In addition, the FCC had adopted content regulations—most notably the Fairness Doctrine—to assure audiences access to diverse viewpoints. This understanding of diversity thus hewed to an interventionist interpretation of the First Amendment, one in which the state had an affirmative role to play in assuring the rights of citizens to hear diverse perspectives.[7]

In response to the social movement activism of the 1960s and 1970s, the FCC revised its understanding of diversity to consider not just how many speakers were in a market but who had the ability to speak. In addition to its EEO rules for its licensees, the FCC adopted three policies in 1978 to expand the number of minority owners of broadcast stations. The minority ownership policies resulted, in part, from the activism of civil rights organizations, namely the National Black Media Coalition (NMBC) and the National Association of Black Owned Broadcasters, who capably persuaded the commission to hold a two-day conference on minority ownership in broadcasting.[8] In its 1978 order the FCC decided that when considering competing applications for a broadcast license, the commission would consider the race of the applicants as one of many factors in its decision; other factors would include past broadcast experience and ties to the community of service. The FCC's distress-sale policy allowed broadcasters susceptible to losing their licenses to sell their stations to a minority-controlled entity for at most 75 percent of the station's value. And the commission developed a tax-certificate policy that allowed broadcasters who sold their stations to minority-controlled entities to defer payment of capital gains taxes. Combined, these policies sought to address the dire imbalance in ownership patterns; at the time that the policies were enacted, minorities owned less than 1 percent of the eighty-five hundred broadcasting stations operating in the United States.[9]

The policies thus had two goals: to address the substantial underrepresentation of minorities as broadcast station owners and to attend to the speech rights of the entire broadcasting public by diversifying the range of viewpoints made available over the air. The rules were not remedial; they were not explicitly meant to address how broadcast regulation had afforded preferential treatment to white applicants in the past. Rather, they were to serve the public interest goal of diversity. As the commission asserted in its statement, "Adequate representation of minority viewpoints in programming serves not only the needs and interests of the minority community but also enriches and educates the non-minority audience."[10]

In this the minority-ownership enhancements echoed the 1978 *Bakke* Supreme Court decision, in which the Court ruled on the University of California's affirmative action program for medical school admissions. *Bakke* divided the Court, which offered six different opinions in the case.[11] The judgment of the Court, penned by Justice Lewis Powell, found that the program was constitutional—so long as race was one factor in admission decisions and so long as universities did not employ quotas—since it contributed to the diversity of the student body and thereby augmented the educational experience of all students.[12] For Powell, however, the policy would not be constitutional on remedial grounds, as a program to address the prejudices of the past. Justice Thurgood Marshall, in his powerfully worded dissent, chastised his colleagues in taking umbrage at a program to redress discrimination even though for more than two centuries it had not prohibited "the most ingenious and pervasive forms of discrimination" against African Americans.[13] That is, although Marshall found the remedial intent of affirmative action programs legitimate and necessary, many of his colleagues on the Court rejected a race-conscious policy but were willing to sanction "diversity" as an appropriate goal, one that, like the minority enhancements, was imagined of benefit to minority and white students alike. In *Bakke*, "diversity" displaced remedial action to address long-standing institutionalized discrimination as a rationale for race-conscious policies.

In the 1980s *diversity* was redefined both within the realm of broadcast regulation and, more broadly, in response to the heated debates over race and culture during the culture wars. The FCC, under chairperson Mark Fowler, reconceptualized the public interest in line with a "marketplace approach to regulation." Fowler understood his role as chairperson as shifting the FCC from a "social agenda to a technical agenda aimed at getting government out of the way."[14] He brought broadcast regulation in line with Reagan-era neoliberal policies, in which maximizing the autonomy of industry and minimizing the role of the state presumably would best serve the needs of the polity. As advocates for minority rights in the media expressed early on, technical policies had social implications, and seemingly neutral regulations could disproportionately hamper the abilities of people of color to participate in broadcasting. Furthermore, "getting government out of the way" also signaled a willingness to leave untouched past regulatory decisions that favored certain groups over others.

This policy shift was best articulated in a 1981 law review article, coauthored by Fowler and Daniel Brenner, "A Marketplace Approach to Broadcast Regulation." This approach, in which the "perception of broadcasters as community trustees" was to be swapped for one that saw "broadcasters as marketplace participants," would rely on "broadcasters' ability to determine the programming wants of their audience through the normal mechanisms of the marketplace."[15] In other words, by trying to maximize their profits, commercial broadcasters by definition would seek the programming of most interest to their viewers. Thus Fowler and Brenner erased any distinction between the consumers broadcasters sell to advertisers and the citizens broadcasters had been required to serve on condition of their license. Though frequently described as deregulation, it perhaps is more accurate to think of the "marketplace approach to regulation" as an alternative model of regulation, one committed to sanctifying the property rights of corporations, preserving the previously awarded advantages to players within various economic sectors, and imagining consumer behavior as the best arbiter for determining the public good. Within this regulatory paradigm the circulation of diverse programming was imagined as something that a robust marketplace yields, not an actionable public interest goal.

The FCC pointed to the rise of cable television and the VCR as necessitating a different approach to regulation; as media outlets proliferated, and especially as radio stations and cable networks targeted specialized audiences, the FCC reasoned that this shift from a presumed media scarcity to an ascending media plenty would allow the commission to remove what it saw as onerous obligations on broadcasters. As Fowler and Brenner wrote, cable and VCRs "provide virtually limitless diversity of scheduling and content," and therefore "no scarcity exists with respect to the television spectrum."[16]

While the number of media outlets would escalate over the course of the 1980s, whether there was more diversity of perspective in the media landscape was an open question. Adoption rates of new technologies varied based on location and income, and for many audiences over-the-air broadcasting remained their primary site of media consumption. In addition, burgeoning cable networks frequently repurposed off-network reruns, packaged for targeted audiences.[17] More media outlets did not necessarily yield more opinions, perspectives, or programming objectives, especially as the FCC would enable greater levels of media concentration as part of its "marketplace approach." Yet from the FCC's perspective, diversity of outlets was synonymous with diversity of perspective.

Deregulation severely hampered the broadcast reform movement. Throughout the 1980s the FCC eliminated broadcasters' ascertainment requirements, repealed the Fairness Doctrine, and lengthened the term of broadcast licenses. Combined, these rulings removed critical instruments from media advocacy groups' tool kits to level license challenges. As it made petitions to deny far more difficult, deregulation also enabled incumbent media companies to amass even more power and control through loosened ownership restrictions. Quite logically, then, the 1980s and 1990s have often been interpreted as dark days for media reform advocacy. However, this context only made media advocacy important for groups like the NAACP, whose work at this time attempted to challenge not only the policy shifts but the ideological assumptions that undergirded them.

Prologue II: Diversity and the Culture Wars

The problem of media diversity intersected with the larger question of the meaning of diversity itself during the culture wars. The culture wars of the 1980s and 1990s were a period of reckoning over broad questions about American identity and especially, as Andrew Hartman has illustrated, over the social and political transformations of the 1960s. Hartman suggests that the culture wars were a period in which "liberal, progressive, and secular Americans" fought their "conservative, traditional, and religious counterparts" over the nation's cultural institutions and over the ideas defining, and especially the challenges to, what he deems "normative America" that were constitutive of the cultural upheavals of the 1960s.[18] The culture wars—fought over public funding of the arts and media, the content of television shows and films, the presentation of history in textbooks and museums, the place of religion in the public sphere, the salience of traditional ideas about gender and sexuality, and the meanings of racial difference in contemporary life—were thus referenda on the 1960s and on whether that decade had opened up American culture to be more inclusive and democratic or whether it had shattered the very meaning of "America" and its values.

The fight over the meaning of racial equality was an important facet of the culture wars. In addition to the battles over multiculturalism in educational curricula, affirmative action programs were a key battleground. Throughout the 1980s race-conscious programs came under attack in the culture at large and especially in the federal courts. Significantly, both supporters and opponents of affirmative action claimed their positions to be consistent with the goals of the civil rights movement. Indeed, what was remarkable about the rhetoric on issues of race and policy in the 1980s and 1990s, as Daniel Rodgers and others have shown, is in how quickly conservatives—who had insisted on the import of racial distinctions in the classical civil rights era—quickly adopted, and inverted, the language of civil rights to fight affirmative action policies in the 1980s and 1990s.[19] Asserting that color blindness was the critical component of racial justice, opponents of affirmative action insisted that to see racial difference, and to continue to seek remedies to racial discrimination, was, on the one hand, to engage in an insidious racial consciousness and, on the other, to trample on the rights of white Americans who were victimized by unnecessary, and unconstitutional, affirmative action programs. For adherents to this position to presume in the realm of broadcasting policy that race mattered to the public interest goal of diversity was to engage in pernicious stereotyping.

Opposition to affirmative action as a form of reverse racism was central to Ronald Reagan's position on racial injustice, both during his presidential candidacy in 1980 and during his presidency. Reagan sought to promote a "truly color-blind society," and he insisted that affirmative action programs "turned our civil rights laws on their head," because they allowed discrimination based on race or sex.[20] Yet as Terry Anderson has argued, this rhetoric did not map onto aggressive action by the Reagan administration, especially given the considerable support for such programs in Congress. Where Reagan's impact on affirmative action was most tangible was in his federal court appointments, which shifted the Supreme Court and the federal judiciary to the right, especially on issues related to civil rights.[21] As affirmative action cases wound their way through the courts, they were increasingly heard by judges who shared the president's conflation of racial consciousness with racism. This shift determined the fate of a number of cases on minority media rights.

On the other side of this battle would be groups like the NAACP, who fought this scripting of the Black Freedom Struggle, as well as the presumption that racial classifications always ran afoul of constitutional protections. As the NAACP leveled efforts to protect the minority enhancement policies and to forestall deregulation in the 1980s and 1990s, it simultaneously engaged in a definitional battle to rescue "diversity" from neoliberal market enthusiasts and culture warriors who denied the significance of racial difference in contemporary American life. In this, like the JCET and NOW before it, the NAACP's media advocacy efforts were material and symbolic; they were fights over the allocation of resources and over the discursive construction of the "public," as well as over the attending consequences of seeing or not seeing racial difference, and of acknowledging or not acknowledging existing forms of racial inequality, to the rights of people of color in American society.

From *Birth of a Nation* to *Beulah Land*: The NAACP and Popular Media

When the NAACP engaged in advocacy efforts in the 1980s and 1990s, it built on a long-standing concern over how popular media depicted African Americans. The NAACP, which formed as an interracial civil rights organization in 1909, had employed multiple strategies, ranging from economic boycotts to direct negotiations with networks to media advocacy efforts to secure, in its view, more responsible images of African Americans. Beginning with its 1915 protests of *The Birth of a Nation*, the NAACP had posited that demeaning and stereotyped images of African Americans, as well as egregious misrepresentations of African American history, could impede African Americans' fight for full citizenship.[22]

The NAACP's media campaigns reflected the organization's commitment to racial uplift and its reformist approach to racial equality. When it launched a protest against the television versions of *Amos 'n' Andy* and *Beulah*, voted on at its national meeting in 1950, it pursued this boycott despite the fact that African American performers objected to the NAACP campaign, as did many African Americans who liked *Amos 'n' Andy* and were just happy to see images of African Americans onscreen.[23] In the 1960s and 1970s the NAACP was attuned to the presentation of African American struggles on television and was especially fearful that radical, separatist groups were becoming more seductive to programmers than reformist organizations seeking racial integration.[24] When NBC planned a 1980 miniseries, *Beulah Land*, which presented slaves as lovingly devoted to their white masters or as sexually predacious threats to them, the NAACP engaged in a sustained campaign to persuade the network to rethink the ethics and politics of the film.[25]

The history of the NAACP's engagement with media is also a history of advocacy. The NAACP had been part of the listeners' rights reform campaigns of the 1940s (see chapter 1)[26] and the broadcast reform movement of the 1960s and 1970s (see chapter 2). In these efforts the organization collaborated with other groups, like the ACLU, unions, and other civil rights organizations, in pursuit of a more responsive, more democratic broadcasting system. Like its media activism the NAACP's media advocacy intended to ameliorate derogatory images of African Americans and enable greater integration of African Americans into positions of power within the broadcasting industry.

The NAACP's goal was to adapt existing structures to be more inclusive of African Americans rather than to overhaul or substantially transform the political economy of broadcasting and the role of commercialism and corporate power within it. Accordingly, though the NAACP was opposed to deregulation in the 1980s and 1990s, it occasionally was willing to accept policies that enabled greater media consolidation if they contained provisions to increase minority participation in broadcasting. For example, the NAACP was very supportive of the Mickey Leland rule, which allowed media companies to exceed current broadcast ownership limits if they had a financial interest in a minority-controlled station.[27] In 1992 the NAACP and LULAC endorsed two policy proposals, one that would allow broadcast networks to own cable systems outright and one that provided an incentive program to encourage networks to invest in minority-controlled MSOs (multiple-system operators). They reasoned that more stable revenue streams would enable networks to take greater programming risks that could benefit minority audiences, who still disproportionately relied on over-the-air television. In addition, they believed stimulating investment in minority-controlled cable systems could benefit people of color, since cable operators exert influence over selecting channels, allocating channel positions, and providing local access programming.[28] This seemingly contradictory stance on deregulation underscores how the NAACP prioritized a civil rights agenda in its media advocacy and was open to finding ways to advocate for people of color that were consonant with the interests of media companies.

Yet more commonly, broadcasting policy in the 1980s and 1990s functioned as an important battleground where the NAACP worked not only to preserve the gains of the previous decades but to fight the whitewashing of racial inequality and the overreliance on marketplace forces to solve social problems. These battles were over not only the dismantling of minority enhancement policies but also the discursive repositioning of citizenship rights, multiculturalism, and diversity.

Petitions to Deny under Deregulation: Equal Employment Opportunities

Equal employment opportunities for African Americans, in broadcasting and in other sectors, was a priority for the NAACP in the Reagan era. Its attention to the EEO rules was consistent with the organization's broader advocacy for affirmative action in the 1980s and 1990s. At this time the NAACP worked against the Reagan administration's Justice Department, which both weakened the power and resources of the Equal Employment Opportunity Commission (EEOC) and made clear that it understood affirmative action programs as unconstitutional "preferential treatments."[29] Countering conservative claims that affirmative action was an unjustifiable "gratuitous advantage," the NAACP asserted that such programs were necessary to address the history of exclusion of African Americans from myriad institutions of American life. As Althea T. L. Simmons, director of the NAACP's Washington Bureau, put it in a 1984 address: "The recent adoption of racially 'neutral' admissions policies, employment practices, and contracting procedures could not suddenly obliterate the consequences of our history and bring about immediate equality of opportunity."[30] In addition to seeking relief in the courts for the performance of Attorney General Edwin Meese on civil rights, in 1989 the NAACP organized a "Silent March" in protest of a string of Supreme Court decisions that gutted affirmative action policies. This march was modeled on the 1917 Silent March in New York, when more than five thousand people had marched silently down Fifth Avenue to protest "Jim Crowism," lynching, disenfranchisement, and race riots.[31]

This concern over affirmative action would structure the NAACP's media advocacy. Throughout the 1980s and 1990s the NAACP, under the guidance of attorney David Honig, filed hundreds of petitions to deny against local broadcasters, based almost exclusively on equal employment opportunity grounds. In 1983, for example, the NAACP challenged twenty-three licenses in Mississippi and Louisiana alone.[32] In 1990 the NAACP was involved in petitions against 181 stations. In 1993 a total of 143 stations were operating under short-term licenses (their conditional renewal due to EEO violations), 133 of which were sanctioned because of an NAACP license renewal challenge.[33] When the organization leveled petitions to deny, it aimed not necessarily to revoke licenses but, much like NOW's advocacy in the 1970s, to win concessions from broadcasters, as well as to push the FCC's hand to act on EEO violations.

These license challenges for the NAACP in the 1980s and 1990s were part of a national reform strategy. Local chapters participated in the petitions yet almost always at the behest of the national office. A few months before stations were up for renewal, Honig would investigate their employment practices and identify the broadcasters who seemed to be in violation of the commission's EEO rules. After gaining permission from the NAACP's executive director and general counsel, he would contact local NAACP branch presidents about participating in a license challenge. Should they agree, these local presidents would be signatories on the petitions to deny. Honig also would provide a list of stations whose employment records were suspect and encourage representatives of local branches to meet with their general managers to see if they could work out an agreement. These agreements typically would include a station commitment to implement policies to enhance the number of African Americans in the station's employ, including using black organizations, media, and educational institutions for referrals when jobs were to open; to hold regular meetings with NAACP branch representatives to discuss minority hiring procedures; and to implement an internship program for African American high school or college students. If the station was unwilling to negotiate or to meet with the chapter, Honig would draft a petition to deny and file it with the FCC, after which he would ask the local NAACP chapter to look over the station's public files and monitor its programming for subsequent comments to be filed with the commission.[34]

Once the NAACP filed a petition, a number of things could happen. Individual stations could negotiate with the NAACP in return for rescinding the petition to deny. Should stations choose not to do so, and should the FCC find that they had been in violation of the EEO policies, the FCC could take any of the following actions: it could admonish the station but still grant it an unconditional renewal; it could grant a conditional renewal and require the station to file periodic reports on its EEO performance; it could give a conditional renewal and impose a fine; it could impose a demerit, to be applied during comparative hearings, on the station if it were seeking additional construction permits; it could revoke the station's license, though the commission historically never had applied this penalty solely for an EEO violation.

In 1990, for example, in response to NAACP and NBMC petitions against broadcasters in South Carolina, the FCC granted unconditional renewal to four stations, granted renewals to four stations but required them to submit periodic reports on their EEO compliance, granted short-term renewals to four stations subject to their subsequent EEO performance, and imposed fines on four stations, two of which were required to submit reports of their current EEO program and documents outlining steps they intended to take in the future to improve its effectiveness.[35] As the *Los Angeles Times* reported in 1990, from 1988 to 1990 more than two hundred broadcasting stations had been the target of petitions to deny on EEO grounds, and since 1990, nineteen stations had been fined up to $20,000 for EEO violations.[36]

These petitions, furthermore, frequently elicited concessions from local broadcasters. In 1989, for example, the Miami-Dade branch of the NAACP reached a settlement with Cox Enterprises, licensee of a number of stations in Florida. In exchange for an NAACP commitment to rescind its petition to deny, Cox agreed, among other things, to establish voluntary goals for African American employment at all levels of station operation, make a reasonable effort to use black vendors for goods and services, meet at least twice a year with representatives of the NAACP to discuss recruitment and programming, create an internship program for African Americans, and adopt a policy that the general manager of the stations was to consult with the NAACP on the station's response to future civil disturbances in the area.[37] The NAACP earned analogous concessions in 1992 from WDKY-TV in North Carolina, in an agreement that included a station commitment to start an internship program for minority students, to contact civil rights organizations when job vacancies opened up, and to meet with the president of the Danville NAACP chapter twice a year to discuss station practices.[38] The NAACP's petitions both insisted on the continued salience of the EEO rules and operated, much as had the petitions to deny filed by groups like NOW, as a means to pressure broadcasters to alter their practices to be more inclusive and attentive to their diverse publics.

Lutheran Church and the Many Faces of Diversity

Perhaps paradoxically, the NAACP's vigorous attention to EEO compliance would ultimately lead to the rules' downfall. In 1998 the U.S. Court of Appeals for the District of Columbia, in its *Lutheran Church Missouri Synod v. FCC* decision, found the EEO rules unconstitutional. The path to this decision began with an NAACP complaint against four radio stations in Missouri. The

NAACP's actions against the Missouri radio stations were consistent with its broader emphasis on ensuring that the EEO rules were enforced. This time, though, as the case wove through the commission and the courts, the NAACP would lose both its fight against the stations and its definitional battle over what constitutes diversity.

In 1990, NAACP chapters in Missouri initiated action against KFUO-AM/KFUO-FM and two other Missouri stations. Honig had investigated the EEO performance of the stations from 1983 to 1989. The KFUO stations, owned and operated by the Lutheran Church Missouri Synod, according to the NAACP's January 2, 1990, petition had the "worst minority hiring record of any station in Missouri throughout the license term," having failed both to employ people of color and to devise an affirmative action program to diversify their employment rolls. Given that there were no facts in dispute, according to the NAACP, an investigation was unnecessary, and the "renewal application should be designated for hearing and promptly denied."[39] The stations, as summarized by an NAACP press release, "had no more than token employment of blacks and other minorities during their current license period, they do not appear to be operating under meaningful equal employment opportunity programs, nor have they proposed meaningful EEO programs."[40] In response to the petition the FCC asked KFUO for additional information, since there was "insufficient information to make a determination that efforts were undertaken to attract Black applicants whenever there were job openings."[41]

The Lutheran Church, in its initial response and throughout the case, insisted that its employment needs were unique. To work at the stations would require knowledge of classical music or theological training in Lutheran church doctrine. Therefore, the station's "highly specialized employment needs make reliance upon overall minority labor force availability meaningless."[42] Accordingly, the NAACP had overstated "the availability to KFUO of minorities with the specialized skills required for most job positions at the station."[43] In addition, the stations' employment and recruitment strategies were tied to this unique mission. The mix of classical music and Lutheran theology made the stations desirable sites of employment for a very small subset of individuals, who had submitted unsolicited applications to the station in the hopes of future job openings. The location of the studios at the Concordia Seminary also required KFUO to employ seminary students in exchange for the free use of the space. Furthermore, the lack of continuity in station managers had made it difficult to devise and implement an effective EEO program.[44]

In 1994 the FCC held hearings on the stations' compliance with the commission's EEO rules. In 1995 the commission's Administrative Law Judge (ALJ) sanctioned the church for its EEO record and for its misrepresentation of its EEO policies to the commission. While the ALJ found no particular instances of explicit racial discrimination against individuals, he ruled that the station had improperly preferred hiring individuals with knowledge of

Lutheran doctrine for positions for which such knowledge was irrelevant. In addition, the ALJ ruled that the church had lacked candor in its description of its minority recruitment program. The FCC required the church to file subsequent EEO reports and to pay a $50,000 fine, a penalty for its lack of candor to the commission.[45] As Honig had stated in a 1990 address, "To the FCC, the only thing worse than a dumb licensee is a dishonest one."[46]

Neither the Lutheran Church nor the NAACP was happy with the results, and both petitioned the commission for redress. The church argued that the FCC had violated the First and Fifth Amendments, insisting that the decision burdened its free exercise of religion and that the EEO program writ large was out of step with current judicial understandings of equal protection. The NAACP, for its part, attacked the credibility of the ALJ, claiming he was incapable of fairly handling a civil rights case and that he disregarded pertinent information that qualified the station for license revocation.[47] In 1997 the commission affirmed its previous ruling, though reduced the fine on KFUO to $25,000.[48] The following year, the appellate court would weigh in.

Throughout the long road that the *Lutheran Church* case traveled, the respective parties understood the core terms of the case—diversity and discrimination—in different ways. For the NAACP, to promote diversity was to facilitate minority perspectives on the airwaves. While the public interest goal of diversity predated the formation of the EEO rules, the rules themselves were born out of the civil rights struggles of the 1960s, the diversity they were designed to promote that of ethnoracial diversity, an inclusion of voices long absent over the airwaves. Furthermore, the NAACP understood discrimination in a broader frame than specific acts of racism against individuals. Discrimination, especially as addressed by the EEO rules, included structural impediments that limited access from the outset.

The church and its supporters, however, recognized an alternate form of diversity. The stations contributed to diversity by providing formats not offered by other stations in the area. Accordingly, listeners wrote to the commission to lambaste the NAACP and its narrow construction of broadcast diversity. Twenty-nine members of the Lutheran Church Missouri Synod sent a letter to the FCC in which they claimed that just as there are "ALL BLACK television networks on the cable network and also all black radio stations!!!!!," it should be permissible to have stations dedicated exclusively to the teachings of the Lutheran Church. Imploring the commission to "stand up to this NAACP organization for once!!!!!," the church members defended the employment record of the stations by suggesting that they did not intend to exclude African Americans but rather to give jobs to students and wives that lived on the seminary grounds.[49] Other listeners echoed the arguments for parity, citing the presence of African American–oriented radio stations as obviating the need for KFUO to integrate its workforce, and made veiled or explicit claims that the NAACP's charges were reverse racism or illegitimate forms of race consciousness.[50] Perhaps the clearest articulation of this alternative understanding of diversity was in a letter to the FCC from St. Louis resident David Wexler, who suggested that "cultural diversity is more than ethnic and racial diversity; without these further dimensions, racial diversity is a hollow sham."[51] Such claims not only called for a more expansive understanding of diversity, but they inverted the claims of injury at the center of the NAACP's petition, as they insisted that it was African Americans that had been the beneficiary of a system of preferences unavailable to other communities.

In 1998 the federal appellate court decided against the NAACP. The *Lutheran Church* decision rested on two premises, one tied to a liberal individualism that refused the notion that race meaningfully affected one's worldview and one linked to an economic determinist rationale that understood the maximization of profits as the primary basis for decision making in commercial broadcasting. The court's decision thus united the neoliberal shift that had taken place in broadcast regulation with the concurrent neoconservative pushback against privileging racial difference in public policy. The court applied the most onerous standard of review on the rules, strict scrutiny, and examined whether they passed the two prongs of the "strict scrutiny" test: did they advance a compelling state interest, and were they narrowly tailored? Insisting that the commission's goal of diversity "seems too abstract to be meaningful," the court surmised that its function was "the fostering of programming that reflects minority viewpoints or appeals to minority tastes."[52] The court ruled, however, that "diversity" was not a "compelling" interest, and it asserted that the "Court never explained why it was in the government's interest to encourage the notion that minorities have racially based views."[53] In this, as in other affirmative action broadcast cases, the court refused to distinguish between the taking of account of "racially based differences" to remedy, rather than propel, racial discrimination. The decision exemplified an embrace of a color-blind jurisprudence in which all recognitions of racial difference were equally suspect.

In addition, the court in *Lutheran Church* argued that the EEO policy clashed with "the reality of the radio market, where each station targets a particular segment: one pop, one country, one news radio, and so on."[54] In this the court refused to see a distinction between diversity of formats and diversity of viewpoints, between speech rights and consumer choice. In intertwining its rejection of affirmative action with its embrace of the marketplace approach to regulation, the *Lutheran Church* decision was in step with other federal court decisions that similarly rejected minority enhancements in broadcasting. The FCC appealed the *Lutheran Church* decision, though its request for an en banc hearing was denied.[55]

The *Lutheran Church* decision presumed a level and equal playing field in the broadcasting sector, one that ignored how the previous sixty years of policy-making decisions had preferred commercial networks and their affiliates, defined the public interest in ways consonant with majoritarian views and perspectives, and facilitated the construction of a public sphere that whitewashed the nation's ethnoracial diversity. An equal playing field where all citizens compete based on their own merit, articulated by the court as an already realized political reality, operated as a cudgel against programs that addressed the continued existence of racial disparities in broadcasting. The minority ownership policies would suffer a similar fate.

"The Communications Act, like the Constitution, Is Color Blind": Minority Ownership Policies under Fire

Throughout the 1980s and 1990s the NAACP was mindful of the precarious position of the FCC's minority-ownership enhancement policies. It worked to preserve them by closely monitoring the FCC's enforcement of the rules and by participating in crucial court cases over their fate. In these actions the organization sought to preserve the material benefits of the minority-ownership enhancements and to challenge the rescripting of race relations and racial prejudice at the center of the attacks on them.

From the outset the FCC's minority-ownership enhancement policies were enmeshed in a debate over history, race relations, and the law. The FCC historically had not considered race as a relevant factor in assigning broadcast licenses. In 1970 the commission explicitly stated that race could not be a factor, announcing that the "Communications Act, like the Constitution, is color blind."[56] In 1973 the U.S. District Court of Appeals disagreed. In *TV9, Inc. v. Federal Communications Commission* the court asserted that the race of applicants should indeed be a relevant factor. Deeming it reasonable that increasing minority ownership of broadcasting stations would introduce even more diverse perspectives into the public sphere, the court ruled that the FCC had erred in denying the import of race in comparative hearings.[57] In response the FCC crafted specific policies to bring more people of color into broadcast station ownership.

Over the course of the 1980s the FCC leveled implicit and explicit attacks on minority-ownership enhancements. In formal petitions to the commission, congressional testimony, and amicus brief filings, the NAACP and other civil rights organizations challenged this turn away from the policies. In 1982, for example, the NAACP and the NBMC got embroiled in a TV station license transfer, the facts of which portended a dubious future for the FCC's distress-sale policy. The FCC approved the transfer of WJAN-TV, a UHF station in Canton, Ohio, from the PTL (Praise the Lord) of Heritage Village Church and Missionary Fellowship Inc. to the David Livingstone Missionary Foundation Inc. Officers of the PTL television network, most notably televangelists Jimmy and Tammy Faye Bakker, had been accused of misappropriating large sums of money donated in response to solicitations on the syndicated show *The PTL Club*. The commission conducted an investigation of these allegations, amounting to more than four thousand pages of witness testimony, which included serious charges of misconduct. The FCC's report included evidence that Jim Bakker had solicited money from viewers for foreign missions to spread the gospel overseas, while in fact using the money himself domestically, and that the Bakkers had spent ministry money to buy a houseboat, a mink coat, and a Corvette.[58]

While the commission forwarded its findings to the Department of Justice for investigation, the majority voted to drop the case and allow the license transfer to Livingstone.[59] Under analogous circumstances, the FCC typically would have designated the licensee for a hearing, and, should the licensee choose, the station could be sold to a minority-controlled entity in a distress sale. In not designating a hearing in this case, the FCC enabled PTL to sidestep a distress sale and sell to Livingstone at full value. The concern for the NAACP and NBMC was that the commission was setting a precedent for future licensees that, when in fear of commission action, it would be permissible to sell quick and get out, without commission penalties or the obligation to engage in a distress sale, and thus sell to a minority-controlled entity. Three commissioners dissented to the FCC's decision and, in a strongly worded articulation about why, echoed the concerns of the NAACP and NBMC. As Commissioners Fogarty and Rivera wrote, "The distress sale vehicle for license relief represents a deliberate Commission balancing of deterrence values with the value of enhancing minority broadcast ownership. PTL's assignment application compromises deterrence values with no discernible countervailing public interest benefit."[60]

After the NAACP and NBMC filed an unsuccessful petition for reconsideration and lost the appeal, they continued to pursue the case while simultaneously courting a settlement with Livingstone and PTL, which they reached in 1985. In exchange for a promise that they would not seek certiorari with the Supreme Court,[61] Livingstone agreed to cover approximately 77 percent of the civil rights groups' legal and research expenses, to meet with community groups to discuss prospective programming, and to obey a principle of nondiscrimination in all station practices. This agreement signaled a victory of sorts; though it did not put the station in minority hands, it did commit Livingstone to be responsive to the African American community of Canton. In addition, as Honig, who had acted as counsel for the case, indicated, the vigilance through which petitioners pursued it "should make it clear to future broadcast policymakers and historians that this case should be treated like the 'purple cow' it really is."[62] If a primary concern of the NAACP and NBMC was that the PTL case would render the distress-sale policy meaningless, then the paper trail of formal legal actions taken by them would hopefully assure that it would be treated as an anomaly rather than a precedent for future cases.

Still, the FCC's willingness to ignore its own policy was troubling, and in following years the commission's resolve to enforce its minority ownership policies continued to falter as it questioned their very constitutionality.

Metro Broadcasting, Minority Ownership, and the Meaning of Diversity

In 1990 the minority-ownership enhancements came under the scrutiny of the Supreme Court in *Metro Broadcasting, Inc. v. FCC* (1990), when the Court delivered a brief victory to proponents of affirmative action. In *Metro* the Court combined two cases, one involving the minority enhancements in comparative hearings, the other the distress-sale policy. The NAACP, NBMC, and LULAC had been involved with both cases since they were tried at the appellate level. Although the NAACP was not directly implicated in the facts of the cases, as it would be in *Lutheran Church*, the outcomes held tremendous significance for both the opportunities of people of color in broadcasting and the viability of future media reform efforts. *Metro* was of significant import both to advocates of affirmative action broadly and to those concerned with diversity in broadcasting specifically.

Metro came on the heels of a series of other decisions in which the Court ruled affirmative action policies unconstitutional.[63] The case thus has been read within the context of affirmative action jurisprudence; it was, in retrospect, a short-lived approval of racial classifications at a moment in which, by and large, the courts embraced a color-blind commitment to antidiscrimination. In addition, *Metro* has been interpreted as a case on the parameters of the First Amendment, one in which the Court signaled a "new judicial receptivity to governmental sound mixing"[64] to policies that allow the state to promote speaker diversity. *Metro*, however, should also be interpreted as a case on the intersections between media policy and civil rights, on the significance of media ownership in the broader struggle over racial justice, and on the appropriate historical narrative to which this struggle instantiates the next chapter. The NAACP would weigh in on all these questions.

The path to *Metro* began with *Steele v. FCC* (1985). The United States Court of Appeals in the District of Columbia Circuit in 1975 (*Garrett v. FCC*) and 1984 (*West Michigan Broadcasting Co. v. FCC*) had affirmed the commission's use of enhancements in comparative hearings. In both cases the decisions emphasized the policy's intention to address the substantial underrepresentation of minority perspectives on air.[65] In *Steele*, however, the court ruled that the FCC, in extending its preferences in comparative hearings to *female* applicants, had exceeded its statutory authority. When the entire appellate court voted to rehear the case en banc, it asked the FCC to submit a brief justifying both its female *and* minority-ownership enhancement policies and indicated its own suspicion over the constitutionality of the minority enhancements.

This suspicion was perhaps most boldly expressed when the court claimed, "There is no reason to assume, for example, that an Italian station owner would primarily program Italian operas or would eschew Wagner in favor of Verdi. Similarly, it is questionable whether a black station owner would program soul rather than classical music or that he would manifest a distinctively 'black' editorial viewpoint."[66] The court further insisted that "to suggest that these dubious, ethnically-determined tastes will outweigh the economic imperative of what the audience wants to hear therefore strikes us as more than a little implausible."[67] Anticipating the *Lutheran Church* decision, the *Steele* court conjoined, as was often the case in this era, a marketplace approach to regulation with a deeply held suspicion of the legitimacy of race consciousness in public policy.

To the shock of the court, Congress, and public interest groups, the FCC did not defend its ownership policies and instead argued they were indefensible based on the commission's current record. Accordingly, the FCC signaled that it was prepared to dismantle its minority-ownership programs. In response the House Subcommittee on Telecommunications held hearings to question the commissioners on the minority enhancements. In his testimony Fowler made four claims to support his position that the minority-ownership enhancements were on shaky ground: a recent court decision (*Wygant v. Jackson Board of Education*)[68] had rendered the policies unconstitutional; the commission had never compiled a factual record to substantiate the presumptions underlying these policies; financing had been the greatest obstacle to minority ownership, and future commission efforts should be focused on this problem; and race-neutral solutions—for example those that targeted small businesses— would be preferable to race-based policies.[69] The FCC subsequently opened up an inquiry on the legitimacy of gender- and minority-ownership preference policies.[70] In 1987 Congress terminated this process in an appropriations bill that forbade the FCC from touching its current ownership programs.[71]

The two cases that were under review in *Metro—Shurberg Broadcasting of Hartford, Inc. v. FCC* (the distress-sale case) and *Winter Park Communications, Inc. v. FCC* (the comparative enhancement case)—were decided in the wake of these developments. In *Winter Park* the appellate court had affirmed the constitutionality of the minority enhancement in comparative hearings. Important to this decision was that race was only one of many factors that provided an enhancement for an applicant.[72] In *Shurberg* the appellate court decided that the distress sale policy was unconstitutional. According to the court, not only was the distress-sale policy not narrowly tailored, but it did not advance a compelling state interest.[73] The *Shurberg* decision, like *Lutheran Church* and *Steele*, united an attack on affirmative action with an embrace of deregulation.[74] These arguments would also wind their way through *Metro* and inform the competing perspectives on the legitimacy of the minority ownership enhancements that the Court was tasked with settling.

To be sure, one of the central questions in *Metro* was what standard of review should apply to the minority enhancements? Answering this question required sussing out whether the rules had been mandated by Congress or by the FCC. In *Fullilove v. Klutznick* (1980) the Court had afforded latitude to race-conscious programs devised by Congress, whereas in *Wygant v. Jackson* (1986) and *J. A. Croson v. Richmond* (1989), the Court had subjected state and local policies to a strict scrutiny standard.[75] Would the minority enhancements deserve greater latitude, or should they be assessed along strict scrutiny grounds?

Though questions of standard of review, congressional intent, and binding precedent were critical—indeed were truly the meat of the case—so, too, were deep disagreements over the meaning of diversity, the role of broadcasting in American life, and the history of racial discrimination in the United States. Opponents of the rules—including the petitioners, the U.S. general solicitor, communication corporations, and a host of conservative public interest law groups—made consistent arguments about these issues in their amicus briefs. They overwhelmingly cast suspicion over "diversity" as a rationale for broadcast regulation. In so doing, they routinely contrasted the diversity sanctioned by *Bakke*—which promoted academic diversity and thus academic freedom and the university's First Amendment right to create a diverse student body that, in turn, would complement the university's educational goals—with the diversity promoted within the ownership enhancements, seen as unrelated to, and in direct violation of, the First Amendment.[76] Some claimed that "diversity" was too vague a concept to legitimate race-conscious broadcasting policies, while many others insisted that diversity was assured by a free marketplace, not by government regulation.[77]

Furthermore, if *Bakke* was to help break down stereotypes, opponents to the ownership rules insisted that their very premise only reinforced stereotypes, premised as they were on the flawed assumption that "Hispanics are likely to program for Hispanics, blacks for blacks and women for women—all of which is absurd."[78] Thus not only were the policies invidious, unnecessary, and unconstitutional, but they relied on reductive and stereotypical notions of race that propelled, rather than undermined, the insidious history of racial stereotyping that had marred the history of the nation.[79] In addition, opponents to the rules cited recent Court decisions on affirmative action—affecting issues like the awarding of construction grants or teacher hiring-and-firing policies—to demonstrate that precedent required the Court to find the minority-ownership enhancements unconstitutional.[80]

If the opponents to the rules drew on assumed inerrant constitutional principles of equality, process, and liberty, and posited the market as the best guarantor of program diversity, advocates for the rules focused on history, both the history of broadcast regulation and the history of racial discrimination in the United States, which often were imagined to be intertwined. They demonstrated that diversity long had been understood by the policy-making community as a public interest goal; program diversity was not, in other words, part of some "frightening and Orwellian"[81] system to justify unjustifiable uses of race-conscious policies, as opponents of the rules claimed, but a long-standing objective of broadcast regulation.[82] In addition, advocates noted how broadcast licenses had been distributed at a time when racial minorities were subject to myriad forms of discrimination that impeded their ability to compete. This, in turn, led to a broadcast sector in which people of color were woefully underrepresented.[83]

This position was articulated in the briefs of many civil rights and social justice organizations and was critical to the amicus brief submitted by the NAACP, in conjunction with the NBMC, LULAC, and the Congressional Black Caucus. That brief asserted that the "distribution of radio and television licenses today is the product of a system of state-sanctioned preferences favoring white males that has existed since the founding of this nation."[84] The 1978 policies countered the lingering effects of state-sanctioned racial discrimination that had produced a broadcasting system in which an African American had not received a license in comparative hearing until 1975. Given that both the FCC and Congress had found that the low levels of minority ownership was related, at least in part, to a history of racial discrimination, affirmative action programs were a necessary means to assure that one racial group—whites—did not maintain near exclusive control over broadcasting. As the NAACP and its partners wrote, "The need for race conscious programs arises in large part from the history of racial discrimination that produced a virtual white monopoly of mass media licenses."[85]

In addition, advocates rejected the notion that race consciousness was racism or that the marketplace was the best mechanism to assure diversity. As the NAACP Legal Defense Fund (LDF), a civil rights law firm that had its origins in the NAACP but operated as a separate body, stated: "Because blacks were not pleading their own cause, the content of the media became a voice to them rather than a voice by them. Because black people had no input into the ownership and decision-making function of hiring, program production, budgeting, promotion and scheduling; the result was a long line of situation comedies on television, 'blaxploitation' films and 'soul' radio stations, which were nothing more than jukeboxes."[86] The politics of distribution, of who is awarded a broadcast license, was important because of its relevance to the politics of representation, of who had the power to depict and define African Americans and to determine the frames through which race relations were distilled within broadcasting content.

The Court found in favor of the commission's policies. In tracing the history of the policies under review, Justice William Brennan's majority opinion cited the history of exclusion of minorities from broadcasting, not only when the rules had been devised but still in 1986, when, according to an NAB study, minorities owned only 2.1 percent of broadcasting stations. The Court also acknowledged that the commission had justified the policies not as remedial but as important to the promotion of programming diversity. This justification, according to the Court, qualified as an important governmental objective, one that honored that an understanding of speech rights that affirmed the "widest possible dissemination of information from diverse and antagonistic sources is essential to the welfare of the public."[87]

In addition, the Court echoed that while individual minority owners may not program differently than white owners do, it was more than logical to assume that a "broadcasting industry with representative minority participation will produce more variation and diversity than will one whose ownership is drawn from a single racially and ethnically homogenous group." Drawing on the same studies quoted by the NAACP and other civil rights and public interest groups in the amicus briefs, the Court found that "as more minorities gain ownership and policymaking roles in the media, varying perspectives will be more fairly represented on the airwaves" (582). The decision suggested that the commission had only adopted race-conscious policies after race-neutral ones had failed; furthermore, the ownership policies were tailored to address the factors that had affected minority underrepresentation in broadcasting.

Importantly, the Court tackled the marketplace objections to the minority ownership policies, those that were articulated in *Steele* and would be reiterated in *Lutheran Church*. "The Commission has never relied on the market alone to ensure that the needs of the audience are met," the Court stated. "Indeed, one of the FCC's elementary regulatory assumptions is that broadcast content is not purely market driven; if it were, there would be little need for consideration in licensing decisions of such factors as integration of ownership and management, local residence, and civic participation" (571). As the Court acknowledged, and the commission's licensing policies demonstrated, the FCC historically had believed that ownership matters and that market forces alone would not be determinative of programming content. To presume that the marketplace would take care of the programming needs of the broadcast audience, in other words, was to fly in the face of the history of broadcasting policy in the United States.

The Court issued four decisions in *Metro*. In addition to the Brennan majority opinion, Justice John Paul Stevens offered a concurring opinion in support of the majority ruling, and Justice Sandra Day O'Connor and Justice Anthony Kennedy penned dissents. In her dissent Justice O'Connor echoed the ruling in *Steele* and anticipated the *Lutheran Church* decision. Reading the equal-protection clause as requiring the government to treat citizens as individuals, not as "components of a racial, religious, sexual or national class," she interpreted the majority decision as indicative of a "renewed toleration of racial classifications and a repudiation of our recent affirmation that the Constitution's equal protection guarantees extend equally to all citizens" (602–603). The notion of a "benign racial classification" to O'Connor was a contradiction in terms.

In his dissent Kennedy drew a comparison between *Plessy v. Ferguson* and *Metro*, claiming that the majority decision moves us from "separate but equal" to "unequal but benign" (638). He reiterated that a "fundamental error of the *Plessy* Court was its similar confidence in its ability to identify 'benign' discrimination." He furthermore argued that he could not agree that "the Constitution permits the Government to discriminate among its citizens on the basis of race to serve interests so trivial as 'broadcast diversity'" (633). He suggested that the majority's logic here would sanction policies like that of Japanese internment during World War II. In sum, Kennedy opined that "history suggests much peril in this enterprise, and so the Constitution forbids us to undertake it" (637–638). This opinion agreed with many of the assertions made by Justice O'Connor in her dissent, especially in its insistence that strict scrutiny was the appropriate standard of review here, but Kennedy phrased his objections in a much more vigorous moral language and drew historical parallels to underscore his condemnation of the decision. It was a view echoed in a *Washington Times* editorial on the *Metro* decision: "Today, 30 years after the civil rights movement broke Jim Crow's back, the old bird is alive and well. His nest is not in Selma, Little Rock, or the Birmingham jail but in Washington D.C., and he bears a strange resemblance to liberal jurists and politicos who use race to enforce an agenda as silly and obsolete as Jim himself."[88] As Patricia Williams has noted about the arguments against *Metro*, "In only twenty-five years, blacks and Bull Connor have become relativized in this soupy moral economy."[89]

In addition, though the *Metro* case must be understood as weighing in on the permissibility of race-conscious policies, it also should be considered as a case on the role of broadcasting in American life. Although Justice Kennedy dismissed broadcast diversity as "trivial," for the *Metro* majority it was consonant with the First Amendment itself—not trivial but crucial to the proper functioning of democracy. The NAACP brief demonstrated, as did its media reform work from this period, a correlation between who has access to the airwaves and who has meaningful citizenship rights. To castigate the purpose of the enhancements was thus not only to adhere to a position of race neutrality, which conflated all forms of race consciousness as equivalent in harm, but also to deny the importance of broadcasting to the construction of the public sphere. Though neither Kennedy nor O'Connor evoked Fowler's infamous definition of television as a "toaster with pictures," their dissents indicated that they did not share the view that broadcasting operated as an instrument of a shared public culture.

Although *Metro* delivered a victory, it was short-lived as the Court over-turned its decision five years later in an affirmative action case, though one not dealing with broadcasting, *Adarand Constructors v. Pena* (1995). Between *Metro* and *Adarand,* Justice Thurgood Marshall retired and was replaced by Justice Clarence Thomas, shifting the balance of the Court decidedly to the right. Justice Thomas's hostility to any preferential policies was clear from his days on the appellate court. Notably, in *Lamprecht v. FCC* (1992) he penned the court's decision, which ruled unconstitutional the FCC's gender enhance-ment in comparative hearings.[90] In his dissent in *Lamprecht*, Abner Mikva accused Thomas of basing his decision on the O'Connor dissent rather than the majority ruling in *Metro*, a case that he saw as the binding precedent.[91] Thus, when the Court heard *Adarand* in 1995, it was no surprise that Thomas joined the majority, which sanctioned O'Connor's position on federal affir-mative action policies and, in overturning *Metro*, cast out the two minority-ownership policies that had been at its center.

Diversity Undone: The NAACP, Fox Broadcasting, and Stealth Deregulation

In the early 1990s the NAACP tangled with Rupert Murdoch's Fox Broad-casting Company. Fox, which had begun broadcasting in the United States in 1986, had grown into a viable competitor to the Big Three broadcast networks out of a combination of many factors: the timing of its entry into the broad-cast market, the cagey maneuverings of its executives, and the willingness—or, arguably, complicity—of the FCC to enable its growth. While the FCC was enthusiastic about the ostensibly enriched diversity over the airwaves that a viable fourth network would provide, civil rights organizations like the NAACP interpreted the concessions made to accommodate Fox as a threat to the diversity it prioritized, one in which the ethnoracial diversity of the nation was reflected in its media.

In 1985 News Corp. CEO Rupert Murdoch had had the opportunity to buy six broadcast stations from the Metromedia group in important media markets (L.A., New York, D.C., Boston, Houston, and Dallas).[92] Since section 310(b) of the communications act prohibited "alien control" of U.S. broadcast stations, Murdoch quickly became an American citizen and created a new entity, Twentieth Century Holdings (THC), to acquire the stations. Fox Tele-vision Stations, a subsidiary of THC, would continue to purchase additional television stations, and the Fox Broadcasting Company, another subsidiary of THC, would go on the air in October 1986. Over the course of the late 1980s and early 1990s the reach of Murdoch's Fox would expand, as would his media holdings in the United States.

Importantly, when Fox emerged in the mid-1980s, the FCC defined a *network* as an entity that broadcast more than fifteen hours of prime-time programming per week and whose affiliates reached 75 percent of U.S. households. Fox strategically stayed below these markers throughout the 1980s, which exempted it from the Prime Time Access Rule (PTAR) and the Financial Interest and Syndication Rule (Fin-Syn): it did not have to limit the network shows and off-network reruns it aired on its stations (PTAR) and was not prohibited either from having a financial interest in its entertainment programming or from retaining domestic syndication rights over its programming (Fin-Syn).[93] In 1990 Fox persuaded the FCC to give it a waiver from both rules, as it was close to qualifying as a network, on the grounds that enforcement would provide a disincentive for Fox to grow and thus would deter the diversity and competition that a fourth network could bring to the television marketplace. When, in 1991, the FCC revised Fin-Syn, it included a loophole specifically tailored for Fox that exempted emerging networks from the new rules. By the mid-1990s both Fin-Syn and the PTAR were repealed, and Fox's previous exemptions from them had contributed without question to the growth and stability of the fourth network.[94]

It perhaps then with good reason that the NAACP feared that, when Fox asked for waivers from the commission's ownership restrictions, the FCC would comply. In 1993 Fox petitioned the Federal Communications Commission for two waivers: one to permit it to purchase the *New York Post* and still retain its flagship television station, WNYW-TV in New York, a sale that would put Fox in violation of the FCC's newspaper-television cross-ownership ban; and one to allow Fox to buy WGBS-TV in Philadelphia, which would put it in violation of the FCC's prohibition against owning two television stations in the same market. The NAACP filed petitions in opposition to both waivers.[95]

In building the case against the waivers the NAACP stumbled on information that broadened the scope of its opposition. In investigating the ownership structure of the stations, Honig found an inconsistency in Fox's reporting to the FCC and the Securities Exchange Commission (SEC). Section 310(b) prohibits a foreign entity from controlling more than 25 percent of a U.S. broadcast station.[96] In its filings with the FCC, accordingly, Fox had insisted that since 1985 Murdoch, through his THC, controlled 76 percent of Fox Television, the Australian News Corp. 24 percent. This arrangement put the station group squarely within acceptable limits according to federal communications law. When filing with the SEC, however, Fox was claimed as an entity controlled by News Corp., a foreign entity, and thus as exempt from paying corporate taxes in the United States.

The NAACP drew on this finding to argue, in both a petition against a waiver and in petitions to deny license renewals of Fox stations, that Fox had not been "completely candid as to the extent of alien influence"[97] and that the true nature of its ownership structure ran afoul of section 310(b). According to the NAACP's petition, and to one that NBC would file the following year,[98] foreign-controlled News Corp. in fact owned 99 percent of the company that owned the Fox stations, thus throwing the legitimacy of the Fox network itself into question. Fox, in response, initially maintained that when the FCC in 1985 approved the sale of the initial stations, it was aware that News Corp. would provide equity to secure the purchase. In addition, despite the tremendous financial interest that News Corp. had in Fox, Murdoch—an American citizen—exercised both de jure and de facto control over the stations.[99] Fox later insisted that even if its ownership structure ran afoul of the limits on foreign control, the FCC had the power to, and in this instance should, permit exceptions to 310(b) when doing so would serve the public interest.

While Murdoch would insist that the NAACP's challenges were evidence of an irrational vendetta against Fox, they in fact were consistent with the civil rights organization's battles over media deregulation during this period. At the core of both petitions to oppose the waivers was a challenge over the meaning of *diversity* and the impact of deregulation on minority media rights. On one hand, the NAACP argued that the granting of the waivers would essentially vacate in practice, if not in letter, the FCC's ownership restrictions. On the other, the NAACP sought to counter a definition of diversity that privileged the number of outlets in a community, or the imagined benefits of a fourth broadcast network, and reassert the importance of ethnoracial diversity in media ownership to serve the communication needs of a multiracial society.

All of the NAACP's challenges to Fox, to its ownership restriction waivers and to the ownership structure of its station group, were tied to its concerns over the evacuation of racial difference from the public interest goal of diversity and over the cultivation of an environment that would make it even more difficult for people of color to break into broadcasting. It opposed Fox's request for a waiver to buy the *New York Post*. In this, it challenged that diversity was consonant with a diverse number of outlets—Fox's position—and insisted that diversity was tethered to the ethnoracial diversity of the community; New York, for example, had more Chinese speakers than the number of total viewers in some markets, as well as a large and heterogeneous black community. Deeming the "fruits of media diversity" as "but a dream for the Black community in New York,"[100] the petition underlined how media outlets underserve the area's African American population, disable black institutions from reaching their publics, and limit the information about African Americans in New York available to the entire community. In addition, the NAACP feared that approval would set a dangerous precedent, one that could render the ownership restrictions toothless. The commission's ownership restrictions had benefited minority buyers, who often were able to purchase stations when proposed mergers ran afoul of them; to grant the waivers to Fox could thus set the stage for an even tougher environment for people of color to penetrate.[101]

Significantly, when the NAACP made accusations of alien control over the network, these, too, were tied to its fears over the precedent it would set regarding media ownership should foreign capital be allowed in the U.S. television station market.[102] Minorities had a hard enough time raising the capital to purchase broadcasting stations, a condition that would only worsen if foreign conglomerates could bid for broadcast stations. The harm, in other words, was not just the consolidation of voices under one corporate entity but the devastating impact that abandoning 310(b) would have on the opportunities for people of color to get a toehold in the media market.

The NAACP challenge perhaps paradoxically targeted a network that by the early 1990s had "fostered a space for black authorship in television."[103] While, on the one hand, the NAACP was pursuing remedial action against Fox and working to prevent the expansion of its media holdings, on the other, and concurrently, it was praising Fox for its representations of African Americans in its prime-time programming. As Krystal Brent Zook has demonstrated, Fox initially adopted a counterprogramming strategy against the Big Three networks by targeting African American audiences who, by the late 1980s, had not migrated in the same levels to cable and who watched 44 percent more broadcast television than nonblack viewers. In the late 1980s and early 1990s, Fox was telecasting situation comedies that not only featured predominantly African American casts but were produced and written by African American creative teams. Though these shows faced their share of interventions by the network and sponsors that curtailed which and how topics could be explored, as Zook demonstrates, the shows provided a platform to explore multiple concerns that African Americans discussed in private spaces but rarely saw depicted onscreen. These shows particularly mattered to African American audiences, not only because of the visibility of black performers but for the integration of themes, idioms, and objects that marked the shows as African American creations rather than shows peopled by black performers that expressed a white creative team's vision of African American life.[104] Fox highlighted its success in this area as it defended itself against NAACP charges. Three days before the NAACP had filed its complaint, the organization had honored Fox with twenty-two Image Award nominations in three separate categories.[105]

The case got stranger. As the FCC held depositions with Murdoch, Fox attorney Thomas Herwitz, and Fox chairman Barry Diller, it increasingly amassed evidence that Fox had not been candid with the commission about the extent of foreign ownership. The commission uncovered an internal memo that revealed that the company intentionally had decided against any form of corporate restructuring in order to avoid FCC scrutiny of its ownership structure.[106] Thus the NAACP's case against Fox seemed solid. The station group was afoul of 310(b), and Fox had not been candid in its dealings with the commission. But in response to its investigation, the FCC found itself on the receiving end of sustained political pressures from Congress to leave Fox alone.[107] In addition, suspicions circulated about the timing of a $4.5 million book deal awarded to Speaker of the House Newt Gingrich, in the midst of the Fox investigation, by HarperCollins, a publishing company owned by Murdoch.[108] The NAACP filed a supplement to its petition to deny, noting the contract and raising the question of whether Murdoch was improperly trying to influence the proceedings.[109]

Fox was victorious in its battles against the NAACP. The WGBS deal fell through, but otherwise the FCC granted Fox's request for a permanent waiver to purchase the *Post*, and in 1995 the appellate court affirmed the FCC's decision.[110] The concerns raised by the NAACP and other petitioners over its impact on media diversity were brushed aside or rendered insignificant in light of Fox's willingness to rescue the *Post* from financial ruin, thus preserving a valued media voice within the community. Similarly, after investigating and determining the veracity of the foreign ownership charges leveled against Fox, the commission arguably jumped through remarkable logical hoops to absolve Fox of any wrongdoing, asserting, for example, that the commission's process of calculating alien control in 1985, when Murdoch applied for Fox's initial six stations, may not have been clear and finding no evidence that Fox intended to deceive the commission. Furthermore, the commission determined that the network served the "public interest" and, as a viable network competitor to the Big Three, offered an important form of diversity.[111]

One could interpret the Fox-NAACP confrontation as does Marvin Kitman, who in a 2011 *Harper's* piece identified it as one of two opportunities to stop Murdoch's incursion into U.S. media and the "cultural revolution in television that overstimulates us with reality shows and undernourishes us with news-lite celebrity 'journalism' and less-than-meets-the-eye reporting" that Fox's rise augured.[112] The second turning point, according to Kitman, occurred a couple of years later when Ted Turner initially refused to carry the Fox News Network on Time Warner Cable in New York. In both instances Murdoch capably secured support from powerful politicians and especially used his newspapers to impugn the character of those seeking to prevent the expansion of his media holdings, including calling Honig a "bloody idealist" and a "communist" and circulating a theory that the NAACP had conspired with CBS in its petitions, in essence acting as a front for the network.[113] The political pressure, in Kitman's view, was a particularly important factor in the outcomes of these incidents, as members of Congress lambasted the FCC for the investigation of Fox's 310(b) compliance.

If Fox's win marked an important step in Murdoch's penetration into the U.S. media market, the NAACP's defeat was consistent with the way the commission had treated the public interest goal of diversity, especially as it related to racial diversity, in this era. Indeed, as the FCC enabled the growth of Fox, it perhaps issued its most bald statement about what kind of diversity it would honor. To transform the three-network oligopoly into a four-network oligopoly was consonant with a vision of the public interest in which marketplace competitors vying for viewers' eyeballs would yield the optimal broadcasting service for the polity. The NAACP's interest in racial diversity, in contrast, was substantially less compelling.

The NAACP would find alternative ways to advocate for the rights of minorities within broadcasting. But throughout the 1980s and 1990s the NAACP's struggles over law and policy tried not only to preserve some semblance of advocacy for minority media rights but also to counter the whitewashing of history that instantiated the fiction of a "level playing field," in broadcasting policy and American culture more broadly. The NAACP's media advocacy during this period demonstrated how media deregulation could not be understood apart from minority media rights and that at this historical juncture a regulatory model reliant on the democracy of the market portended a broadcasting system unjustly wedded to its own undemocratic past.

Media Deregulation and the Culture Wars

Diversity, as a plank of broadcasting policy, was not a panacea. Much as Justice Marshall opined in the *Bakke* decision, to legitimate race-conscious policies under the rationale of "diversity" was to disavow how affirmative action had sought to remedy deep, long-standing, structural forms of inequality; diversity, instead, valued a multiculturalism of benefit to all, premised on the assumption that the mixing of different groups of people would diminish societal tensions. Still, for groups like the NAACP, appeals to diversity—a long-standing public interest goal of broadcast regulation—were a means to retain policies that at least recognized the paucity of minority participation in broadcasting. Though these policies were not explicitly remedial, and thus were somewhat unmoored from the history of discriminatory practices that necessitated their creation, they signaled an effort to redress the profoundly inequitable distribution of resources within the broadcasting sector and to recognize how this distribution affected the images, narratives, and perspectives to circulate over the airwaves.

Diversity for the NAACP, therefore, was inseparable from the long history of racial injustice in the United States. This was a point that the organization made in its myriad attempts to slow the tide of deregulation and to demonstrate the interconnection between media policy and civil rights. This history, for the NAACP, could not be swept away by assumptions of an already realized level playing field or by an embrace of a liberal individualism that sought to deny the import of racial difference in how people make sense of the world and their place within it. This history necessitated continued consideration of racial difference in media regulation, even or especially in the face of a neoliberal faith that free markets, unfettered by state intervention, would better serve the needs of broadcast audiences.

This history also offered a potential retort to the claims of people like the KFUO listeners that to reduce diversity to racial diversity was to misunderstand the contours of American pluralism, which included diversity of faiths, diversity of educational backgrounds, and diversity of taste and interests. To focus only on race as a vector of difference was to diminish other forms of diversity and to continue to privilege a group of people who had borne the fruit of interventionist government policy—of a minority rights revolution—for more than two decades. What of people of faith desirous of broadcasting stations serving their needs? Was not religious diversity a meaningful form of diversity as well? While the NAACP may claim that Lutherans had not been subject to the same historical forces as African Americans, and had not borne the brunt of analogous forms of oppression, such claims by the 1980s were wearing thin on populations who since the 1970s had begun to resent the affirmative uses of state power to address racial—and gender—inequality. The *Lutheran Church* case most pointedly pitted racial diversity against religious diversity, the station and its listeners feeling especially aggrieved that African Americans continued to make claims of injury in the context of a media landscape that seemed to privilege African American tastes and interests, while ignoring those of communities like their own.

Indeed, if the NAACP faced a regulatory environment in which conservative ideas—about markets, about racial difference—structured policy outcomes, it did so at a moment in which conservatives themselves also felt aggrieved by both television programming and television policy. If a battle line in the culture wars was over racial diversity in a post–civil rights society, another front was over the values and mores of popular culture itself, understood by conservatives to gleefully trample on traditional family values and to foment a lack of respect for traditional sites of authority. As the NAACP fought a system that it found too conservative in its understanding of media and civil rights, conservative advocacy groups mounted a fight against what they saw as a television system controlled by a constellation of liberal elites who evinced no regard for the values or beliefs of conservative Americans. This concurrent culture wars battle, discussed in the next chapter, offers an alternate window into media advocacy in an era of deregulation, as well as onto how the mobilization of a particular scripting of the past can legitimate a vision of what television—and broadcast regulation—should do in the present.

5

Fighting for a Safe Haven

///

The Parents Television Council and
the Restoration of the Family Hour

In his memorable address at the 1992 Republican National Convention, Patrick Buchanan announced that the country was divided between "us" and "them" in the fight over "who we are" as Americans. The country was mired, as Buchanan saw it, in a "culture war as critical to the kind of nation we shall be as the Cold War itself. But this war is for the soul of America." Of the many battle lines in the culture war—which included gay rights, women's reproductive rights, and voluntary prayer in the public schools—was the "raw sewage of pornography that so terribly pollutes our popular culture" and undermines the values of socially traditional Americans.

Buchanan was not alone. In his polemic about the decline of American civilization, *Slouching toward Gomorrah*, Judge Robert Bork characterized films and television programs as "propaganda for every perversion and obscenity imaginable."[1] Film critic Michael Medved summarized in his *Hollywood vs. America*: "Hollywood no longer reflects—or even respects—the values of most American families"; furthermore, "popular entertainment seems to go out of its way to challenge conventional notions of decency."[2] As television shows increasingly included risqué jokes and double-entendres, allusions to premarital sex, and outwardly gay characters; as they seemed to cast aspersion on traditional gender roles and on the family as an institution;

and as they tended to treat American institutions—the law, industry, the church—with derision, they signaled, in Buchanan's dyad, the triumph of the "them" over "us" mentality and a fundamental disregard for the values of conservative Americans. The America of the conservative imagination, one that had been on display in 1950s family sitcoms like *Leave It to Beaver* and *The Adventures of Ozzie and Harriet*, had given way, in the realm of cultural expression, to an America that had been called into being by the liberation movements of the 1960s and 1970s. Indeed, as one TV critic noted, "Ozzie and Harriet would be amazed by how many erection jokes modern TV can fit in the family hour."[3]

The attacks on the "raunchiness" of prime time during the culture wars signaled how some of the loudest voices decrying the "marketplace approach to regulation" were those of social conservatives. The FCC under Mark Fowler, consistent with its belief that an open marketplace, unfettered by government intervention, would yield the optimal communications system for consumers, initially had not enforced its indecency regulations, assuming that consumers—"voting" with their listening and viewing preferences—would best convey to broadcasters what was or was not acceptable content.[4] Yet an array of family-values advocacy groups, like the Parents Television Council (PTC), would argue that there had been a market failure; the broadcast networks' pursuing of "desirable" consumers had led to TV shows that assaulted American families. They saw television not as a "toaster with pictures," as Fowler did, but as a guest in families' homes and a site of moral instruction for their children. If the FCC in the 1980s defined the "public" of the "public interest" as consumers in a marketplace, social conservatives conceived of the "public" as traditional families seeking to inculcate good morals in their children.

The media advocacy of the PTC, much like social conservative activism during the culture wars, amplified a conservative discourse, ascendant since the 1970s, of the endangered family. As Robert Self has demonstrated, conservatives had opposed the gender and sexual liberation movements of the 1960s and 1970s through a discourse that positioned the American family as in peril, harmed by "not economic hardship, but moral assault."[5] Women's expanded entrance into the workforce, the adoption of no-fault divorce laws, the legalization of abortion, the increased visibility and social acceptance of gay men and lesbians—these represented to conservatives not the steady march of progress, in which notions of citizenship and its benefits became more egalitarian, but rather a narrative of steady decline, facilitated by the state, which unmoored and destabilized the bedrock social formation, the traditional family, within society. Conservative media advocacy became a site in which groups like the PTC reasserted an archetypal definition of the "family," defined in opposition to the prime-time content in which it was derided or attacked, and constituted by the imagined audience for whom such content was "dangerous." Television's status as a domestic medium only accelerated the safety/danger dyad that had structured conservative discourse on the family, broadcasting literally having become a "home invader,"[6] one that could corrupt the family within the confines of its own sanctum.

Television, for the PTC as for other social conservative media groups during the culture wars, operated not as a public sphere, a space in which the diversity of the nation was to be affirmed through national publicity, as it had for liberal reform groups like NOW and the NAACP. Rather, the PTC positioned television as a forum of moral instruction for protocitizens—children—whose future contributions to civil society hinged on their respect for traditional sites of authority, their embrace of the virtue of the heterosexual family, their understanding of the marital bed as the only site of sexual relations, and their belief that homosexuality is an immoral lifestyle choice. For the PTC, the only way to excise the threat to American families was to return to the past, both to forms of industry self-regulation that had capably constrained the excesses now on display in prime time and to the programming of television's imagined past, which had operated as a locus of traditional values, reified the nuclear family, and kept homosexuality in the closet.

As this chapter demonstrates, the PTC's chosen strategy to "clean up" the airwaves in the 1990s was advocacy for the restoration of the "family hour," a period in prime time set aside for family-friendly programming. In this the PTC's campaign tried to square a circle that had bedeviled conservative media activists since the 1960s. The proindustry disposition of conservatism had for decades run up against the perception that broadcasting—like the culture industries broadly—was controlled by liberal elites; to provide more power and autonomy to broadcasters was thus to strengthen the control of these elites over the instruments of an incredibly powerful form of communication. Thus, some conservatives had sought a regulatory response, from a more robust enforcement of the Fairness Doctrine to a more robust enforcement of the FCC's indecency regulations, to combat the ideological imbalance of the media. Other conservatives had seen broadcast *regulation*—like broadcasting itself—as a tool of liberals and as an unjust interference in free enterprise. For some conservatives, in other words, media regulation could address the problem of liberal bias; for others, media regulation had created—and propelled and codified—the overwhelming liberalism of the media.[7] The PTC's family-hour campaign, along with its attacks on regulatory and legislative fixes to the problem of indecency in the 1990s, thus allowed the organization to address what it saw as the liberalism of prime time while casting suspicion on solutions that involved a more interventionist state in regulating the broadcasting industry.

Prologue: Regulating the Family—The Family Hour and Indecency Regulations in the 1970s

Alongside the formation of the PTC, critics in multiple publications noted the "coarsening" of prime-time content and frequently evoked the "family hour" to underscore just how different American broadcast television of the 1990s seemed to be from the prime time of the past. They juxtaposed the "adult" situations and comedy of contemporary television with a more wholesome television past, a period when networks honored a "family hour" of viewing by scheduling shows like *The Waltons* or *Little House on the Prairie*.[8] Throughout the 1990s, newspaper and magazine articles identified, and often decried, the "sex jokes, bathroom jokes, and body-part jokes"[9] that overwhelmed the dialogue of situation comedies airing at 8 P.M. Significantly, though, such pining involved a reimagining of the history of the "family hour" and the purchase it had had on network scheduling practices.

The histories of the "family hour," and of the FCC's indecency regulations, serve as important context for the media reform battles leveled by social conservative groups like the PTC during the culture wars. The family hour, a form of industry self-regulation encouraged by the FCC, and the indecency rules, adopted as official FCC policy, were departures in how the FCC historically had approached broadcast regulation.[10] By and large the FCC previously had justified both structural regulations (ownership restrictions, for example, or licensing decisions) and content regulations (most notably the Fairness Doctrine) via an appeal to the scarcity of the broadcast spectrum. Given that there was a limit on how many "speakers" could have access to the airwaves, and given that broadcast licensees were granted a special privilege to use a scarce public resource, the commission had the authority to impose regulations on licensees to assure that they met their obligations to serve the public interest, convenience, or necessity. When the Supreme Court weighed in on the constitutionality of FCC regulations, from the restrictions it imposed on network-affiliate relationships in 1938 to the Fairness Doctrine itself, it, too, pointed to the scarcity rationale to affirm the policies. As the Court opined in its *Red Lion* decision, finding that the Fairness Doctrine did not violate the speech rights of broadcasters but rather protected the speech rights of listeners: "In view of the scarcity of broadcast frequencies, the Government's role in allocating those frequencies, and the legitimate claims of those unable without governmental assistance to access those frequencies for expression of their views, we hold the regulations and ruling at issue here are both authorized by statute and constitutional."[11]

When in the 1970s the FCC tackled the issue of violent and sexual content, it justified its policies not on scarcity grounds but on the imagined relationship between broadcasting and children. In its encouragement of the family hour and its adoption of specific indecency rules, the FCC reconceptualized the "public" as private families, its own role as their protector, broadcasting as unique in its location in the private space of the family home. Importantly, at the time, the FCC's efforts to address broadcast morality were interpreted—by broadcasters, media producers, and dissenters on the commission and on the courts—as cudgels to silence politically or culturally minoritarian perspectives. Thus when the issues of broadcast decency reemerged during the culture wars, a rhetorical and regulatory framework was in place to legitimate restrictions on broadcast speech to promote the welfare of families, as were the traces of resistance to these practices in the name of cultural pluralism.

The "family hour" had been a short-lived form of self-regulation adopted by the broadcast networks and the National Association of Broadcasters (NAB) in the mid-1970s. Concerns had accelerated in the 1970s over the impact of televisual violence on children, spurred by the Surgeon General Scientific Advisory Committee on Television and Social Behavior's report on television and violence, which had been commissioned by the Senate Subcommittee on Communications in 1969. After the release of the report in 1972, Congress repeatedly turned its attention to how, when, and whether violent programming had a negative impact on young viewers. In 1974 Congress required the FCC to investigate the commission's ability to address "violence and obscenity" on the air, especially given the effect of such content on children. Should the FCC not comply, it would risk a cut to the agency's budget.[12] Out of this threat the family hour emerged.

The family hour resulted from private meetings among FCC chairperson Richard Wiley, the broadcast networks, and the NAB. It was not an official FCC policy, nor was it provisioned by an act of Congress; the wisdom or efficacy of this approach was not subject to public comment, expert testimony, or administrative review. Rather, it was a voluntary system of self-regulation adopted by the networks and codified in the National Association of Broadcasters' television code, at the encouragement of the FCC's chairperson. Under the family-hour system broadcasters agreed to set aside the first hour of prime time (8 P.M.), as well as the hour that preceded it, for programming safe for families to view.[13] Although crafted in response to anxieties over televisual violence, the family hour became a much more expansive program to redirect or censor, depending on one's view, the more controversial content that was part and parcel of the relevancy prime-time programming of the 1970s.

The implementation of the family hour occurred against the backdrop of another significant change in broadcast regulation, one that had facilitated a shift in the content politics of prime-time programming. In 1970 the FCC had adopted the Financial Interest and Syndication Rule, also known as Fin-Syn. Fin-Syn restricted networks from having a financial interest in programming outside of news and from holding domestic syndication rights for entertainment programming; it thus prevented vertical integration by separating ownership of production from ownership of distribution. Its goal was to combat the monopsony power of the Big Three broadcast networks—in which they constituted a set of very limited, and therefore very powerful, buyers of content—over independent producers. The FCC's hope was that Fin-Syn would redirect networks to purchase diverse, quality programming rather than to contract with producers from which they were able to secure the most favorable terms, including syndication rights.[14]

Fin-Syn was implemented alongside other shifts in the TV landscape. The broadcast networks, seeking the young audience so desired by advertisers, abandoned many of its high-rated shows, which had been successful with the "wrong" demographic of older, more rural viewers, and replaced them with programming intended to appeal to a young, educated, urban audience. This turn toward seeking a "quality" audience rather than a "mass audience,"[15] coupled with Fin-Syn, promoted the growth of programming by independent television production companies like Norman Lear's Tandem and MTM, which created prime-time series—such as *All in the Family*, *Maude*, and *The Mary Tyler Moore Show*—noted for their relevancy and quality, their discussion of the taboo and controversial, and their engagement with issues like racial discrimination, women's liberation, gay rights, and abortion. Though shows like *All in the Family* were polysemic, enabling viewers both to laugh at and laugh with Archie Bunker as he lobbed racial epithets and ethnic slurs, its creators were noted liberals who sought to use television to address the exigent issues of the day.[16]

The family hour became a particular problem to this kind of programming. It seemingly gave the broadcast networks license to impinge on independent producers' freedom to address certain topics, to reject scripts based on vague and nebulous concerns about the family viewing audience, to stall production while the appropriateness of an episode's content was assessed, or to move shows to later times of the broadcast schedule and, in deeming them not acceptable for the family hour, severely diminishing their syndication potential. For example, Tandem's *All in the Family* was moved from its Saturday 8 P.M. slot to Monday at 9 P.M. Since the most lucrative time to broadcast syndicated shows was in the hour right before prime time, series deemed inappropriate for the family hour during their first run would have a very hard time being picked up for rebroadcast by local stations. In addition, the family-hour policy could slow production and raise production costs given that, as writer Larry Gelbart noted, it became "costly for a cast to wait and not be filmed while you run to the phone and find out children aren't supposed to know what virgins are."[17] The family hour also was having a chilling effect on prime-time content, exemplified by a CBS executive's recommendation that producers limit their material to that which would avoid upsetting the most "uptight parent that could be imagined."[18] The creative community in Hollywood accordingly filed suit against the networks, the NAB, and the FCC.

In *WGA v. FCC* (1976) the court avoided ruling on the legitimacy of the family hour and instead insisted that the "question is who should have the right to decide what shall and shall not be broadcast and how and on what basis should these decisions be made."[19] The problem with the policy, according to the court, was that it robbed local licensees of the power to determine how best to schedule for their local communities; the FCC and the NAB had no right to coerce them into conforming to a rule that had been developed "in closed-door sessions" and outside "legislatively mandated administrative procedures."[20] This decision was reversed by another appellate court in 1979, which remanded the charges brought against the family hour for the FCC's consideration. The FCC issued its opinion on the WGA charges in 1983, determining that Wiley had not coerced the networks and the NAB to adopt the family hour.[21] However, since 1979 the policy had fallen into disuse, and by the time the commission reached this conclusion, the NAB had dissolved its television code as part of an antitrust settlement with the Justice Department.[22] Thus the family hour was quite short-lived in practice, though it would be evoked by television's critics long after it had been abandoned as a formal policy.

The formation of the family-hour policy coincided with the FCC's formulation of specific policy to address broadcast indecency. Both hinged on marking out particular times of the broadcast schedule as safe for families. The family-hour policy positioned the networks in the role of surrogate parent, or parental ally, determining what kind of programming would be appropriate for families with children to see. The indecency rule would give this kind of authority to the FCC, when it similarly positioned its prohibitions on indecent content as an intervention on behalf of parents to assure that their children did not stumble on programming harmful to them. And if the creative community understood the family hour as an obstacle to their ability to address controversial topics, many critics of the indecency policy would read it as a tool to silence dissenting and minoritarian voices under the guise of "decency" and child protection.

Dating back to the Radio Act of 1927, and codified by Title 18 Section 1464 of the U.S. Code, Congress had forbidden the utterance of "obscene, indecent, or profane" language over the airwaves. Yet for the first few decades of broadcasting, the FCC had had little need to enforce this prohibition. As Lili Levi has demonstrated, up until the 1950s, whether out of fear of FCC condemnation or out of their own self-interest, broadcasters by-and-large did not engage in sexually explicit talk over the airwaves. In the 1950s and 1960s, alternative, listener-supported radio stations especially became targets of early rumblings of FCC interest in indecency, as they were sanctioned for broadcasts, for example, of discussions of homosexuality or for readings of poetry and novels that contained four-letter words. At this point the FCC did not develop a cogent policy on indecent speech but rather justified its sanctions on the stations as part and parcel of its assessment of their public interest performance.[23]

In the 1970s the FCC formalized its approach to broadcast indecency. Borrowing from contemporary obscenity law, the FCC initially defined *indecency* as speech that was "patently offensive by contemporary community standards and wholly without redeeming social value." As it had with its earlier wrist-slaps for indecent content, the FCC initially targeted, as Levi writes, "relatively powerless non-commercial stations and alternative counter-cultural programming" in its application of its new indecency standards.[24] The commission sanctioned nonprofit radio station WUHY, for example, for a broadcast of an interview with Grateful Dead guitarist and songwriter Jerry Garcia, who sprinkled the word *fuck* in his answers. While "patently offensive" to the majority of the FCC, Commissioners Kenneth Cox and Nicholas Johnson saw the commission's response as an attack "not on words but a culture, a lifestyle it fears because it does not understand."[25] In the early 1970s the commission would also target commercial "topless radio" broadcasts, which included frank discussions about sex and sexuality, in its application of its indecency policy.

The FCC would reconfigure its indecency standard once again in response to a broadcast on Pacifica's WBAI, in the middle of the day, of George Carlin's comedy routine satirizing the "seven words" you could not say on the airwaves. The FCC here defined indecency as "language that describes, in terms patently offensive as measured by contemporary community standards for the broadcast medium, sexual or excretory activities and organs, at times of the day when there is a reasonable risk that children may be in the audience." At the core of indecency regulation was the need to address the "exposure of children to language which most parents regard as inappropriate for them to hear."[26] As a result the commission opined that "patently offensive language" should be regulated like a public nuisance and channeled to a time of day when children are less likely to be in the audience. The FCC reasoned that such a restriction was merited by the peculiar conditions of broadcasting as a mode of communication to which children may have unsupervised access; in addition, broadcasting is received in the home, "a place where people's privacy interest is entitled to extra deference."[27] The commission created a safe harbor—from 10 P.M. to 6 A.M.—in which indecent content could be broadcast. In the first of what, by the end of the case, would be a string of pig analogies, the commission suggested that the restriction of indecent language was just a rezoning, not forbidding one to have a pigsty but simply preventing its location in a place where it does not belong.[28]

The Supreme Court, in its 1978 *FCC v. Pacifica* decision, affirmed the constitutionality of the policy and argued that broadcast media are subject to different First Amendment protections than are other forms of speech. Again, the particularity of broadcasting lay here, not as it had in the past, with the scarcity of the airwaves, but in broadcasting's location in the home. Broadcast media, according to the Court, is "uniquely pervasive," and accordingly because "the broadcast audience is constantly tuning in and out," prior warnings regarding content cannot really protect the viewer from encountering indecent content.[29] In addition, broadcasting is "uniquely accessible to children," and, consistent with other rulings in which the Court permitted the restriction of content appropriate for adults to be withheld from children, the indecency rules were justified.[30] It affirmed that the indecency rules were in fact like public nuisance laws and that indecent content, to quote a ruling in a public nuisance case, "may be merely the right thing in the wrong place,—like a pig in the parlor instead of the barnyard."[31]

In his dissent in the *Pacifica* case Justice Brennan echoed Commissioner Johnson's concern that the commission's indecency rules were an attack on the speech of cultural minorities and dissidents. He warned that the majority decision would sanction the "dominant culture's efforts to force those groups who do not share its mores to conform to its way of thinking, acting, and speaking," and he accused his colleagues of an "ethnocentric myopia," the *Pacifica* decision itself an imposition of the justices' own "fragile sensibilities" on a culturally pluralistic society. Identifying that the "visage of the censor is all too discernible here," he argued that the Court's ruling "permits majoritarian tastes completely to preclude a protected message from entering the homes of a receptive, unoffended minority."[32] Invoking his own pig metaphor, Brennan quoted a line from Justice Frankfurter's decision in *Butler v. Michigan*, a case in which the Court outlawed banning books, by noting that the indecency policy was "to burn the house to roast the pig."[33] He also suggested that with this policy the FCC usurped the power of parents to determine what was appropriate for their children while simultaneously reducing the speech that adults can hear to that which is imagined to be acceptable for children.

Most centrally, Brennan's concern was that the commission's indecency policy, and the Court's affirmation of it, was a way to eliminate speech that offended their own sense of decorum, expose taboos they would prefer to remain hidden, articulate political and social values they found unpalatable. However, the majority of the Court, along with the FCC, in these instances did not imagine broadcasting, as the Court had done in its 1969 *Red Lion* decision, as a mediated public square; instead, it configured broadcasting as a guest in families' homes that must curtail what it says accordingly. The needs of the rest of the public, and the diversities across American families, here were subordinated to the imagined concerns of a normative American family, one that perhaps ironically had been propelled and codified by television programming itself.

In practice, however, the FCC had limited its definition of indecent speech to those very seven words Carlin had identified in his monologue. As long as broadcasters avoided using them, they avoided being sanctioned by the commission on indecency grounds.[34] Accordingly, broadcast content in the 1970s could, as Elana Levine has argued, wallow in sex[35]—from *The Love Boat*'s Lido Deck and its promise of sexual assignation to the discussions on *The Newlywed Game* about young couples' preferences in "making whoopee"—without incurring the attention of the FCC, so long as they avoided the indecent words uttered by Carlin.

What would be so important about the precedent of the family hour and the FCC's policy on indecency was the way that they codified, in practice and in policy, a definition of the public as normative families, private citizens raising families rather than public citizens whose First Amendment rights hinge on their exposure to diverse perspectives and viewpoints. While the FCC throughout the 1960s and 1970s was asked by participants in the broadcast reform movement to recognize diverse publics, and to eschew the idea of a unitary general public, its indecency regulations returned to the notion of a monolithic public, here conflated with a universal "American family," whose values and understandings of injurious content were univocal. Such an imagined family seemed under threat during the culture wars, not only by broadcast content but by the "marketplace approach to regulation," which for a number of conservative groups had allowed the networks to privilege the values of viewers aligned with liberal causes, while ignoring the interests of the American family.

The freedom of broadcasters accelerated in the 1980s, when the FCC evinced little desire to enforce indecency regulations at all, preferring to let the marketplace determine the parameters of acceptable broadcast speech. Social conservative groups responded in turn in three ways. They leveled boycotts against sponsors of programming deemed antifamily. Under the leadership of the Reverend Donald Wildmon, for example, social conservatives launched in 1980 a "full-scale holy war over who should decide what sort of programs prime-time America sees."[36] In this campaign Wildmon and Jerry Falwell's Coalition for Better Television monitored the broadcast networks to identify the sponsors of the most offensive shows in preparation for a threatened but never launched boycott.[37] Throughout the 1980s and into the 1990s, social conservatives routinely deployed the sponsor boycott to protest offensive prime-time content.[38]

In addition, conservative groups pressured the FCC and Congress to make the indecency regulations more robust. In a "final plea" to conservatives in 1987, as he left his position as director of communications at the Reagan White House, Buchanan implored that conservatives "demand of that toothless lion, the FCC, that it begin pulling the licenses of broadcasters who flagrantly abuse the privilege."[39] This was in the spirit of what members of Morality in Media and the National Federation for Decency had done when in 1986 they protested Fowler's renomination via pickets at the FCC and sent letters to senators opposing the nomination. Fowler was an unacceptable chair because, as per Wildmon, he had done "nothing, zero, zilch" about broadcast indecency.[40] In response the FCC reversed course, working with socially conservative groups to find test cases to extend the parameters of what "indecent" content was, as well as to expand the FCC's enforcement power. In this, the commission would be joined by members of Congress, most notably Sen. Jesse Helms (R-N.C.), who pushed through legislation to expand the scope of the commission's indecency regulations. Though the federal courts would find unconstitutional attempts to diminish or get rid of altogether a "safe harbor" for indecent content, they would allow the commission's more robust definition of what indecency is, which in practice included double-entendres, shock jock potty humor, and discussions of rape.[41]

The third path, taken in the PTC's family-hour campaign, focused on compelling industry self-regulation. While other conservative groups at the time focused on consumer boycotts, demonstrating the economic power of "traditional families," and others pressured the FCC and Congress to amp up the commission's indecency enforcement mechanisms, the PTC in the 1990s focused on creating a rhetorical scaffolding through which politicians, the networks, and the public would view television and its threat to the family. In this it drew on and adapted the strategies of the Media Research Center from which it sprang.

The MRC, the PTC, and Media Advocacy Strategy

The PTC was founded in 1995 by L. Brent Bozell III, initially as the entertainment arm of Bozell's Media Research Center (MRC). Bozell was a scion of sorts to a conservative aristocracy. He is the nephew of William F. Buckley Jr., one of the leading conservative intellectuals in post–World War II America. Bozell's father, also named Brent Bozell, coauthored with Buckley a defense of Joseph McCarthy, ghostwrote Barry Goldwater's seminal *The Conscience of a Conservative*, and was one of the first editors and contributors to Buckley's *National Review*. While Buckley and the elder Bozell substantially fostered the growth of the postwar conservative movement through their writings, especially through the *National Review*, the younger Bozell had been, and is, a critical player in more contemporary conservative politics through his media activism, cohering and galvanizing the right through the PTC's and MRC's critique of mainstream media institutions.

The MRC, Bozell's first media activist group, was founded in 1987. Bozell, and many of the people who would join the MRC's staff, had worked at John "Terry" Dolan's National Conservative Foundation (NCF), which had formed to promote conservative candidates for office. In the early 1980s the NCF would set its sights on the problem of liberal bias in the media. The NCF embraced a range of tactics in its media activism, from hosting conferences on the conservative movement and the liberal bias in the media, to producing bumper stickers that read "I don't believe the liberal media," to campaigns targeting television series that evinced, to the NCF, a liberal bias. Perhaps most important, the NCF would produce *NewsWatch*, a newsletter edited by Brent Baker, which would provide the template for *MediaWatch*, also helmed by Baker, the MRC's first signature publication. After Dolan died in 1986, Bozell, who fundamentally disagreed with Dolan's sister over the future of the foundation, put his energies into creating the MRC, taking much of the NCF staff with him.[42]

The MRC, too, focused on the issue of bias in news reporting. Since its founding in 1987, the MRC collected data, statistics, and direct quotations to corroborate its claims of liberal media bias. Much like many other media advocacy groups, from educators in the 1950s to feminists in the 1970s, the MRC privileged the monitoring study to make its allegations of media misconduct credible and legible. Its monthly newsletter *MediaWatch* consisted of "News Bites," short stories that documented instances of liberal bias in the news; a "Revolving Door" section that charted the flow of personnel between political appointments and positions in the media; a "Study" that looked in-depth at one particular issue's coverage in the media, including statistical data and direct quotations from the news sources studied; and a "Janet Cooke Award," which honored the news story of the previous month that the MRC deemed most unconscionably biased. Cooke, the award's namesake, had been a reporter for the *Washington Post* and a recipient of the Pulitzer Prize for a feature she had written on a heroin addict. Cooke later returned her prize and lost her job at the newspaper after admitting that the subject of her article was a fake—not an actual person but a composite of many people she had met. In evoking Cooke in its awards for more than ten years, the MRC implicitly called its winners liars, biased reporters shirking their professional responsibilities. Though this charge was often hyperbolic, between 1988 and 1998 the MRC continued to find some unlucky recipient to single out as especially biased and irresponsible.

However, unlike other media advocacy groups, the monitoring studies for the MRC were not a tool to persuade policy makers and legislators but the public at large. Its use of humor and name-calling, much like that of radio talk-show host Rush Limbaugh, expressed its incredulity at the performance of the media and induced its members and readers to view the mainstream media not as a legitimate site of news and information but as a joke of a public sphere, one run by charlatans, ideologues, and liars. The Cooke award exemplified this strategy, as did the MRC's list of "Notable Quotables," direct quotations it found especially slanted and/or funny, and its annual banquet honoring the journalists who—in its estimation—made silly or especially slanted remarks, for years referred to as "The Linda Ellerbee Awards for Distinguished Reporting." According to Bozell, the MRC had named the award after journalist Ellerbee because she "epitomizes a liberal blowhard who has nothing to say."[43]

Though the MRC had subscribers who paid for its publications, two-thirds of its circulation was to groups and individuals who received the publications for free, including conservative foundations, magazines, think tanks, talk-show hosts, public figures, members of Congress, and the major mainstream news organizations. According to Baker, a goal of the MRC was to provide "ammunition" to other conservative organizations and figures who may seek to make a compelling case for media bias. At its height of popularity *MediaWatch* was distributed to more than twenty-five thousand readers. The MRC publicized its work through advertisements in magazines like the *National Review* and through direct mail campaigns.[44] Its work would provide data to conservative media outlets, which routinely lambasted the mainstream media for its liberal media bias, and would pave the way for denunciations of the liberal media by conservative pundits like Bernard Goldberg and Ann Coulter, the latter of whom, in the acknowledgments to her 2002 *Slander: Liberal Lies about the American Right*, wrote, "Novenas should be said to Brent Bozell and the Media Research Center, who have been on the case long before I was."[45] If, as Kathleen Hall Jamieson and Joseph Capella argue, conservative media has constituted an "echo chamber" that emphasizes how the mainstream press distorts coverage of current events to advance a liberal agenda,[46] this frame—along with the evidence to support it—was, and is, greatly advanced by the work of the MRC. In addition, through this work the MRC gained both reputational capital as a leading conservative watchdog group and strong political allies, in conservative members of Congress and in conservative media personalities, who drew on the group's findings.

The MRC sought to correct the problems of the liberal media not by extending the power of the state to intervene in the broadcast marketplace but through a steady informational campaign to persuade the public to see the mainstream media as it sees it. The MRC was a great believer in deregulation—as Baker said, "We are free-market oriented here"[47]—and has rejected the notion that the government, through regulatory action or legislation, should redress the problems of the televisual public sphere, even as its reports document its failures. The MRC did not, as had other conservatives like Reed Irvine and Phyllis Schlafly, advocate for the retention of the Fairness Doctrine when it was on the chopping block in the late 1980s. Indeed, as the organization matured, its opposition to federal regulation of the airwaves intensified, and it worked actively against the implementation of new policies in the public interest.[48]

In 1989 the MRC turned its sights to entertainment programming. Its *TV, etc.* would "examine the political biases of the entertainment world"— analyzing the content of television, motion pictures, and music—and would provide "in-depth reporting on the political activities of the stars themselves." Its first issue, for example, lambasted the sitcom *Head of the Class* as "a study of leftist programming at its worst," identifying star Howard Hesseman as "a liberal activist" who appeared in pro-labor advertisements; the issue also included quotations from series such as *Family Ties* and *Designing Women* as examples of anticonservative, proliberal sentiments.[49] A 1990 issue warned parents that MTV operated as a "powerful weapon to advance the Hollywood Left's political agenda."[50] For the MRC, what was dangerous about entertainment programming was the values that it fostered, not primarily its sexual or violent content. As Bozell noted, "We've found that parents are to be questioned, businessmen are to be suspected as greedy, dishonest, or murderers. Religion is to be ridiculed or feared and conservatives are to be reviled. Culturally, it shapes a generation."[51]

TV, etc., according to Baker, never found much of an audience.[52] But the MRC would continue to adapt its focus on entertainment programming and, much like it did in its analysis of news content, assess its ideological slant. Bozell's syndicated columns routinely flagged the liberal bias of entertainment shows, from their sanctioning of gay rights to their sanctioning of abortion rights to their sanctioning of single-parent family structures. His columns also sought to make visible the politics of entertainment television and to redirect how fellow conservatives defined the medium, imploring them to see it not as "mindless junk" but as the "greatest shaper of our culture." If conservatives were to combat the gains made by the left on social issues, they would have to take on the television industry.[53] In addition, in 1994 the MRC created a resource for conservatives in its "Parents' Guide to Prime Time Television Programming," which rated prime-time television shows from a conservative perspective, using a traffic-light system: green-light shows were acceptable; yellow ones may "contain anti-conservative content or adult material inappropriate for children"; red shows "frequently attack conservative views and traditional values."[54] This traffic-light taxonomy would become central to the PTC's resources for parents, though it would omit explicit references to conservatives and address its findings to parents.

The PTC emerged in 1995 out of the MRC's interest in entertainment programming, yet it would examine not the political leanings of the actors and writers but rather its content and its presumed assault on American families. The PTC claims to have been formed as a response to the state of American television in the 1990s, when, in its own words, "decency took a nose dive."[55] Much like the MRC, the PTC emphasized its extensive research activities, especially its monitoring of prime-time television content. In addition, the PTC positioned itself as a resource, much like the MRC, that provides informative material to interested parties on the state of the media. Yet rather than pitting a politically liberal and elitist news media against an aggrieved public, the PTC has juxtaposed an immoral and elitist entertainment media against embattled private citizens, American families whose homes are unjustly invaded by inappropriate content that undermines moral parenting goals.

Throughout the second half of the 1990s the PTC both leveled a public relations campaign and formed strategic alliances with members of Congress to reassert the crisis of the family hour, position the family as the ur-category of civic life, and normalize its own particular definition of family values as common sense, universal, and shared by all parents. At this time the PTC cast suspicion on government solutions to the problem of indecency (much as did the MRC), focusing instead on compelling the industry to serve the needs of parents. The PTC's early media advocacy framed an interventionist state response as misguided and counterproductive, incapable of effectively addressing the problem of broadcast indecency and paradoxically only providing more power to the very corporations responsible for it.

Restoring a Vanishing Haven: The PTC, the Family-Hour Campaign, and Gay Visibility

The family-hour campaign in the 1990s was a response to a perceived market failure, in which the broadcast networks' pursuit of a desirable demographic had pushed them to abandon their commitments to the American family. This abandonment was evident not only in the uptick in coarse language and sexual references but, importantly, in the increased visibility of gay characters on television. Yet rather than ask for greater government regulation, the campaign asked for greater corporate responsibility. In this the family hour sought a return to a past, both of more wholesome programming and of industry restraint, when the creators of culture recognized their moral obligations to their publics. To save the family was thus not to ask for an expanded role of the state—whose own actions the PTC saw as ineffective and counterproductive—but to compel the industry to do the right thing by making clear how its actions threatened the American family.

While the PTC was concerned with a number of facets of prime-time content in the 1990s, its family-hour campaign targeted the increasing prevalence of gay characters on television. Gay visibility, by definition for the PTC, was antifamily. For conservative media groups the visibility of gay and lesbian characters in the media was a critical political issue, especially in this period. The battle was part and parcel of a longer history, outlined by Tina Fetner, of the intertwined political struggles of the religious right and gay and lesbian activists. In the 1990s, when the PTC emerged, gay rights were a crucial juridical and cultural battleground, propelled into the national spotlight by, for example, controversies over gay and lesbian service in the military, public funding for the display of Robert Mapplethorpe's homoerotic photographs, and the fate of legal prohibitions against discrimination targeting gay and lesbian individuals. These battles, as Fetner puts it, "brought lesbian and gay issues from the margins of political discourse to the center. In the contests over the hearts and minds of the American people, the stakes were as much over symbols as policies."[56] Television's depiction of gay and lesbian characters throughout the 1990s was critical to these "contests over the hearts and minds" of the public; thus, it was an especially important arena of conflict for organizations like the PTC.

If, as Martha Nussbaum has argued, the expansion of gay legal rights has hinged on a shift from a "politics of disgust" to a "politics of humanity," then sympathetic representations of gay men and lesbians within the media could have political and legal consequences.[57] The flip side of this coin—that derogatory representations of gays and lesbians also had political and legal consequences—had animated gay rights activism since the 1970s.[58] The PTC's family-hour campaign, in which the organization labeled even the inclusion of a gay character as antifamily and implicitly dangerous to children, thus sought to erase gay people from the (televisual) public sphere, shoring up culturally what a number of conservative culture warriors sought to gain politically.

The PTC adopted a four-pronged campaign in the 1990s to restore the family hour. It compiled and circulated reports, based on analyses of prime-time content, that demonstrated the extent and kind of inappropriate content that circulated on network television during prime time; in addition, it rated individual programs based on the appropriateness of their content for children, which it also distributed. It used this analysis for its second prong, the enlistment of support of members of Congress to agitate for a restored family hour. The PTC also ran advertisements, both in the mainstream and trade press, to popularize its family-hour campaign and to flex its political muscles; Bozell's syndicated columns further promoted the PTC's family-hour efforts, as well as the framework of the "imperiled family" on which they rested. Finally, the PTC's critique of the television ratings and V-chip system mandated by the 1996 Telecommunications Act (discussed in more detail in the following section) became a platform for it to privilege the restoration of the family hour as the better way to protect families.

Given its origins in the MRC, the PTC's campaign for the restoration of the family hour began, perhaps expectedly, with monitoring studies. The PTC routinely selected a four- to six-week period, frequently the "sweeps" period, and assessed the content of programs on the broadcast networks. The results were compiled and circulated as reports, published under titles like *A Vanishing Haven: The Decline of the Family Hour* (1996), *The Family Hour: Worse Than Ever and Headed for New Lows* (1999), and *The Sour Family Hour: 8 to 9 Goes from Bad to Worse* (2001). The reports provided an introduction, which read as an executive summary of the studies' findings, before they turned to their data. Broken down by broadcast network, the reports provided statistics on the frequency of uses of obscenities and references to sexual behavior; while the reports acknowledged that violent content would also be inappropriate for children, they repeatedly indicated that vulgar language and sexual references were far more common in the programs studied. Their quantitative statistics would be complemented by examples from individual shows of the kind of content being telecast during the first hour of prime time. In addition, the reports often featured pie charts and bar graphs that highlighted the PTC's central findings and concluded with recommendations, which, expectedly, called for the restoration of a family hour in prime time.

In assessing whether content or language within a program posed a problem, the PTC used "this common-sense barometer: Would family members speak to one another this way at the dinner table?"[59] This question spoke to the orientation of the PTC, as well as to the politics of its reports. First, it reminded readers that television was a domestic medium, consumed in people's homes, much as their family dinners may be. Accordingly, it was like a guest at the family table and, especially when children may be around, should address its audience accordingly. Second, it presumed a singular model of an American family, with shared norms of decorum, ways of interacting, and views of what was and was not appropriate content. Third, in evoking the "dinner table," the PTC drew on a nostalgic site of imagined familial bonding— one visible in the kind of television content they wished the networks would return to—that underlined the organization's presumption of a normative, middle-class family.

In its reports the PTC did acknowledge that the "official" family hour had been struck down in 1976. Yet it claimed that the first hour of prime time "has always been the unofficial family hour," as it was home to "wholesome series such as *Little House on the Prairie, Happy Days, The Cosby Show,* and *Full House.*" While certainly much of broadcast networks' programming between 8 and 9 P.M. had offered domestic sitcoms, the slot also had been home to programming that would fall outside of the PTC's definition of content appropriate for children. NBC scheduled its short-lived *The Richard Pryor Show* (1977) during that period, and the same network was home to *Bosom Buddies* (1980–1984), a situation comedy about men who dress as women to live cheaply in an all-women's residence and "be surrounded by women in various stages of undress,"[60] as well as to a number of shows like *Magnum, P.I.* (1980–1981) and the somewhat macabre *Fantasy Island* (1978–1984), which made reference to sexual conduct outside the marital bed.[61] Even *Happy Days* (1974–1984), a show repeatedly identified as emblematic of the kind of "wholesome" programming that networks used to offer, was a series focused on the sexual desires of its young characters.[62]

In addition, television's critics had been decrying the loss of the "family hour" for more than a decade before the PTC published its first report. In the 1980s a series of articles noted the increased visibility of violence during the family hour, and in the early 1990s a flurry noted how it had become racy; both takes indicated that the notion of a family hour still resonated after it had been deemed unconstitutional but also signaled a perennial anxiety that it was not operative.[63] For the PTC the "family hour" was a touchstone, a nostalgic yearning for an earlier time of not only wholesome content but corporate responsibility. This rhetorical family hour was central for the PTC to the implementation of an actual family hour, one that would provide a "safe haven" to families negotiating the "raw sewage of pornography," in Buchanan's phrase, that characterized American popular culture in the 1990s.

The PTC's reports were informative and pedagogical, instructing readers to assess the morality of television programs through the PTC's own prism. In assembling charts and statistics, the PTC presented its case for a failing family hour in the language of social science, using metrics of assessment in which value is assigned based on a show's fidelity to "traditional values." The PTC's first report, *A Vanishing Haven*, penned by Thomas Johnson, a senior writer at the MRC's entertainment division, provides a good illustration of the PTC's claims and methods. The findings were based on a monitoring of four weeks of prime time in September and October 1995. Its first section, "Language: Has It Hit Bottom Yet?," quantified how many times particular "curse words and vulgarities" were used during the family hour and offered examples of how they would appear in a program. *Ass*, for example, was the "leader by far," with twenty-nine instances, in which characters made statements like "Kiss my ass" or "Drop his ass in the trash out back." Other tracked terms included *bastard*, *bitch, suck, piss*, and *bite me*. The report also included a bar chart that indicated how many obscenities during the family hour each network had telecast.[64] Importantly, none of these terms would qualify as "indecent" and thus were not subject to FCC action.

The report provided brief contexts for selected uses of terms ("Told a member of a wealthy family had passed away, a character on the 8 P.M. *Wings* snapped, 'That rat bastard.'") but did not indicate tone, response, or broader circumstance in which the vulgarities were uttered; as cited, they read predominantly as insults or expressions of discontent ("I just suck"). But the PTC made clear that utterance itself was the problem. The report lacked a discussion of why these expressions were harmful for children, assuming a self-evident parental disapproval in children's hearing statements like "The Ebola virus. That's gotta suck, right?"[65]

The second part of the report, "Sex: Almost Anything Goes," detailed instances of sexual content in family-hour programming. In this part of the report, however, Johnson made clearer why such content is objectionable. The PTC was concerned not only with references to nonmarital sex but with its condoning. The PTC found that premarital sex was common and condoned, extramarital sex was "treated" but not endorsed, and that marital sex was sometimes portrayed "lasciviously." The report also found treatments of "homosexual issues," including a story line on *Melrose Place* in which a gay man sued his supervisor for firing him, an issue that was presented in a "definitely pro–gay rights" manner. The report also identified "suggestive one-liners" and provided another bar chart tracking sexual content by broad-cast network.[66]

Perhaps obviously, the PTC was concerned not only with the inclusion of sexual content but with the stance taken within a show's diegesis about its acceptability and its morality. This is evident in a 1997 report, *A TV Ratings Report Card* (discussed more fully below), that commended an episode of *Clueless* for its "pro-abstinence" message when the topic of teen sex arose.[67] In addition, it is important that the PTC included discussions of gay rights in its "Sex: Almost Anything Goes" section, a story line about fighting job dis-crimination on sexual orientation grounds being located in the same category of harm as the promotion of premarital sex. The organization's objection to homosexuality on the screen was to its visibility and, within the confines of the shows, its acceptability. That characters identified as gay, regardless of their conduct onscreen, was for the PTC in and of itself inappropriate for children's consumption. This would be a recurring trope of the PTC's reports, in which it would characterize gay visibility as harmful to children.

This characterization of gay visibility as antifamily was present in the PTC's family-hour reports, but it was most strenuously voiced in its other publica-tions. The PTC since 1996 had monitored and assessed prime-time content based on a traffic-light system of classification. In the PTC's version green-light shows were safe for families, yellow-light shows contained some objec-tionable content, and red-light shows should be shielded from children's eyes. Based on this taxonomy, the PTC compiled lists of the ten best and worst family shows on network television. In these evaluations the PTC routinely identified any story line that reflected positively on gay rights as dangerous to families. *Melrose Place*, for example, made the top-ten worst shows list of the 1996–1997 season not only for the premarital and extramarital sex in its sto-ries but for coming out in favor of gay adoption.[68] *Dawson's Creek* topped the 1998–1999 worst list for both its frank discussions of teen sex and for "teen self-identification with homosexuality" as "given a thumbs-up" on the show. *Will and Grace* unsurprisingly also made the list of worst shows for that sea-son, offensive to the PTC for its "disingenuously saccharine presentation of the homosexual lifestyle."[69] Indeed, in each list of worst shows from 1996 through 2000, the PTC identified gay or bisexual characters, or references to homosexuality, within a series as unsuitable for and a threat to families.[70]

This understanding of gay visibility on television as, by definition, anti-family, is in no way surprising. Since the 1970s, as gay rights groups sought greater visibility and political protections, they were met with a powerful antigay backlash frequently reliant on a framing of gay people as immoral and sick, extrinsic to the civic body and therefore outside legal protection, and a threat to families, especially children. This antagonism between the "rights of parents" and gay rights underlay how the PTC would examine gay visibility on television: the presence of gay characters was an affront to the rights of parents to keep their kids safe from harmful content. And if, as Self has characterized the 1970s, "visibility produced liberation and backlash in equal measure,"[71] by the 1990s, as visibility was on the uptick on prime-time television, efforts by groups like the PTC became part of a new stage of the backlash against it.

Indeed, part of what the PTC was resisting was a shift in prime-time programming strategies in the 1990s that, as Johnson astutely notes in *A Vanishing Haven*, derived from the "networks' rush to appeal to the 18–49 demographic coveted by advertisers" and abandon children and their parents.[72] While demographics had mattered to networks since the late 1960s, when they sought a "quality" rather than merely "mass" audience for their programming, definitions of what constituted a "quality" audience would shift over time, though it would consistently skew young. Ron Becker has illustrated that in the 1990s, as broadcast networks had to compete with the expansion of cable for audiences, they increasingly sought to attract an upscale demographic to sell to advertisers. This demographic—what Becker labels SLUMPY (socially liberally upwardly mobile professional) but which also resembled David Brooks's Bobo (bourgeois bohemian) or Richard Florida's creative class—understood itself as socially liberal, as it embraced a multicultural rhetoric of inclusion, while also somewhat fiscally conservative, as it embraced neoliberal tenets of personal responsibility, the efficacy and virtue of free-market capitalism, and the existence of a meritocracy that structures the distribution of resources.[73] On television, as Becker argues, networks sought to appeal to the SLUMPY audience through an increased visibility of gay characters whose presence rewarded the open-mindedness of SLUMPY viewers and whose lifestyles, as depicted onscreen, resembled that of the upscale demographic so sought by the networks.

Gay characters on television in the 1990s, however, frequently were asexual or were denied intimate lives, or they operated peripherally within the narrative as opportunities for straight characters to demonstrate their valiant open-mindedness and tolerance as they defended gay men and lesbian women from intolerant bigots.[74] Gay characters on scripted TV shows in the 1990s often blended seamlessly within and ultimately served to reinforce heterosexuality, as they were both sanitized of any difference and frequently reinforced a cultural stereotype that could only imagine gay men as white and affluent with impeccable consumer tastes. Increased gay publicity, according to Eric O. Clarke, came at a price, one in which visibility codified a particular construction of homosexuality that synced with the values of straight citizens and, through these safe-for-straights characters, structured permissible expressions of gay identity.[75] Importantly, though, gay characters on television in the 1990s were presented largely favorably. Within scripted television, gay characters more frequently functioned as the target of uncivil and antisocial behavior than as perpetrators of it.

It was this increased visibility and acceptability of homosexuality that the PTC was responding to in its reports. But while other conservatives in the 1990s would frame their complaints with the media in terms of balance, the PTC would position its own within an imperiled family discourse. Groups like the Gay and Lesbian Alliance against Defamation (GLAAD) would tangle with conservatives over whether there was an "other side" to the issue of gay rights. Conservative organizations throughout the 1990s would argue that, in the name of balance, the networks have an obligation to present an opposing viewpoint on homosexuality, whereas organizations like GLAAD understood such claims to be not a legitimate position on a controversial issue but an expression of bigotry, not unlike racism or sexism, that spreads dangerous untruths that sanction myriad forms of violence—legal, physical, psychological, symbolic—against gay men and lesbian women.[76] The MRC's own analysis of television's coverage of gay rights throughout the 1990s would accuse journalists of selective reporting, of providing more time to a pro–gay rights agenda than to its detractors, and of a reliance on selective exclusions and omissions to hide the more controversial and objectionable positions and predispositions of gay leaders and their objectives.[77] Thus, for some conservatives gay rights on television was positioned as a public issue, subject to political debate, whereas for groups like the PTC it was a moral issue, equivalent to extramarital affairs, from which children should be shielded.

The funding of public television also would land in the crosshairs of these battles over gay visibility on television, especially in response to its telecasts of Marlon Riggs's *Tongues Untied*, an experimental documentary that explores the lives of gay black men, and *Tales of the City*, a miniseries adapted from Armistead Maupin's 1978 novel of the same name, which celebrated gay life in San Francisco in the 1970s. As William Hoynes has argued, the telecast of these programs united economic conservatives—who viewed public television as an unnecessary federal expenditure, especially in a diversified media landscape so different from that of the time (1967) when the Public Broadcasting Act was passed—and social conservatives, who viewed this programming as part of television's assault on American families, in a common battle to defund public broadcasting.[78] Conservative media activist stalwarts like Bozell and Wildmon vilified the broadcasts and inflamed public pressure against public broadcasting.[79] While PBS would survive these threats of defunding, the service would assume, as James Bennett has suggested, a far more cautious approach to its programming in their wake.[80]

Much as in the period of the original formation of the family hour, in the 1990s the PTC's family-hour campaign raised the slippery issue of whether efforts to protect families were, in practice, means to erase minoritarian perspectives from the public sphere. As the PTC positioned the visibility of gay characters as, by definition, antifamily, it sought to compel broadcasters to ignore the substantial, if also at the time controversial, progress on the cultural and political rights of gay people in the 1990s. In so doing, the PTC appealed to a long-standing concern over vulnerable audiences and asserted a normative understanding of the televisual public, conflated with a normative definition of the American family, for whom any exposure to homosexuality marked a crack in the moral fiber of the nation.

The Family Hour versus TV Ratings: Battling for Industry Self-Regulation

Appropriately, when Bozell testified at Senate hearings in 1997 to discuss the problem of prime-time television, he evoked the Hays Code.[81] The Hays Code, also known as the Hollywood Production Code, had been adopted by the major motion picture studios in 1930 and would be enforced by their Production Code Administration beginning in 1934. The Code not only restricted things that could not be uttered or shown—vulgar language, nudity—but provided a moral code that had to be followed. Evil always had to be punished; no religion could be mocked or attacked; representations of sexual perversion (homosexuality) were forbidden. The Code had been under revision since the 1950s, and in 1968 it was replaced with a movie ratings system. The latter enabled filmmakers to address more sophisticated and difficult topics, to include in their films nudity and forms of violence previously forbidden, and to present a more cynical worldview, in which murderers got away with their crimes, adultery could go unpunished, and traditional sites of authority were exposed as corrupt.[82] The parallels between what the PTC advocated, a return to the self-regulation of the family hour, and what it saw as potentially making the problem worse, a ratings system mandated by Congress as part of the 1996 Telecommunications Act, were clear, as was Bozell's pining for the kind of content that had been produced during the era of the Hays Code, in which popular media served as a moral compass, not a site of moral decay.

The family-hour campaign increasingly took shape in opposition to other fixes to the problem of broadcast "raunch." Throughout the 1980s and 1990s, as the FCC and Congress embraced a neoliberal faith in broadcast markets, they simultaneously tempered it with the consistent reregulation of broadcasting to protect children and aid parents. They amped up the enforcement and scope of the commission's indecency regulations; the 1990 Children's Television Act, in part, reversed the deregulation of children's programming adopted in 1984; and, importantly, the 1996 Telecommunications Act—which, as Patricia Aufderheide has characterized, "boldly articulates, at long last, that a competitive environment is equated with the public interest, is convenient, and is a necessity, and is to be facilitated by deregulation"[83]—included provisions for greater regulation on behalf of children, namely the V-chip and the ratings system.

Indeed, regulators and legislators at this time addressed libertarian objections over an intrusive administrative state and social traditionalist concerns over moral decay by embracing a somewhat internally contradictory approach to regulation that deemed the market the best arbiter of the public interest, except with regard to public morality, where the heavy hand of the state was needed. Social conservative media activism had played a big role in this.

Yet the PTC routinely framed the V-chip and the ratings system not as effective solutions but as devices that would only exacerbate the problem. Bozell's public opposition to the V-chip and the ratings system dated back to March 1996, immediately after the law's passage. In a syndicated column he depicted the technology as part of the "nanny state at work"; if Congress turned Democratic, the provisions could dangerously extend to sex and violence, as well as to "politically correct nonsense" like considerations of race, gender, ethnicity, and religion of the characters onscreen. More important for Bozell, the V-chip and the ratings did not solve—in fact, only exacerbated—the problem; they would sanction offensive shows and provide legal cover for those who sought to create more. State solutions, in other words, would make the problem worse. "The pollution on television can be eradicated only with a national outcry, a resolve to raise television's values out of the sewer."[84] His PTC, through its advocacy, would lead the way via its family-hour campaign.

In this the PTC would secure important allies. Though the PTC was especially proud of its celebrity supporters, like Steve Allen and Shelley Winters, arguably its most important allies were in the U.S. Congress. Senators Joseph Lieberman (at the time, D-Conn.) and Sam Brownback (R-Kan.) and Representative Lamar Smith (R-Tex.) in particular routinely endorsed the work of the PTC and adopted its mission as their own. Lieberman and Brownback frequently appeared with Bozell at press conferences on the release of a new PTC study.[85] The release of the PTC's reports garnered a good deal of press attention accordingly, and the organization quickly became a site of expertise on the issue of the television networks' performance during the family hour.

In addition, members of Congress lent their signatures to open letters to the broadcasting industry penned by the PTC, frequently in the form of advertisements published in the mainstream or trade press, calling on the networks to restore the family hour. In April 1996 the PTC ran a full-page ad in *Daily Variety*, a primary trade publication for the entertainment industries, urging the networks to restore the family hour through an open letter that was signed by seventy-four members of Congress. Legislators from across the political spectrum, from Paul Wellstone (D-Minn.) to Jesse Helms, lent their signatures to this initiative.[86] In May 1997 the PTC again ran an ad in *Daily Variety*, calling for the return of the family hour, this time signed by one hundred members of Congress and endorsed by Speaker of the House Newt Gingrich.[87] In July 1996 members of both houses of Congress proposed a nonbinding resolution to compel the broadcast networks to return to the family hour. In so doing, they acted not as legislators, per se, but as "concerned citizens" fearful of the destructive impact of television, which in the words of Smith, was "corrupting the morals and corroding the minds of a generation of Americans." He asked, "How can we be surprised at record numbers of teenage mothers, divorces and violent relationships?"[88]

In a 1996 cover story in *Policy Review* Lieberman, who had pushed for the V-chip, amplified Bozell's claims and drew on the PTC's (identified here as the MRC) research to support his own skepticism about the efficacy of the 1996 act's provisions. In his article "Why Parents Hate TV" Lieberman positioned the V-chip not as a technological fix to the problem of television content but as a surrogate for a more widespread "sense that our culture is not only out of touch with the values of mainstream America, but out of control as well." This sense has created a fear, in which families see television as a "threat to their children," in which television is "not only offensive, but on the offensive, assaulting the values they and most of their neighbors share." Much like the PTC, Lieberman posited a market failure because the industry's "zealous pursuit of the prized demographic cohort of young adults" has led it to "shut out the rest of the public." Lieberman suggested that social violence and unrest have their source in the "collapse of fundamental values," and he drew a connection between the "erosion of morals and the explosion of social pathologies around us." He then made the next logical connection, between the collapse of values and the "plummeting standards of decency on television and in our culture." Conceding that single television series cannot account for moral decline, Lieberman insisted, given the overwhelming power of the media, that the airing of "degrading" programs contributed to the "moral and social breakdown we are suffering." Embracing the central claim of the PTC, Lieberman insisted that the "most disturbing" facet of television programming's "slide into the gutter" was that much of it happened during the family hour. Thus, he implored the TV industry to see the V-chip as a "symbol of discontent" and, like the PTC, implored it to get its own house in order so that television would cease to be a "pariah in American living rooms."[89]

In 1997 the PTC's research and reports would further link its advocacy for the family hour with its criticisms of the ratings system. In the process the organization implicitly castigated Congress for its misbegotten effort to protect families and the television industry for its abrogation of its responsibilities to families. Its February 1997 study, *A TV Ratings Report Card: F for Failure*, determined that the ratings system was not working. "As applied, it is liberal in its definition of what kind of material is suitable for children."[90] The PTC likely meant *liberal* in two senses of the word: as not strict and as in line with leftist beliefs. Indeed, the report, also penned by Johnson, concluded that the "central flaw of the ratings system is permissiveness," in which the networks have a far more "liberal definition of what's fine for children than does the average parent."[91] If the ratings system had asked the networks to act as parental allies, as surrogate parents determining what was appropriate for children, they had failed because they were, metaphorically, bad parents, entertaining a level of permissiveness with regard to sexuality that "average parents" would reject.

The PTC, in studying two weeks of rated programming, determined that the ratings were assigned inconsistently. The industry had adopted the age-based ratings system used by the film industry, assigning shows the rating of G, PG, TV-14 (a variation on PG-13), and TV-M (a variation on the R rating). The PG rating in particular, assigned to three-fifths of the programming in the study, was "applied with abandon to shows containing sexual material and vulgar language and shows containing neither."[92] The problem was both the inconsistency—sometimes the rating was appropriate; sometimes it was not—as well as the fact that shows broadcast under the PG rating had featured "an outrageous level of raunch," including references to couples having sex on cars or a man masturbating in public. For the PTC there was one of two responses. The industry could assign content-ratings, which would better let parents know what to expect in an episode; however, this could, ironically, "encourage even racier programming since they could carry a clear content rating." The other alternative, preferred by the PTC, was "self-restraint," a "more wholesome prime time." As PTC executive director Mark Honig commented, "garbage labeled is still garbage, and that is the real problem."[93]

The PTC's next report explicitly conjoined its advocacy for the family hour with its attack on the television ratings. The "Family Hour": No Place for Your Kids, released in May 1997, analyzed the content of rated shows during the first hour of prime time. The report underlined that this time slot, "once a safe haven" for all viewers, may now be "the most dangerous time slot for families," especially since parents may still erroneously believe that turning on the TV would deliver shows analogous to the "favorite TV series of their childhood," when in fact programming is now "inundated with filthy language, sexual innuendo, and perverse storylines."[94] The report confirmed that the family-hour picture was bleak, the ratings system "badly misapplied." The PTC again suggested that a better ratings system was not the solution but rather that networks needed to air family-friendly shows during the family hour.

By June 1997 the television industry agreed to integrate content ratings, this concession a response both to the drumbeating of groups like the PTC and especially to threats of congressional action against the industry should it resist this more specific rating system. At this time a more robust ratings system was more palatable to broadcasters than a bill, supported by Democrats and Republicans alike, to mandate a violence safe harbor, analogous to the indecency safe harbor, from 6 A.M. to 10 P.M.[95] In addition, members of Congress threatened to deny spectrum to broadcasters for the development of digital telecasting unless they revised their ratings system. They also had floated legislation, cosponsored by Lieberman and Brownback, to provide an antitrust exemption to television networks to adopt an industry-wide code of conduct that would address sexual activities and innuendo on the airwaves. The bill was modeled on an analogous exemption from 1990 to 1993 to the television industry to address violence in programming. Bozell testified in support of the bill, using the PTC's studies as evidence of the harm to families posed by broadcast television. His testimony, in which he invoked the days of the Hays Code, also signaled that the medium of television in the past had been a "force for good," and his goal was to have TV "go back to what it once was, which was a force for good in a very troubled time."[96]

But despite the PTC's work, broadcast programming did not seem to "clean up" in the family hour. Bozell's columns and the organization's reports continued to chart the assault on American families, defining television in homes with children as "radioactive,"[97] but the organization's commitment in the 1990s to industry self-regulation and pressure, rather than regulatory action, did not seem to be delivering results. Especially in the realm of gay visibility, from the PTC's perspective the situation only got worse, in which by the end of the decade, for example, "lesbian motherhood becomes mainstream, and conventional morality is relegated to the fringe."[98] By 2000, Bozell announced that in regard to prime-time content the "libertarian in me resigns." If Hollywood refused to get its house in order, he—and his PTC—would support a "federal crusade" that in the realm of the entertainment industry would have "more merit" than other sectors.[99]

Throughout the 1990s the PTC propelled the trope of the family-in-danger, beset upon by immoral and inappropriate content during a time—the family hour—when it should presume to be safe from such an assault. Drawing on the strategies of the MRC from which it emerged, the PTC used research and reports to authenticate the group as the expert on television raunch and to mainstream its framing of televisual content as another source of threat to traditional families. For much of the 1990s the PTC would try to find industry solutions to the problem, eschewing government action as making things worse. In this it sought to balance the PTC's concerns over decency with the MRC's free-market orientation in its advocacy. Yet if, as Bozell had stated, it would only be through "the politics of shame" that the "industry will get the message,"[100] its concerted shaming campaign—through research, through publicity, through denunciations by members of Congress—had not done the job. Accordingly, in the following decade it would prioritize its cultural conservatism over its economic libertarianism and become the leading organization to fight for more robust indecency regulation of the airwaves.

The PTC and the Fight against Indecency

The family hour would continue to make an appearance in PTC research and reports. Yet it would play second fiddle to what has been, since the early

2000s, the PTC's priority: greater enforcement of the FCC's indecency regulations.[101] The PTC built into its website a form through which members and visitors can easily submit an indecency complaint to the FCC. The PTC became the organization most responsible for the deluge of indecency complaints filed with the FCC, as well as a strident voice in legal challenges to the constitutionality of the FCC's indecency rules as enforced.[102] The PTC is the organization credited with lobbing the FCC with complaints over Bono's claim that his Golden Globe Award was "fucking brilliant"; over Nicole Richie's query on the live broadcast of the Billboard Awards, "Have you ever tried to get cow shit out of a Prada purse? It's not so fucking simple"; and, of course, over the very momentary baring of Janet Jackson's breast during the halftime show at the 2004 Super Bowl. Through its indecency efforts the PTC has enlisted hundreds of thousands of people to get involved in media advocacy through the filing of complaints and, from the organization's perspective, educated them in their rights as members of the public, a public that owns the airwaves that deliver the "raunch" into their homes, as to how they can fight back.

The PTC's efforts to combat broadcast indecency through its copious indecency complaints marked a shift in strategy from the 1990s, one that enfolded the FCC in the group's designation of threats to the American family. The FCC's lack of action on indecency complaints, its timid sanctions for indecency violations, and its unwillingness to dedicate staff and resources to monitor the airwaves for indecent content had made it a large part of the problem. As Bozell put it in testimony before Congress in 2004, not only was the FCC a "toothless lion"—the very phrase Buchanan had used in 1987—but its inaction had allowed the networks to be "laughing at the public because they know they can do or say whatever they want to over the broadcast airwaves and the FCC won't lift a finger to penalize them."[103] The FCC's inaction, for Bozell, had rendered it more than an ineffective steward of the public's airwaves; it had made the commission an accessory to the assault on American families.

The PTC turned its attack on the inefficacy of the FCC at the very moment in which its chair, Michael Powell, was furthering the marketplace approach to regulation begun by Fowler in the 1980s. In 2002 Powell and the Republican commissioners on the FCC voted to repeal or loosen existing media ownership restrictions, which would enable even greater levels of media consolidation within the broadcasting industry. The 1996 act, which had mandated the ratings and V-chip, otherwise deregulated broadcasting, cable, and telecommunications, enabling high levels of horizontal and vertical concentration in its wake. Powell not only intended to pursue greater deregulation but, like Fowler, also indicated initially his desire to abandon content restrictions on broadcasters, viewing the differential affordance of speech rights to broadcasters—as opposed to cablecasters or magazines—as unjustifiable. Importantly, in both he would be met by strenuous opposition from social conservative groups like the PTC, who saw in myriad forms of deregulation potential danger to American families.

The PTC would join a broad coalition in 2003 and 2004 to protest the revision of the FCC's ownership restrictions. It was an odd coalition, one that united the National Rifle Association with Code Pink Women for Peace, the PTC and NOW, in a shared effort to resist this next step in the deregulation of American broadcasting.[104] Of the many concerns over an even more deregulated mediascape—which included fears of a reduction in diversity of perspective, an erosion of localism, an uptick in commercialism, and a penchant for formulaic programming—was the fear that putting even more power and control into existing media conglomerates would only accelerate "the raw sewage of the ultra violence, the graphic sex, the raunchy language that is flooding into their living rooms day and night through the television screen and poisoning the minds of an entire generation of youngsters whose parents' concerns are dismissed by an industry that admonishes them instead to stand guard over the TV sets, perhaps with a baseball bat, to keep impressionable children away."[105] Deregulation and media consolidation, in other words, posed a threat to the American family.

It would be this confluence of social conservatives and progressives, fighting economic conservatives, that would most effectively, if temporarily, resist the neoliberal logics that had governed broadcast regulation since the 1980s. Congress would temper the FCC's new rules, and a federal appellate court in 2004 would issue a stay on them, remanding the rules back to the FCC for more careful and thorough consideration of their public interest benefits or harms.[106] As it had in the culture wars, media reform exposed fissures across conservatives over the politics and efficacy of broadcast regulation, as well as the understanding of the public interest at its center.

Throughout the 1990s the PTC had sought to have it both ways, viewing the problem of television through the lens of social conservatives while seeking solutions compatible with a libertarian worldview. It was a strategy premised on the notion that the group could compel a return to the past, not only of *Ozzie and Harriet* but of the networks that saw fit to telecast it, through the steady exposure of television's harms to the American family. But much like, in Hartman's phrase, the normative America conservatives sought to recover, this era of television practices was long gone. The PTC's shift in tactics reflected this recognition and signaled that in the fight for the American family all options were on the table to excise the threat of more "raw sewage of pornography" entering into its home.

6

The National Hispanic
Media Coalition,
Spanish-Language
Broadcasting, and
Latino Media Advocacy

Media consolidation, for the PTC and for a wide range of public interest and civil rights organizations, was an issue of tremendous concern in the early 2000s. While FCC chair Michael Powell put great faith in the commission's online commenting system to gauge public support for revising media ownership regulations, Democratic commissioners Michael Copps and Jonathan Adelstein insisted that public hearings in local communities were critical to understanding media consolidation's impact on the everyday lives of Americans. In September 2006 Adelstein came to Austin, Texas, to assess what deregulation had meant in the Texas capital. Many of the Latino participants in the hearings drew a connection between low levels of minority ownership in a deregulated environment and myriad harms to the local community, from the absence of any radio station that played Tejano music to the inability of local businesses to advertise on stations run by media conglomerates with no local ties. In addition, one of the consistent complaints was that local Spanish-language broadcasters ignored the needs of the local Latino community. The speakers at the hearing made a distinction between serving Mexican nationals, as they accused the local Univision station of doing, and meeting the needs of the Chicanos and Tejanos living in Austin, who did not see their interests or concerns reflected in either English-language or Spanish-language programming. Their outrage stemmed from the media's misguided conflation of "Spanish-speaking" and "Latino," and the disregard of both broadcasters and the commission for the speech rights of Latinos in cities like Austin.[1]

This was a fight that organizations like the National Hispanic Media Coalition (NHMC) had been engaged in for almost two decades, in which it had been motivated by very similar concerns to those that arose that evening in Austin. A consistent issue for the NHMC since it formed in 1986 had been that the large Spanish-language television networks, which overwhelmingly serve a Latino population, had not been under the control of Latino ownership and frequently had not even employed Latinos in influential decision-making positions. In their advocacy battles over Spanish-language broadcasting, the NHMC faced the limitations of the minority media rights paradigm created during the height of the civil rights era, which did not conceive of linguistic diversity as an essential component of minority media rights. Accordingly, Spanish-language broadcasting fell outside of regulatory policies addressing the media needs of minority publics. As Hector Amaya has argued, U.S. media policy has operated simultaneously as a national language policy, one that has naturalized English and treated Spanish as "foreign." Accordingly, U.S. broadcast regulation routinely has diminished the cultural and political role of Spanish broadcasting for Latinos even though this has been the sphere in which Latino communication needs frequently have been met.[2]

This chapter examines battles over Spanish-language broadcasting via the NHMC's long engagement with the ownership structure of Spanish-language television network Univision. Over the course of thirty years the NHMC worked to compel Univision to be responsive to the interests of its Latino audience. In this, the NHMC's advocacy work would adapt to a changing regulatory environment, one that increasingly embraced a neoliberal understanding of markets and diversity, except in the realm—as the work of social conservatives had assured—of broadcasting's relationship to children. The NHMC's tactics capably responded to its own history of success and failure in its media advocacy, as well as to its increased sophistication in how to navigate the contemporary regulatory landscape to assure that broadcasters met the interests of the Latino community. In these efforts the NHMC would find itself allied with and also opposed to other Latino organizations who similarly saw Spanish-language broadcasting as a critical Latino public sphere but who pursued alternative paths to secure its responsiveness to Latino communities.

Prologue: Spanish-Language Broadcasting, Media Regulation, and the Public Interest

In 1976 representatives of the Spanish International Network (SIN), Spanish International Communications Corporation (SICC), and Televisa made a deal. Televisa, a Mexican television network run by the Azcarraga family, would offer twenty to twenty-five hours of original programming, originating from Mexico, for broadcast on SICC stations via the SIN network, which operated in the United States. Televisa would offer advertisers the opportunity to simultaneously address viewers in Mexico and in the United States. Televisa would pay SIN a fee to distribute the programming, which in turn would pay a fee to its affiliated stations to carry it. SIN's affiliates, including the SICC station group, would be able to sell two minutes of advertising per hour. The concept, the simultaneous broadcast of programming in Mexico and the United States, one especially lucrative for the Mexican Televisa, was called Univision.[3] Univision—"one vision"—well summed up the Azcarraga family's ambitions for its cross-border television service, uniting viewers in Mexico and the United States around its programming and cultivating a cross-national audience to sell to advertisers.

Latino media advocacy groups would seek to disrupt the "one vision" of transnational viewership at the center of Televisa's business model. In so doing, they frequently had to destabilize for the FCC its "one vision" of Latinos in the United States and to decouple the interests of Latinos from that of the Latin American media companies that historically had been the engine of the Spanish-language broadcast sector. This had been the concern of Austinites in 2006, who saw in the confluence of media consolidation and a long-standing devaluation of the political import of Spanish-language broadcasting by the FCC the basis for their own communication needs being dismissed in the local media landscape.

Indeed, while all Latino media reform efforts have intended to secure the cultural rights of Latinos—by, for example, bringing more Latinos into decision-making positions or challenging derogatory depictions of and narratives about Latino characters—the political stakes in efforts targeting English-language and Spanish-language media have differed. Much like the battles of other identity-based communities, Latino efforts to reform English-language media have been struggles for visibility, access, and control. Such participation has been necessary to assure the inclusion of Latino persons and perspectives within the televisual public sphere, to challenge a long history of exclusion and demeaning representations, and to push back against the structural impediments to Latino ownership of and employment in broadcast stations. Like other forms of media advocacy, these efforts also have been crucial in exposing how extant conditions fail to serve the interests of Latinos.

Struggles over the regulation of Spanish-language broadcasting have mattered differently. Their goal has been less to assure Latino visibility in a majoritarian public sphere than to persuade policy makers that Spanish-language broadcasting was critical to the communication needs of Latino citizens. Part of the struggle has been to puncture the conflation of "Spanish" and "Latino." Not only is the Latino "community" heterogeneous, but its communication needs extend beyond Spanish-language programming imported from Mexico or Venezuela. The presumption that imported programming was sufficient has spoken not only to the particular development of Spanish-language broadcasting in the United States, a sector historically dominated by Mexican television interests, but to the devaluation of Spanish as a "foreign language" and therefore as not a legitimate instrument of civic communication and participation.

This devaluation of Spanish-language media has been part and parcel of a broader construction of Spanish as a "foreign" language in the United States. As Amaya reminds us, this "is not a historical claim; it is a claim about the preferred histories we enjoy using to justify our present. It is a myth."[4] This myth has long and powerful roots, ones that speak not only to ethnoracial constructions of U.S. citizenship that have cast suspicion on Latinos as threats to—rather than members of—the civic body but also to the complex place of Spanish within American culture and within advocacy for Latino civil rights within the American past.

The vehemence with which advocates of "English only" laws insist that English is the sole national language of the United States belies a complex history in which other languages—notably German, French, and Spanish—have been spoken by large numbers of U.S. citizens and have been used as languages of instruction in schools and official languages in states with large populations who speak languages other than English. While the adoption of English has been associated with the assimilation process, as part of the immigrant's tale of embracing his or her new homeland, as Juan Gonzales makes clear, this narrative speaks only to those who came to the United States as immigrants willingly and who adopted English as the primary language of the public sphere. Omitted from this story are the enslaved peoples forcibly brought to the United States and required to give up their native languages and the people already living in what would become the territorial boundaries of the United States, whose lands were either conquered or acquired by the United States, such as Native Americans, Mexicans, Puerto Ricans, and French Creoles. The languages of these peoples, as Gonzalez put it, were relegated to "the margins of American experience," dismissed as "either primitive or nonexistent."[5] Whitewashing the histories of linguistic diversity in the United States not only has improperly naturalized English as *the* language of U.S. citizens but has codified an exclusionary narrative of American identity and history, one that has marked other languages, and their speakers, as pollutants to the integrity of the civic body.

Accordingly, Spanish historically has occupied a contested space within constructions of Latino identities and Latino struggles for justice and equality. It has been imagined as a welcome and unwelcome marker of difference, interpreted alternately as an impediment to acceptance within American culture and American institutions or as a significant marker of cultural identity. Bilingualism, and legal provisions for bilingual education, for some have been necessary to enable Latino social mobility and civic participation, for others as central to Latino cultural citizenship. Spanish also has been the starting point for the creation of the "Latino," a designation of a singular ethnic category that covers and collapses a diverse range of peoples within the United States. Spanish was the means by which a "Latino audience" was constituted, one that could be sold to advertisers, addressed by in-the-know marketing executives, and courted by Spanish-language stations.[6]

In the ferment of the 1960s, Chicano activist groups would shift the place of Spanish within political advocacy for Latino rights. The gains, strategies, and tactics of the African American civil rights movement became a template for Latino rights advocacy groups. Their efforts put pressure, for example, on the Equal Employment Opportunity Commission (EEOC) to tend to employment discrimination cases against Latinos, but they also put the issue of linguistic difference in the center of considerations of Latino citizenship rights. By the early 1970s bilingual education was a central element of public policy recommendations for Latinos. The Bilingual Education Act of 1974 provided for federal support of bilingual education as a means not only to help transition students to speak English and to provide effective instruction to non-English-speaking students but to allow for the maintenance of linguistic and cultural diversity. Maintenance of language, in other words, was understood as an important facet of cultural identity, one that the federal government supported as part of its broader program to secure citizenship rights for its multicultural public.[7]

Paradoxically, just as in the realm of education Spanish instruction was recognized as important to the social and cultural rights of Latino students, in the realm of media policy Spanish-language broadcasting was politically devalued by the FCC. Non-English programming, as America Rodriguez and Dolores Inés Casillas, respectively, have documented, had been a part of radio broadcasting since the 1920s. While there were no immigrant-oriented radio *stations* at this time, non-English-language programming would be broadcast on commercial stations. On the one hand, Spanish-language programming also could attract Anglo audiences; imagined as the language of the exoticized South, Spanish was tied to narratives of adventure and romance.[8] On the other hand, when addressing local Latino audiences, Spanish-language radio was perceived by station owners as filler programming consumed by audiences of little economic value to them. Spanish-language media producers had tremendous freedom in shaping their programming and in injecting political advocacy in their public-affairs content. In addition, Latinos in the United States in the 1930s were predominantly Mexican in nationality and resided in borderland states. Thus, as Mexican media mogul Emilio Azcarraga began to dominate Spanish-language radio programming in the United States, the Mexican nationalist inflection of his programming and the idealized construction of Mexican life at its center interpellated the Latino population then living in the United States.[9]

Significantly, though Spanish-language broadcasting had been part of the American media landscape since the 1920s, it fell outside the parameters of how the FCC understood and constituted minority media rights in the 1960s and 1970s. These policies took shape in response to the African American freedom struggle yet were applied to other "disadvantaged groups"—women, Native Americans, Asian Americans, and "Spanish surnamed" Americans. While African American struggles over media regulation would provide a model for other civil rights battles, like those of both feminists and Latinos, and would lend the moral and juridical language for other communities to articulate their own injury with regard to broadcasting policies and practices, they also would structure and arguably delimit how the commission and the courts constructed minority media rights. Though the minority enhancements were intended to assure that the communication needs of a racially diverse society were met, they formed primarily to address the impact of broadcasting on African Americans and derived from the claims of discrimination, in license challenges like the WLBT and especially in the pages of the Kerner Report, over broadcasting's complicity in racial inequality. As such, they proved insufficient to conceive of linguistic difference as a critical component of minority media rights, the availability of Spanish-language media as critical to the speech rights of Latinos. Such an approach to broadcast diversity casts out linguistic diversity from a notion of the public interest modeled after racial, not ethnolinguistic, difference. This would be the fate of Spanish-language broadcasting, which instead has occupied an ambiguous location in regulatory frameworks.

Spanish-language broadcasting, since the 1970s, had been classified as a broadcasting format, analogous to classical music or Golden Oldies. In the 1970s, as the FCC grappled with how to promote broadcast diversity, it considered whether the promotion of entertainment format diversity lay within its regulatory authority. A series of appellate court decisions had decided that, under certain circumstances, the commission could not rely solely on marketplace mechanisms to assure that the diverse needs of the public, within the realm of entertainment formats, would be satisfied. In 1976 the FCC issued a policy statement on this topic, affirming its commitment not to regulate or intervene with format diversity. In 1981 the Supreme Court affirmed the FCC's decision.[10] Though, as Amy Jo Coffee and Amy Kristin Sanders argue, the FCC on occasion departed from its designation of Spanish-language broadcasting as an entertainment format, it was as an entertainment format that the commission officially recognized Spanish-language media.[11] Accordingly, if the minority ownership rules were to assure diversity of perspectives on issues of public import, the format policy was to rely on the marketplace to provide sufficient diversity of entertainment programming; Spanish-language media was understood as only as vital to the First Amendment needs of the polity as was, say, country music. In addition, while at the time *who* owns a broadcasting station was considered important to the diversity of perspectives offered by English-language media, the market was presumed to be sufficient to assure the diversity of "entertainment."

The FCC's relegation of Spanish-language broadcasting as a "format" has structured how it has regulated this sector of U.S. broadcasting, as has the shifting location of Spanish within the political imaginary of the nation. To be sure, over the course of the twentieth century and into the twenty-first the political valence of Spanish has shifted both among Latinos and within the broader public sphere, changes that map onto ebbs and flows of domestic racism and xenophobia. Paradoxically, just as Spanish became a target in the political sphere, it and its speakers were recognized as a valuable market by media corporations and advertisers. Its value, however, was understood to be in its capacity to deliver audiences to advertisers, not in its political or cultural significance to Latino citizens. Within the realm of media policy Spanish-language broadcasting would continue to be treated as distinct from, and less politically valuable than, English-language broadcasting. Accordingly, the regulation of Spanish-language broadcasting has been an important battleground for Latino rights organizations, as has been the ownership structure of Spanish-language networks. The NHMC would be one of many organizations to take up this fight.

The NHMC: Origins

Founded in 1986 by attorney Armando Durón, journalist and television producer Esther Renteria, and television producer Alex Nogales, the National Hispanic Media Coalition formed to advocate for Latino media rights. Like the NAACP, the NHMC linked its own community's visibility in the media, and its capacity to structure how it was seen in the public sphere, as critical to its ability to achieve equality in other spheres. The NHMC used an array of strategies to bring more Latinos into positions of authority behind the camera and into greater visibility in front of it. In addition, its work targeted derogatory images and discussions of Latinos in the media, from caricatured constructions of Latinos in advertisements and entertainment programming to hate speech against Latinos on talk radio and newscasts. For the NHMC, as for other Latino media reformers, such actions were pivotal to the cultural work of assuring Latinos' presence and participation in the media and to the political work of reshaping discourses about Latinos so that broader discussions over public policy are inclusive of Latino perspectives and experiences.

When Durón, Renteria, and Nogales formed the NHMC in 1986, they did so, on the one hand, on the heels of two decades of efforts to integrate more Latinos into production and decision-making roles and, on the other, in the midst of widespread media deregulation, as the FCC and federal courts displaced public interest regulations with a faith in the mechanisms of the marketplace. The NHMC initiated its media advocacy during what was a hostile era toward media reform activity, in which diversity was imagined to be secured via the market and in which race-conscious programs were under attack as invidious forms of reverse discrimination. Intending to address the paucity of Latinos in broadcasting, as well as in film and print, to challenge negative stereotypes of Latinos, and to assure that media policy decisions served the interests of Latino publics,[12] the NHMC deployed a range of strategies to transform the media ecosystem. As Chon Noriega has argued, the NHMC's founders were well aware of the obstacles to media advocacy and presumed that its challenges—to license renewals or to corporate mergers—would not necessarily alter outcomes but would slow down the process. This stick, that its advocacy could cause delay in a globalized deregulated environment that valued speed, would be the basis for the NHMC to secure concessions from media companies to address the needs of Latinos.[13] In this the NHMC built on a long-standing strategy, one visible in NOW's and the NAACP's local license challenges, to use regulatory challenges as the means of entry into negotiations with entities that would otherwise dismiss one's claims.

When it first formed, much of the NHMC's media advocacy was focused on English-language media. Like the NAACP in the 1980s and 1990s, the NHMC filed or threatened to file petitions to deny, largely on EEO grounds, in order to pressure local stations to increase the number of Latinos they trained and hired. In 1988 the NHMC identified local stations in Los Angeles that had low levels of Latino employment and, in keeping with a well-worn media advocacy strategy, first tried to negotiate with station managers to raise the number of Latinos, especially in decision-making positions, only to file petitions to deny when such negotiations fell through.[14] As one of its first victories the NHMC successfully pressured KCBS-TV in Los Angeles to attend to its low levels of Latino employment, resulting in the appointment of a Latino to assistant news director at the station.[15] It also reached a settlement agreement with KABC in L.A., in which the station's concessions to the NHMC included commitments to increase its number of Latino employees and especially to hire a Latino department head, to expand coverage of the Latino community in Los Angeles, to seek Latino vendors, and to consult with the NHMC on the use of minority-based media for recruitment advertising.[16] After its successes in Los Angeles, where the organization was based, the NHMC filed petitions against stations in communities across the nation, especially those with substantial Latino populations.

The NHMC also took stock of the practices of Spanish-language stations. It specifically tried to make clear, for example, to Telemundo executives that there is a need for Latino participation in Spanish-language stations that serve, almost exclusively, local Latino communities. It supported a petition to deny against KVDA in San Antonio, a station serving a city that, at the time of the petition, was 58 percent Latino, yet its general manager was an Anglo and its board of directors had only one Latino serving on it; the NHMC took particular exception to Telemundo's claim that it could serve the Spanish-speaking community without representatives of that community participating in leadership positions.[17] The NHMC also successfully negotiated with KVEA, Telemundo's Los Angeles station, to hire a general manager who *actually spoke Spanish* and was a Latino. Such a concession was achieved through constant negotiation with the station and a campaign to pressure advertisers not to buy time on a station that did not seem invested in representing and serving the Los Angeles Latino community.[18]

In addition, like the NAACP, the NHMC's Durón in 1987 would get involved in a larger-scale media advocacy battle that, much like the NAACP's challenge to the PTL/Livingstone transfer, sought to rescue the distress sale from FCC actions that seemed to render it meaningless. In this instance, however, also at stake was the ownership of the largest Spanish-language television network in the United States, which the FCC had determined had run afoul of its foreign-ownership rules. Thus the activity of Durón, as well as other Latino rights organizations, was oriented to at once preserve a plank of the FCC's minority-ownership rules and to make the case for Latino ownership of a network that played such a pivotal role in the political and cultural life of its community. The battleground was the first of many over the sales of Univision.

Stage I: Hallmark and Distress-Sale Violations

The NHMC took great interest in the NAACP's battle with Rupert Murdoch's Fox network. Its founders kept in constant contact with the NAACP's Honig about the case's progression. Renteria, for example, sent Nogales an excited fax in January of 1995, reporting news from Honig that Thomas Herwitz, who had been responsible for all legal activities for the Fox station group, had been caught perjuring himself in his depositions with the FCC, which seemed to portend, in retrospect misleadingly, that the NAACP was poised to win its challenge.[19] Though the NHMC was not a signatory on the NAACP's petition, it had opposed Fox's request to buy the *New York Post*;[20] additionally, the case's outcome would affect the Latino organization's own media advocacy efforts. Like the NAACP, the NHMC was committed to fighting for greater inclusion of people of color in broadcasting and for the retention, and enforcement, of minority media policies. This case also would have been of interest to the NHMC because of what it would convey about the FCC's position on section 310(b) of the Communications Act. The NHMC had been involved in its own 310(b) fights, once waged over the ownership of Spanish-language television stations.

The origins of these fights date back to the 1960s, when Emilio Azcarraga, a Mexican media mogul, sought an outlet for his programming in the United States. Azcarraga had two U.S. connections: Frank Fouce, whose business operations included Spanish-language theaters, and Rene Anselmo, who had worked for an Azcarraga subsidiary in Mexico in the 1950s. In 1961 the FCC granted the Spanish International Broadcasting Company, which would become SICC, a permit for a television channel in Los Angeles. Fouce and Anselmo, along with Azcarraga employee Julian Kaufman, would own the SICC stations.[21]

In 1962 Azcarraga formed the Spanish International Network (SIN) as a Spanish-language network that would distribute Spanish-language programming in the United States. The affiliated stations of this network would come from SICC, as well as two other station groups, Bahia de San Francisco Holding Company and Seven Hills Television Company. Anselmo was the president of both SIN and the station groups.[22] Though SIN, for all intents and purposes, was a subsidiary of Televisa, and though the stations in its network primarily telecast programming produced by a non-U.S. company, technically the structure of SIN and SICC was on the legal side of U.S. communications law. From the 1960s through the early 1980s the FCC routinely renewed SICC and SIN affiliate licenses and evinced no interest in investigating the relationship between these broadcasters and the Mexican media company from which so much of its programming originated.

Over the course of the 1960s, SICC received licenses for stations, primarily in the UHF band, in markets with large Spanish-speaking populations. The SIN network would also expand over the next two decades from a network addressing Mexican and Mexican American viewers in the American Southwest to one that imagined a panethnic, Spanish-speaking public across the United States. As the number of Latinos rose in the decades after World War II, most notably as the Puerto Rican and Cuban populations expanded on the East Coast, SIN constructed an audience for its programming and its advertisers on the premise that these diverse groups were in fact united under a shared set of interests and concerns tied together by their shared use of the Spanish language. As America Rodriguez put it, the expansion of SIN was rooted in a "primordial understanding of ethnicity: that the Spanish language (and other common cultural attributes such as religion) is an essential tie that binds U.S. Latinos to each other."[23] By 1982 SIN reached 90 percent of Latino households via broadcast stations and cable outlets. In the early 1980s SIN began to produce programming in the United States, especially news and public-affairs shows.[24]

The FCC had acted in the 1970s to support the expansion of SIN and SICC. The commission, for example, exempted SIN/SICC from its policy that restricted affiliated television stations from using an organization owned or connected with a broadcast network as a national spot-advertising sales representative for the sale of nonnetwork time. National advertising took two forms: time purchased to advertise on an entire network (network advertising) and time purchased on television stations on an individual basis for either a spot announcement or an entire program (national spot advertising). The FCC rule, adopted in 1959, prohibited networks from negotiating the latter on behalf of its affiliates. The goal of the policy was to protect the autonomy of individual licensees and to promote competition in the sale of advertising.[25] Seeing SIN and its affiliated stations as struggling entities, and asserting the public interest value in encouraging the growth of Spanish-language broadcasting, the commission granted SIN/SICC a waiver.[26] Additionally, the waiver to the spot-advertising rule signaled that the FCC saw that, with regard to advertising, Spanish-language and English-language broadcasters operated in different markets. As Nicole Serratore has documented, the SIN/SICC waiver was granted in part because the FCC surmised that the competition the rule intended to promote in the English-language sector was inapplicable to a sector that, at the time, only involved one firm selling Spanish-language advertising.[27]

The fortunes of SICC and SIN would shift in the 1980s, when Fouce initiated a lawsuit against SICC. He, along with Metropolitan Theatres Corporation (which held a 2.2 percent share in SICC), contended that the controlling officers and directors of SICC had conducted the company's business in a way that benefited them, but it had done so at the expense of shareholders. Around the same time, the Spanish Radio Broadcasters of America (SRBA), a trade association for Spanish-language radio stations, filed an informal objection against SICC on the grounds that SICC was subject to foreign control and thus in violation of 310(b). In this action SRBA was joined by those upset with the 1978 spot-advertising waiver, which had invested much power in SIN over advertising on Spanish-language broadcast stations.[28]

In 1983 the commission designated a hearing on the extent of foreign influence over the SICC station group and over SIN-affiliated stations owned by Bahia de San Francisco Holding Company and the Seven Hills Television Company. In January 1986 Administrative Law Judge John Conlin issued his findings. While underlining that the stations, according to their ownership structure, complied with 310(b), he found that Televisa held de facto control over the stations; thus, they were in violation of the rule. Conlin determined that not only had an "abnormal relationship" been established, "whereby the stations were dependent on foreign subsidiaries," but that SIN and SICC functioned essentially as a single company.[29] Conlin stated, "Indeed, the findings show that personnel transfers among the licensees and SIN occur with such ease and regularity that the entities would seem to function as divisions of the same company. In the circumstances, it is not surprising that SICC and SIN share the same headquarters in New York and even with the same telephone number."[30] The linchpin of these relationships was Rene Anselmo, longtime associate of Azcarraga, who was a chief management official for both companies and, in this capacity, functioned primarily to advance the interests of Televisa and SIN.[31] Conlin cited the Univision agreement as evidence of the subordinated interests of the stations to the network, as it provided optimal conditions for SIN at the expense of the financial interests of the stations.[32]

Conlin made two assertions that would have a major impact on subsequent events. First, he underlined that the arrangements between SIN, SICC, and the other parties had not been hidden, obscured, or misrepresented to the FCC. They had been known to the FCC, which for two decades had renewed SICC's, Bahia's, and Seven Hills' licenses. In addition, though finding a 310(b) violation, Conlin characterized license revocation as having a "draconian element" to it and encouraged that his review be the first, rather than final, step in the proceeding. He suggested that a "less drastic remedial solution," such as "corporate restructuring," could clear the problems he discerned in the relationships among the stations, SIN, and Televisa.[33]

As appeals to the ALJ decision unfolded at the FCC, SICC reached an agreement to sell its stations. A federal district court in California supervised the sale. Via this process SICC and Bahia arranged to sell their stations to Hallmark Cards Inc., the greeting card company behemoth. Such a sale would provide the very sort of corporate restructuring gestured to by Conlin to remove the 310(b) violations identified in his hearings and would settle the legal wrangling once and for all. But it also would elicit tremendous outrage from Latino groups and would initiate a four-year legal struggle over the operation of Spanish-language broadcasting in the United States.

The Hallmark sale galvanized Latino media activists. Six groups, for example, filed a petition with the FCC in an attempt to persuade the commission not to approve the sale. Durón, who recently had founded the NHMC along with Renteria and Nogales, penned the petition on behalf of these organizations.[34] Their concerns spoke to the complexity of the communication needs of Latinos, as they both mirrored and diverged from those of other minority communities in their struggles for a media system hospitable to the nation's multicultural population.

The Hallmark sale elicited anger for its departure from stated FCC practices and policies. Typically, the FCC had operated under its *Jefferson Radio* precedent, which held that a licensee whose qualifications were under investigation could not sell its stations until the FCC had concluded its investigation.[35] Additionally, under commission rules, a licensee found in violation of administrative rules or afoul of the law would not be allowed to sell its stations. Such a policy, logically, intended to deter misconduct by depriving licensees of financial remuneration should the commission find them no longer qualified to operate a station. The FCC, however, historically had allowed station sales under particular circumstances, such as when a physical impairment affected a licensee's capabilities or when a station had filed for bankruptcy.[36] And, importantly, the FCC had adopted in 1978 the minority distress sale policy, which allowed licensees to sell their stations for at most 75 percent of their value to a qualified minority-controlled entity. The distress sale provided a deterrent to broadcasters (the diminished remuneration for their stations), as well as an opportunity to minority owners to get a toehold in the broadcasting sector.[37]

For the Latino individuals and groups protesting the sale, allowing the Hallmark purchase would be in essence to nullify the distress sale policy and thus to diminish what had been an important tool for minorities to become station owners. In addition, they argued that to allow a nonminority-controlled entity like Hallmark to buy the stations—an entity with no discernible commitment to the Latino community—was to perform a disservice to Latino viewers who were in need of programming attentive to their interests and concerns. This latter concern dovetailed with another argument made in the petition to deny, which centered on the long-term provision of Spanish-language broadcasting on the stations. Although Hallmark had committed to air Spanish-language programming for two years, the petitioners feared that the company may decide to shift to English-language broadcasts should this prove more attractive over time. Such fears only underscored the central argument of the petition, which was that a station group serving a nearly exclusive Latino viewership should be controlled by a Latino entity. As Durón stated in a letter seeking financial support to prevent the Hallmark sale: "Our effort is designed solely with the intent to have Latinos be awarded the license. We believe that such control is key to the economic, educational, and cultural progress of the Latino community in this country."[38]

Unfortunately for the petitioners, the timing of the Hallmark sale lined up with a broader reconsideration—at both the commission and in the federal courts—over the constitutionality of the distress-sale policy itself. Indeed, in clarifying why the distress-sale policy did not apply to the Hallmark-SICC sale, the FCC pointed to looming questions over the legality of the policy as rendering it inoperative. The challenge to the sale thus occurred at a moment when the FCC itself was unenthusiastic about the need and legitimacy of the distress-sale policy and, more broadly, tended to shy away from using its regulatory authority to promote viewpoint diversity. While the Latino petitioners insisted that the 310(b) violations rendered SICC an unqualified licensee, and therefore—sans distress sale—not legally viable to make this sale, the FCC disagreed, insisting that precedent empowered the commission, as did the particular findings of Conlin's hearings, to sanction the sale to Hallmark.

In 1987 the FCC approved the sale to Hallmark. It issued two Memorandum Opinion and Orders (MO&O) on the case. The first focused primarily on whether SICC and Bahia *could* sell at full market value. In essence the FCC determined that the case was unique and therefore unlikely to alter the deterrence function of FCC policies; in addition, the commission insisted that the 310(b) violation was "technical," not the result of "character violations" or other misconduct, obviating the need for more harsh treatment. Deeming Hallmark a qualified buyer, and identifying myriad public interest benefits in approving the sale—from assuring immediate compliance to the law to terminating adjudicative proceedings and relieving the labor and uncertainty they had generated—the FCC dismissed the concerns raised by the petitioners and granted approval to the settlement. The FCC addressed the legitimacy of the sale itself and ignored the specific concerns regarding a non-Latino entity gaining control over the largest Spanish-language television group operating at that time.[39]

The second MO&O more directly addressed the concerns of Latino advocacy groups, yet it also dismissed their arguments. In summarizing the charges of the Latino groups, and the response by Hallmark, the FCC underlined the fundamental disagreement structuring much of this case. In arguments that echoed the very debates in which the NAACP was mired, the Latino groups maintained that a relationship exists between ownership and diversity of viewpoint and that the only way to assure that stations would remain committed to Spanish-language broadcasting was for a Latino entity to be the licensee. Hallmark, in contrast, argued that "it is not the ethnic background" of the licensee that will determine the format but marketplace conditions.[40] The arguments of the Latino groups, to Hallmark, were rooted in faulty assumptions about how ownership and incentives operate. This was the very argument offered by the FCC and the federal courts in the late 1980s; thus, Hallmark's claims resonated with the "marketplace approach to regulation" adopted by the commission. Furthermore, though section 310(d) of the Communications Act instructed the FCC to consider the public interest qualifications of buyers and sellers of stations, these investigations rested on whether the buyer and seller were qualified, not whether an alternative buyer, for example, would better serve the public interest.[41] Finding Hallmark to be qualified, and refusing to characterize SICC and Bahia as unqualified despite the 310(b) violations, the FCC approved the sale.

A pivotal part of the settlement agreement between Hallmark and SICC and Bahia was a preclusion of any of the principals of the station groups from participating as officers in the assigned stations. In addition, they were forbidden from having any equity interest in them for two years and from acquiring more than a 5 percent equity interest in them thereafter.[42] Thus, the settlement not only removed profitable stations from the licensees, but it substantially curtailed their capacity for future involvement with them. Hallmark, which also acquired SIN, renamed the station group and network Univision. Though the largest Spanish-language television system in the United States was in the hands of a non-Latino group, Hallmark continued to offer Spanish-language telecasts and increased domestic production of programming. And though

Latino media advocacy groups had hoped that the initial ruling had provided an opportunity to wrest control over this powerful outlet of Spanish-language media, the FCC rejected that Latino control was desirable or that a more firm commitment to Spanish-language programming than Hallmark was willing to provide was necessary.

A number of organizations sought to overturn the approval of the settlement. TVL Corporation, a company made up of Latino investors and had been a finalist in the bidding process for the SICC stations, filed a petition to deny the transfer to Hallmark, claiming that the bidding process had been discriminatory. Much of TVL's complaint hinged on the FCC's unlikely decision to allow a full value sale, rather than a distress sale, of the stations. Presuming a distress sale had meant that TVL had assumed that a company like itself would be eligible to acquire the stations and that the stations would be sold at most at 75 percent of their value. TVL thus had had to scramble to secure financing to compete with Hallmark and was unable to have firm financing commitments in place by the time the court settled on a bidder.[43] Other organizations that appealed the FCC decision included the Coalition for the Preservation of Hispanic Broadcasting, Hispanic Broadcasting Systems (HBS), and the Hispanic Broadcasting Limited Partnership (HBLP).[44]

The FCC rejected the petitions to deny on standing grounds and the competing applications on procedural grounds. In 1991 the U.S. Court of Appeals, which initially reversed the FCC's decisions, decided *en banc* that the petitions were untimely and that the advocacy groups lacked standing. The court's decision hinged on an interpretation of section 310(b), in which it suggested that "the entire nation," not local viewers and listeners, was the intended beneficiary, the section's goal to prevent the "hazards of alien propaganda."[45] In other words the only reason why foreign companies could not control broadcast stations was that they may use their stations to threaten the security of the United States. This was not a public interest issue; it was a national security issue. The Latino groups were denied a right to be heard on the issue because they had made the mistake of thinking that the control of the sector primarily serving, and profiting from, their community, either by non-U.S. corporations or non-Latino entities, involved the rights of Latino publics.

At the core of the tensions between Latino advocacy groups and the FCC, the courts, and the parties to the sale was a fundamental disagreement about whether this case was about minority media rights. For the petitioners the 310(b) violation clearly marked the stations for a distress sale, which would enable Latino buyers to secure control over a part of the broadcasting sector directly serving Latinos. To put the stations under the control of a corporation that was non-Latino, and did not commit to Latino communication needs, seemed logically to pose harms to the public interest goal of diversity. For policy makers and the entities involved, this case had nothing to do with media diversity or the rights of minorities. Rather, it involved a corporate restructuring to bring broadcast licensees into accordance with communication law. That the stations provided Spanish-language content, that they served Latino audiences, and that the new owner had no demonstrated ties to the Latino community were, from this view, immaterial to the questions to be resolved. The promotion and health of Spanish-language media, in other words, was not considered part of the FCC's commitment to minority publics. And in its approval of the Hallmark sale the FCC transformed the treatment of Spanish-language broadcasting paradoxically into a cudgel to further erode minority media rights policies, quelling the efficacy of the distress-sale policy by sidestepping it.

Stage II: The Perenchio Sale and the Return of Transnational Programming

For Latino rights organizations it only got worse. This 1991 court decision would be the final word on the Hallmark purchase, yet paradoxically, the following year Hallmark would put its stations up for sale, its prospective buyers including the Azcarragas. In 1992 the regulatory battles would begin again as Hallmark decided to sell the Univision stations and network to Perenchio Television Inc. (PTI), an entity owned by A. Jerrold Perenchio, a non-Latino media mogul who had been in charge of Tandem Productions and had made a short-term purchase of the Loews theater group from the Tisch family. In the late 1970s and early 1980s Perenchio had also owned and operated Spanish-language stations in Los Angeles and New York. Of concern to Latino groups were two facets of this purchase: the sale would once again put the leading Spanish-language television network in the control of non-Latino entities, and, more important, Perenchio's two primary partners were Televisa and the Venezuelan company Venevisión. Under their proposal Perenchio would own 75 percent of the station group and 50 percent of the network; Televisa and Venevisión each would own 12 percent of the stations and 25 percent of the network. In addition, under this deal, for twenty-five years Univision would have the first opportunity to air Televisa and Venevisión programming, essentially giving the network a lock on two of the most popular sources of Spanish-language content in the United States.[46]

Multiple groups—including the NHMC, LULAC, Telemundo, the American G.I. Forum, the National Puerto Rican Coalition, and the Executive Intelligence Review—tried to stop the purchase. The rationales marshaled to persuade the FCC to rule against the merger were fourfold. First, the deal seemed to violate the terms of the Hallmark deal, in which Televisa had been restricted from having more than a 5 percent interest in the Univision station group. Second, they argued that the sale would reduce domestic production of Spanish-language programming; this would constrict employment opportunities for Latinos and would displace content that spoke to the concerns of

Latinos with programming produced outside the United States. In addition, should the merger go through, Galavision, a Televisa-owned Spanish-language cable network that also had broadcast stations, would phase out its broadcast business, which would reduce diversity of content in the Spanish-language sector. In this vein a third charge was leveled over the shady conduct of the bidding process. Joaquin Blaya, a top-ranking executive at Univision and prospective buyer of the Hallmark stations, was suspiciously kept in the dark about the pending sale and routinely misinformed about it. That a qualified Latino buyer was poised to buy the stations, and that the parties involved actively worked to disable his ability to bid on them, spoke both to the missed opportunity to put the station group in Latino hands and to questions of character regarding the parties in the merger. This last point dovetailed with the fourth charge: that Televisa and Venevisión were not qualified to be partial owners of U.S. broadcasting stations on character grounds. The American G.I. Forum alleged that Televisa had engaged in malicious and immoral business practices to defame and undermine artists working with competing companies. The Executive Intelligence Review charged that the Cisneros family, which controlled Venevisión, was involved in the international drug trade and money laundering.[47]

At issue were not only competing understandings of the terms of the Hallmark deal but competing understandings of the political value of Spanish-language broadcasting to Latino audiences. The NHMC and others argued that what the FCC was imagining as permissible in the Spanish-language sector—two foreign companies controlling a major network—would be unimaginable, say, if it were British and German companies seeking control over NBC.[48] In response to claims like this, Perenchio's attorneys accused the Latino advocacy groups of "an extreme xenophobia," that it was these organizations, in their anxiety over "the dominion of an alien business empire," who expressed alarming positions out of step with the precepts of a democratic society.[49] In addition, while the Latino groups feared that the merger would impact the diversity of perspectives available to Latino audiences—a speech-rights concern—Perenchio's attorneys reassured the commission that the merger would not pose competitive harms, as the high rates of bilingual Latinos in the United States would mean that advertisers unsatisfied with Spanish media rates could advertise with English-language broadcasters—an economic concern.[50]

In September of 1992 the FCC approved the sale. In its Memorandum Opinion and Order the commission asserted that the petitioners did not make a persuasive case that the sale would violate 310(b) and that there was no evidence that Televisa and Venevisión would exercise de facto control over the stations. In so ruling, the FCC emphasized that 310(b) applied to stations, not networks, and that indeed its own regulatory power is over stations, not networks.[51] The commission conceded that the new arrangement would be a vertically integrated company but suggested that common ownership of networks, stations, and productions was a long-standing practice in the history of U.S. broadcasting.[52] The commission also found that diversity would not be threatened, pointing to more than thirty sources of Spanish-language programming.[53]

Perhaps most important, the FCC adopted the creative logic advanced by the parties in interest that explained why this merger was not in violation of the Hallmark agreement. Perenchio and Televisa had argued that the earlier settlement had prevented the Azcarraga family from holding more than a 5 percent interest in the *buyer* of the SICC and Bahia stations, that is, from holding this interest in Hallmark. In *this* transaction, however, Hallmark was the seller, and Televisa would gain an equity interest in a different entity, not in Hallmark. Ergo, there was no violation in Televisa's having an interest in the stations purchased primarily by Perenchio because Perenchio was not Hallmark. In its MO&O the FCC embraced this logic, insisting that the terms of the Hallmark deal did not apply to subsequent sales.[54]

In the Perenchio buyout, as in the Hallmark deal, the FCC rejected arguments that who owned the most important outlets for Spanish-language programming had anything to do with minority media rights or the public interest goal of diversity. The commission dismissed out of hand the claim, made repeatedly by Latino advocacy groups, that media targeting Latinos should be controlled by Latinos. In the case of the Perenchio sale the FCC comfortably allowed Mexico's Televisa and Venezuela's Venevisión to provide the lion's share of programming over Univision. It similarly was not swayed by claims that the sale would reduce diversity of viewpoint. The FCC's rulings on the ownership of Spanish-language broadcasting, here and in the Hallmark sale, belied not only a commitment to the logic of deregulation, and the fracturing of the nexus between ownership and viewpoint at its center, but also a dismissal of the significance of Spanish to the linguistic and cultural identities of Latinos.

The NHMC and LULAC both filed appeals. While these cases were pending, the NHMC also met with representatives of Univision to resolve some of its concerns regarding the public interest implications of the sale. The deal that they struck focused exclusively on provisions for the production and airing of quality Spanish-language educational television. Univision made programming commitments and agreed that, should it fail to meet those commitments, it would make $50,000 contributions to scholarship programs. In the fall of 1995 Univision donated $100,000 to an array of scholarship funds, a concession that it had failed to meet the educational television standards it had set with the NHMC.[55] This deal was indicative of what was becoming the NHMC's pragmatism, one that other civil rights organizations had adopted. Though opposed to the sale, it was perhaps clear to the NHMC—reading the disposition of the courts and the commission in the 1990s—that its appeals would not deliver the desired result. Accordingly, the NHMC sought to garner the best outcome for its community, given what now seemed like the sale's inevitability. Negotiating with Univision was perhaps the most efficacious way to assure that the network was committed to its Latino audience. The threat of continued legal action, rather than the regulatory process itself, had proved to be a more productive way to assure Univision's service to local Latino communities.

Stage III: The Univision-HBC Merger and the Politics of "Separate but Equal" Broadcast Regulations

The battle over Univision's merger with the Hispanic Broadcasting Corporation (HBC), proposed in 2002 and approved in 2003, differed demonstrably from the previous fights over Univision's ownership. Latino organizations, members of Congress, and the FCC itself split over the merger's consequences. At stake were competing understandings of the social and political role of Spanish-language media in the United States, the impact of the merger on Latinos, and the desirability of viewing the Spanish-language sector as a distinct sector within the broader media landscape. Both camps claimed to be on the side of Latinos, the merger itself a Rorschach test of how one understood the contours of Latino cultural and political rights. Two of the NHMC's founders, Nogales and Renteria, would find themselves on opposite sides of this issue. Nogales, writing on behalf of the NHMC, supported the merger; Renteria, by 2003 the president of Hispanic Americans for Fairness in Media, was opposed.

The Univision-HBC merger came on the heels of NBC/GE's purchase of Telemundo, the second-largest Spanish-language television network in the United States. In October of 2001 NBC announced that it would purchase Telemundo for $2 billion, as well as its two cable services, Mun2 and Telemundo Internacional. As Bob Wright, NBC CEO, explained, Latinos were the "most dynamic TV market in the U.S.," one that was expanding rapidly.[56] The merger would allow NBC/GE access to this valuable market. In addition, there were other benefits to the purchase, such as allowing NBC to save by combining back-office operations in cities where there was overlap between the two networks. Neither Telemundo nor anyone writing in the trade presses or major newspapers anticipated any trouble with regulatory approval on economic competition grounds.[57]

The NHMC along with seven other Latino advocacy organizations filed a petition to deny the Telemundo purchase.[58] They argued that NBC/GE had not demonstrated that the sale would be in the public interest. Given that review of these proposals at the FCC was one of the few arenas in which public interest concerns, rather than solely concerns over economic competition, could be addressed, the Latino organizations asked that the FCC either request more information from NBC/GE or deny the petition. At the core of their concern was that, though NBC/GE had insisted the merger would benefit Latinos, *how* this would happen was unclear to the Latino groups. While NBC/GE suggested that the sale would enhance diversity, the petitioners stated that in fact "attaching the market runner-up to a larger company only ensures that the public will be served by two monoliths."[59] In addition, they asserted that the merger could lead to the dilution of programming diversity, a concern not at all irrational given that in press reports on the merger—though not included in the petition—NBC had indicated that it intended to create Spanish-language versions of English-language programming for Telemundo.[60] They further expressed concern over the fate of Latino workers after the merger. Given that mergers frequently result in the shedding of duplicative workforces, the petitioners feared that the primarily Latino workers at Telemundo would lose their jobs.[61] The petition also asked the FCC to deny NBC's request for a twelve-month waiver from complying with its ownership rules and allowing it to own three television stations in the L.A. market.[62] At the time, FCC policy allowed entities to control no more than two television stations in a broadcast market.

Not unexpectedly, the FCC approved the merger, approved NBC's waiver request, and dismissed the concerns of the Latino groups. In its approval of the waiver, the commission signaled its view that English- and Spanish-language stations served different audiences; therefore, given the vagaries of the ownership arrangement—and the immense size and diversity of the Los Angeles market in which the three stations operated—there would be no public interest harm in allowing NBC to take a year to find a viable buyer for its station. Accordingly, in this deal the FCC asserted that Spanish-language stations and English-language stations competed in different markets.[63] This question of the distinctness of Spanish-language broadcasting would be central to the debates over the Univision-HBC merger.

The approval of the Telemundo-NBC merger was consistent with FCC decision making since the 1980s. Since the Hallmark purchase, the commission had routinely rejected Latino advocacy groups' concerns over who controlled Spanish-language media. On the one hand, the logic applied to these sales was consistent with the neoliberal approach to policy making ascendant at the commission after the 1980s. If, according to this logic, it was unregulated marketplace conditions that best provided for the communication needs of the public, then questions of ownership were beside the point: media companies, regardless of who owned them, sought the greatest audience for their programming and thus were incentivized to provide the programming most desired by the public. It was this logic that enabled the repeal of content-based regulations, gutted minority media-ownership policies, and sanctioned the diminishment of ownership restrictions.

This logic was premised on the presumption of diversity of outlets, of a competitive marketplace. While critics of deregulation would make a distinction between diversity of outlets and diversity of ownership—that, in other words, a proliferation of outlets is not necessarily a measure of media diversity if they are collectively owned by a handful of conglomerates—advocates of deregulation were dismissive of such accusations, positing that such arguments belied an ignorance of how market mechanisms operated. But if advocacy of deregulation relied on an assertion of abundance, media advocacy over Spanish-language broadcasting had tried to make visible and meaningful the scarcity of companies controlling Spanish-language outlets. It was in this context that the Univision-HBC merger would seem so threatening to a number of Latino groups.

In June of 2002 Univision announced its intention to buy HBC. The merger would bring the largest Spanish-language television network (Univision) and the largest Spanish-language radio network (HBC) under common ownership. In some communities, after the merger, 80 percent of Spanish-language broadcasting would be under the control of the one company. Given the companies' holdings in websites, recording labels, publishing, cable, and concert promotion, the merger also would mean that this new entity would control approximately 70 percent of Spanish-language media in the United States. At the time of the merger Univision owned two additional television networks (Telefutura and Galavision), fifty television stations, a vibrant website, and the leading Spanish-language music label. In addition, Univision had a financial interest in Entravision Communications Corporation, which owned and controlled eighteen television stations and fifty-two radio stations.[64] In purchasing HBC, Univision would, in the words of its president, Ray Rodriguez, "offer our national and local advertisers unprecedented activities."[65]

The Univision-HBC merger was controversial from the outset.[66] As in the PTI-Hallmark sale a decade earlier, the Univision-HBC merger raised questions over non-Latino ownership of a media company that had such enormous reach to and impact on Latino communities. In addition, given the outsized influence this new entity was to have within the Spanish-language sector, and thus on Latino publics, concerns arose over the political commitments of Univision's leadership and its alleged privileging of conservative perspectives in its programming. Yet to some, this merger, along with NBC's acquisition of Telemundo in 2002, conferred greater visibility on the Spanish-language sector as a thriving market segment of the American media landscape.

Approximately eighty-five Latino organizations contacted the FCC to support the merger, submitting virtually the same letter to the commission. These groups routinely gave three reasons the commission should approve the Univision-HBC merger. First, they emphasized how Univision had been an important ally of local Latino communities, from its philanthropic contributions to its inclusion of public service announcements and media segments on issues of especial import to Latino audiences. They also stressed the company's record in training, employing, and promoting Latino employees. Second, they identified the benefits of the merger to Latinos, from the expansion of jobs for Latinos in broadcasting to the increased visibility it would afford to the Spanish-language sector. The merger would put Univision on more equal footing with English-language conglomerates, demonstrating the importance of the Spanish-language sector and thus potentially increasing capital investments in and advertising support for Spanish-language media in the United States. Third, these letters attacked the presumption that Spanish-language media constituted a distinct sector from English-language media as insulting and discriminatory, as an unjustifiable form of segregation. Insisting that Spanish-language media effectively competed with English-language media, they read appeals to think of the sectors as different as a racist affront, one that "segregated" Spanish-language media as "substandard." In this vein they pointed to FCC approval of mergers in the English-language sector and asked if this special attention to Univision-HBC constituted a form of discrimination that held Spanish-language media companies to standards not applied to English-language companies. To not approve the merger, from this vantage point, would be to give an unfair advantage to English-language media conglomerates that had a growing market share in the Latino community.[67]

The NHMC supported the merger, its letter to the FCC echoing many of these points. Nogales, writing on behalf of the NHMC, stressed how Univision, in comparison to English-language media companies, had a strong record of employing Latinos. Though Univision was not owned by a Latino, Nogales labeled it a "Hispanic company" given that its management, programming, and community service contributed to the Latino community; thus, that Univision was not Latino owned, for the NHMC at this time, did not impede its ability to meet its public interest obligations to Latinos. Nogales made clear that the NHMC was concerned with high levels of media concentration yet questioned, given the approval of other, larger media mergers, why there was a seemingly "double standard" applied to this one. The letter of support furthermore stressed that the NHMC support came from Univision's record in serving the Latino community and its creation of job opportunities for Latinos that did not exist at other media corporations.[68]

It is important to note that at this very moment media concentration in the English-language sector was viewed by many as a significant problem. After the 1996 Telecommunications Act passed, which had opened the door to vertical and horizontal concentration, a merger mania ensued uniting, for example, ABC with Disney, CBS with Viacom, and AOL with Time Warner.[69] The deregulation of radio in particular had enabled Clear Channel to dominate in many local markets. The coalition that the PTC joined in 2003 to fight greater media deregulation was evidence of widespread discontent, shared across the political spectrum, that media consolidation had posed harms to public interest goals of localism, competition, and diversity. At the moment that Latino organizations were extolling the benefits of this merger, and insisting that it should be treated analogously to English-language mergers, many communities were gearing up to fight media consolidation in the English-language sector and to defy the very logic, which conflated diversity of outlet with program and viewpoint diversity, upon which it had been justified.[70]

And the Univision-HBC merger had its opponents. Renteria, cofounder of the NHMC but by 2002 the president of Hispanic Americans for Fairness in Media, split with her former colleague Nogales. In this she inverted the claims made by the merger's advocates. To approve the merger, for Renteria, was not to treat Spanish and English broadcasters equally but to subject Spanish-speaking audiences to a level of media consolidation that would be unacceptable in the realm of English-language broadcasting, in which one company was allowed to "have 80% of the U.S. market as its own monopoly."[71] Perhaps most important, Renteria put the merger in the broader context of media deregulation and its impact on Latino media ownership. This merged company would propel the paradox that had been in place for decades, that of non-Latino ownership of media systems serving Latinos. Implicitly arguing that Spanish-language programming is not synonymous with programming for Latinos, Renteria lamented that the diminished presence of Latinos in ownership positions, coupled with the increasingly consolidated nature of the broadcast industry, has meant that "no one really speaks for the Latinos living in the United States. No one discusses the issues of concern to our people."[72]

The most extensive opposition to the merger was filed by the National Hispanic Policy Institute (NHPI), which filed an official petition to deny and became the most public face of public interest group opposition to the merger. The NHPI argued that Univision and HBC had not been candid about the corporate structure of the proposed new entity. Specifically, it insisted that Clear Channel had an attributable interest in HBC and that Univision held a much greater interest in Entravision than it had indicated in its application. Accordingly, the merger under review, according to the NHPI, was between Univision, HBC, *and* Clear Channel and Entravision. Thus the FCC should oppose the merger, both for the lack of candor evidenced in the application and for the public interest harms that this highly consolidated company would pose.[73]

The Univision-HBC merger also attracted the interest of members of Congress, who were similarly divided over its advisability. Advocates of the merger emphasized how it would increase public service to and enhance the provision of programming for Latino audiences. They similarly utilized the language of "segregation" to argue for approval, insisting, as did Congressman Martin Frost (D-Tex.), that notions that "Hispanic-formatted stations be segregated from other media are offensive to many of my Latino constituents who have worked hard to be part of the American experience." Maintaining that "Hispanics should be treated equally" in this schema meant considering Spanish-language media as a part of the larger media landscape and assessing levels of concentration accordingly.[74] Or, as fourteen members of Congress put it, "Creating an artificial 'Spanish-language market' would establish a double standard by treating those broadcasters who choose to serve Hispanic audiences differently than those who choose other program formats."[75] This point was put perhaps most forcefully by Congressman Jose Serrano, who expressed alarm at "the efforts of some to segregate by regulation those broadcast stations that choose to serve Hispanic audiences." He continued: "The idea of creating a 'separate but unequal' category of Spanish-formatted stations is one that I wholeheartedly oppose."[76]

This position was most publicly taken by New Mexico governor Bill Richardson. In Richardson's view the merger would allow Spanish-language media corporations to compete with English-language corporations for ad dollars. Richardson, like many other advocates of the merger, made appeals in the language of parity and equality. He wrote, "Federal authorities have traditionally allowed the English-language television networks to purchase radio stations—and they recently allowed General Electric to buy the #2 Spanish-language television network when it already owns NBC, the #1 English-language television network. Why should Univision be barred from doing what the English-language media giants have done? Why shouldn't a Hispanic media company get a chance to compete on an equal footing against Disney, Viacom, News Corporation, AOL Time Warner, and the rest of the media establishment?"[77] While consistent with other arguments in favor of the merger, Richardson's enthusiasm for the deal likely also was informed by the fact that Perenchio had donated $200,000 to Richardson's campaign when he ran for governor in 2002.[78]

Other members of Congress opposed the merger. A group of eight progressive members of Congress feared it would diminish the already paltry levels of Latino ownership of broadcast stations. They insisted, contra prevailing assumptions, that minority ownership mattered, even in the face of increased visibility of minority programming on nonminority-owned outlets. "Actual minority ownership thus results in a significant increase in sensitivity to the needs and wants of minority media audiences and minority employment in the industry."[79] They insisted, drawing on the Justice Department's review, that Spanish-language media constituted its own distinct media market, one that already was far more concentrated than the English-language market. Inverting the language of injury used by advocates of the merger, they asked that Latinos, and the unique market they constitute, be given the same consideration as other publics similarly deserving of diversity of ownership, viewpoint, and format. This issue of differential treatment was raised by then senator Hillary Clinton (D-N.Y.), who flagged how the merger would put 70 percent of control over Spanish-language media in the hands of a single company, a situation that in the English-language sector would not be seen as inconsistent with the public interest.[80] Nancy Pelosi's (D-Calif.) concerns echoed those of Clinton's, as she raised issues of consolidated control and of the meanings of such an influential media conglomerate being controlled by non-Latinos. She furthermore implored the FCC to see the Spanish-language market as distinct and to assess the public interest hazards in this light.[81] (Democrats also were concerned that the deal would give Perenchio, a registered Republican, control over a phenomenally influential media conglomerate, which could shape the political views of Latinos, the largest growing minority group in the nation. Perenchio and many other top executives of both Univision and HBC had made large contributions to Republican candidates.[82]) As John Dunbar of the Center for Public Integrity summed up, "Democrats are looking at this and thinking, 'You are going to turn all our Hispanic Democrats into Republicans.'"[83] Thus the concern of the politicization of Univision-HBC was twofold: there was anxiety that the new Univision would tilt Latinos to the political right through its programming, and there was the fear that its executives had purchased political favor for the approval through campaign contributions to prominent Republicans.

The FCC split along partisan lines in its decision on the merger. Perhaps the majority's most important finding was that the merger posed no harm to the public interest goal of diversity. In this, the FCC argued that the proper measure of diversity was not diversity across Spanish-language outlets, but that it "must encompass all of the media outlets available to purveyors of viewpoints presumably targeted to Hispanics."[84] Insisting that Latinos have a "wider palette" of options than the general population, as they can watch both English and Spanish broadcasting, the FCC rejected the notion that the merger could threaten media diversity. The FCC pointed not only to the expansion of Spanish-language radio stations in local markets but also to the increased use of Secondary Audio Program (SAP) broadcasts of English programming in Spanish. The FCC concluded, "There is, in sum, no shortage of media outlets available to Spanish-speaking audiences in the United States. Given the wide variety of programming alternatives described above, as well as Hispanic viewing habits and the ease of entry into the Spanish-language format, we simply cannot conclude that the market or Spanish-speaking audience constitutes a separate, insular 'diversity' or competition market."[85]

Democratic commissioners Michael Copps and Jonathan Adelstein dissented, adopting the position of the merger's opponents. They positioned approval as discriminatory toward Latinos because it would allow a level of concentration in this sector that far exceeded even, in their view, the repulsively high levels of concentration in the English-language sector. They specifically addressed the discrimination charges leveled at treating this merger differently by reappropriating the language of equality and justice: "If the Commission were to give special consideration to Spanish-language broadcasting, this does not banish Spanish speakers to a regulatory second-class status tantamount to segregation, as some wrongly—and perhaps mischievously—claim. Instead, it secures them the same consumer protections against excessive consolidation that should be afforded to all the public. The Spanish-speaking population deserves to have localism, competition and diversity in their news, information and entertainment. The Commission is required to safeguard the rights of these Americans just like the English-speaking population."[86] In approving the merger, the majority in actuality was subjecting Latinos to speech conditions vastly inferior to those of Anglos, denying them access to diverse opinion, local and resonant programming, and an array of media outlets that capably can compete in the sector.

The FCC majority's predisposition to sanction this merger was entirely consistent with how it had treated ownership questions. Where this case differed was in the schism across Latino groups over its desirability and in the rhetorical frames deployed in the debate. For advocates of the merger, the increased economic power of Univision and Telemundo brought Spanish-language broadcasting, and Spanish-language broadcasting audiences, out of the cultural margins and into the cultural mainstream. To be desirable as a market was to be legitimate as a public. If, for years, Latino audiences and Spanish programming had been diminished politically by the FCC, they also had been devalued economically by advertisers who either paid lower rates to advertise on Spanish stations or adopted a "no urban/no Spanish" policy in which they avoided stations addressing communities of color.[87] The expanded economic power of Spanish-language broadcasting, achieved through these mergers, thus signaled a recognition of the value of Latino audiences. In addition, a steady concern for groups like the NHMC, in both the English- and Spanish-language media, had been employment and training opportunities for Latinos. If the Univision-HBC merger extended the scale of Spanish-language media, it could as a consequence expand lines of participation for Latinos in the media industries. Opponents of the merger, in contrast, posed concerns that had been central to Latino media activists for well over a decade. They identified increased obstacles to Latino control over a sector that primarily serves Latino publics and impediments to Latinos having their communication needs met, from the reliance of imported programming to, now, the diminishment of diversity in the Spanish-language sector.

What also distinguished this merger was the adoption of the language of injury that had structured attacks on identity-conscious policy making since the Reagan era by mainstream Latino rights groups. While a wide range of actors had claimed for decades that laws that recognized race were in themselves discriminatory—that, for example, affirmative action was analogous to Jim Crow segregation in its acknowledgment of racial difference—mainstream civil rights groups had rejected this discourse as pernicious, as specious in its logic and its false equivalences, and as willfully evasive about the existence in the present of the consequences of historically sanctioned forms of discrimination. This pattern was as true in fights over minority media policies as it was over race-conscious admission policies at universities. Yet in the case of the Univision-HBC merger it was a number of mainstream Latino organizations that likened seeing difference as a form of discrimination, as creating "separate but unequal" treatment based on ethnoracial identity. Their support of the merger, along with the discursive appeals they used to advocate for it, could be read as both a capitulation to the neoliberal conflation of consumerism and citizenship—of the slippage between economic value and political value—as well as an embrace of the rhetorical framework that had served to diminish remedial policies for people of color in the name of racial equality.

The NHMC's support for the merger was inconsistent with how it previously had approached the Spanish-language sector. Indeed, more than a decade later, Nogales and his staff at the NHMC could not recall why they had supported the deal and expressed surprise that the organization had lent its approval, especially given the NHMC's history of working toward greater diversity in, and Latino control over, the Spanish-language sector.[88] It also was an about-face from the NHMC's opposition to the Telemundo-NBC deal, in which the purchase of the Spanish-language network signaled to the NHMC not the "arrival" of Latinos as a valuable consumer demographic but a threat to the speech rights of Latinos. Its own inconsistency, though, was emblematic of this split across Latino groups over what Spanish-language broadcasting meant to its community and over whether being desirable as a target of advertising, and whether the increased economic power of the media companies that serve the Spanish-speaking public, was equivalent to the political and cultural equality sought by Latinos for decades in their media advocacy.

Stage IV: The Saban Buyout, Spanish-Language Broadcasting, and Children's Media Regulation

In 2007 Univision would be sold once again, this time to Broadcasting Media Partners Inc., a consortium of private equity firms assembled by Haim Saban, a highly successful Israeli American media producer. After the 2006 announcement that Univision was for sale, Televisa, Venevisión, and a consortium of American firms seemed the most likely purchasers. After Televisa lost three of its investors, it was outbid by Saban's team; the FCC approved the sale in March of 2007.[89] This sale faced opposition from public interest groups, including the NHMC. While Rincon and Associates, a Texas company that does research on multicultural markets, filed the most extensive petition to stop the Saban sale, it would be the NHMC's charges that would hold the greatest sway over the FCC.

The Rincon petition covered familiar territory with regard to Latino concerns over ownership and control in the Spanish-language sector. In addition to underscoring that the company was already in violation of the FCC's ownership restrictions, Rincon asserted that Univision's reliance on foreign and syndicated programming did not meet the needs of local communities in the United States. Given the import of Univision to the Latino community, given the company's "extraordinarily poor record of stewardship" in serving the interests of that community, and given the particular background of the Saban group—which in no way indicated it was able to correct Univision's programming deficiencies—Rincon reasoned that the sale would not be in the public interest.[90] When the FCC ruled on the sale, it rejected Rincon's complaints. The FCC insisted that it deferred to the editorial discretion of broadcasters regarding programming decisions; if Univision relied heavily on imported content, or if it, as per Rincon, perpetuated a "racial caste system," this was not the FCC's concern.

What the FCC did care about was Univision's record on children's programming, the particular issue raised by the NHMC and the United Church of Christ. By 2007 the NHMC took as a given, based on twenty years of unsuccessful interventions in this arena, that the FCC would probably approve the sale and instead tried to secure benefits from it for Latino groups. Thus the NHMC did not protest the sale per se but initially had worked to assure that there would be tangible benefits to Latinos. Representatives from the NHMC met with Saban and asked that 1 percent of the total sale price be put into a fund that would allocate monies to entities that support Latinos.[91] Not gaining traction with this effort—indeed, Perenchio hired a lawyer who accused the NHMC of extortion—the NHMC focused its efforts on Univision's fallacious claims about its adherence to the Children's Television Act. This act required broadcasters to telecast three hours of informational or educational programming for children each week. Prior to the proposed sale, Univision had met its obligations to program three hours of educational programming for kids with telenovelas that, as the NHMC claimed, could not be considered educational or informational for children.[92] In approving the sale to the Saban group, the FCC imposed a $24 million fine for the company's failure to provide children's programming, the largest fine to date in the history of American television.[93]

In filing the Children's Television Act complaint, the NHMC accomplished two things, beyond securing a hefty fine against Univision. First, although it did not take action to prevent the sale, this move expressed that it would monitor Univision's performance and would file with the FCC when it ran afoul of actionable public interest violations. It was a means to convey to Univision the NHMC's continued status as an important Latino advocacy group. In addition, the action asked the FCC to hold the Spanish-language sector to the same standards as the English-language sector when it came to the few remaining content-based regulations that it enforced. Its win, with the enormous fine, demonstrated to the NHMC that it could persuade the FCC to consider the public interest performance of Spanish-language television when it comes to protecting the rights of children, if not of adults.

Thus, a primary site of advocacy work for the NHMC in the recent past has been in this area. In 2009 the NHMC petitioned the FCC to research whether the parental controls established by the 1996 Telecommunications Act to empower parents to restrict from children's view sexual and violent content had made inroads in Latino households.[94] In addition, it offered support for the current ratings system and requested its translation into Spanish. In 2011 the NHMC jointly filed with the Gay and Lesbian Alliance against Defamation (GLAAD) an indecency complaint against KRCA-TV, part of the EstrellaTV Network owned by Liberman Broadcasting Inc. (LBI), against its series *José Luis sin Censura*, a Jerry Springer–style talk show. The show, which aired on the station at 11 A.M., routinely contained visible nudity, highly suggestive sexual conduct, and the use of profanity and especially derogatory epithets against gay men. Since it was broadcast in the middle of the day, it aired outside the "safe harbor" set aside for indecent programming as established in the late 1970s. The NHMC and GLAAD enlisted more than thirty organizations to file a complaint with the FCC about the show and pressured advertisers to remove their support. LBI removed the series from its schedule in 2012 and in 2013 accepted a fine of $110,000 for violating the FCC's indecency rules.[95]

After decades of Latino media advocacy, of organizations like the NHMC and its allies underlining the political and cultural harms posed by non-Latino control of Spanish-language broadcasting on the rights of Latino publics, of fights over appropriate levels of consolidation in the sector, what provoked the FCC to do something other than rubber-stamp the proposals before it regarding the Spanish-language sector was service to children. Spanish-language broadcasters, from this vantage, have the discretion to provide imported programming to its audiences, to perpetuate color-based hierarchies of value in their casting decisions, and to be part of enormous conglomerates that exercise exceptionally high levels of control over the Spanish-language sector. The adults who rely on Spanish-language media for news and entertainment, or the adults who understand the retention of Spanish to be central to their cultural identities despite their fluency in English, have no acknowledged right to access diversity of views and locally specific perspectives. These broadcasters *do* have an obligation to program for Spanish-speaking children while they are children but cease to have actionable public interest obligations to them once they become adults. Much like in the English-language sector, in the FCC's regulation of the Spanish-language sector, it would honor the Latino family, if not the Latino citizen.

Conclusion

//

Many histories of U.S. media reform campaigns offer narratives of decline. Kathryn Montgomery's *Target Prime Time*, which charts the range of strategies used by myriad activist groups in the 1970s and 1980s to alter prime-time programming, ends with the prediction that deregulation will gut future opportunities for meaningful reform.[1] Elizabeth Fones-Wolf's study of the labor movement's media reform politics and Victor Pickard's analysis of media democracy efforts in the 1940s both end with stories of decline as the anti-communism of the early Cold War neutralized reform campaigns.[2] Robert Horwitz's interview with Everett Parker, a long-standing media reformer and one of the petitioners in the WLBT case in the 1960s, celebrates what Parker was able to achieve but suggests that the broadcast reform movement that his efforts launched was unable to secure structural changes, and thus its long-term impact was limited.[3] Robert McChesney's seminal study of the battle against commercial hegemony in the lead-up to the Communications Act of 1934 concludes with the claim that the battle "provides the sole instance in modern U.S. history in which the structure and control of an established mass medium would be a legitimate issue for public debate," and it was a debate that advocates for public ownership lost.[4]

Others, informed by critical legal studies scholars' skepticism toward the state, have offered even harsher assessments of media advocacy in the United States, noting the limitations of what advocacy could do or dismissing advocacy itself as "ritualistic theater" in which reformers become "captured by the theater's rules, with little hope of affecting the end of the play."[5] Part of the problem, as Thomas Streeter has noted, has been that "the peculiar arena in which advocacy groups operate has been circumscribed by the broader goal of corporate organization for which the arena was originally created."[6] That is, engaging in media advocacy has required accepting the basic premises of broadcast regulation and the role of corporations within it, while trying to alter key concepts, most notably the "public interest," to make broadcast regulation more inclusive and responsive to the needs of diverse publics. These battles can resist how much power is invested in media companies and promote greater restrictions on or requirements of them, but they cannot fundamentally alter the centrality of corporate control. Thus, media advocacy can sometimes look like a fiddling around the edges of broadcast regulation for small concessions that do not really achieve the sort of structural reform necessary to democratize the media.

To some degree the advocacy campaigns at the center of *Public Interests* bear out these criticisms. In the context of the Cold War, the JCET had to fight for noncommercial television reservations in a way that always presumed that television would be dominated by commercial interests. Black activists in the 1960s and early 1970s had to file petitions to deny licenses to broadcasters individually, a process that was costly and time-consuming and resulted in only a few broadcasters losing their licenses. NOW objected not to the fact that television was ad-supported but that advertisements—along with the programs they sponsored—trafficked in harmful stereotypes of women. The NAACP, though striving to demonstrate the harms deregulation posed to communities of color, was willing to accept mergers and higher levels of concentrated media when they included provisions for minority ownership or employment. The PTC initially sought industry solutions to the problem of broadcast indecency and only engaged in regulatory battles when this strategy proved fruitless. The NHMC has objected to the predominance of non-Latino owners of Spanish-language networks but not to their embrace of the same profit models as their English-language counterparts.

In addition, many of these struggles failed to achieve their stated objectives. As the approach to broadcast regulation, especially from the 1980s onward, has signaled, the primary arena in which policy makers could most consistently be compelled to act was in response to the asserted communication needs of children. In this they have embraced a view of public morality tethered to notions of sexual propriety and bourgeois norms of respectable discourse—one that is divorced from and often opposed to considerations of racial justice or gender equality. In other words, the FCC, Congress, and the courts since the 1980s primarily have been willing to recognize a variegated public based on age but often not on any other vector of difference. This points to the relative success of social conservatives in advancing their advocacy agenda in comparison to identity-based groups, as well as to a fissure in the marketplace approach to regulation that recognizes a market failure only when it comes to securing the interests of parents and children. Thus, the efforts for minority media rights, which persisted in the face of deregulation, raised substantial public interest concerns that ultimately did not have much purchase in the realm of broadcast regulation.

Although none of the campaigns examined in *Public Interests* aimed at substantive structural reform that directly challenged the power of corporate broadcasters as a class, they did offer important forms of resistance to the escalating sanctification of markets that has been constitutive of neoliberalism. Indeed, as advocacy groups worked within the "peculiar arena" of broadcast regulation, they consistently reconstituted the "public interest" to direct regulators to value nonmarket concerns, to see the diverse needs of broadcast publics, and to recognize television as a central site of public culture whose stories, images, and perspectives determined the contours of the contemporary public sphere. While these television advocacy campaigns did not fundamentally challenge the corporate underpinnings of American broadcasting, they did routinely challenge the neoliberal logics ascendant since the 1970s, in which, as Wendy Brown has stated, "everything is 'economized'" and "human beings become market actors and nothing but, every field of activity is seen as a market, and every entity (whether public or private, whether person, business, or state) is governed as a firm."[7] Media advocacy has decoupled the corporate interest from the public interest and challenged the tendency to see every field of activity through the lens of market relations. Accordingly, it has been a consistent site of resistance, for liberal and conservative groups alike, against the "everything is 'economized'" rationalities of neoliberalism.

Perhaps more important, many of these advocacy campaigns were produced in response to exigent concerns—like racism and sexism—that bore directly on the distribution of citizenship rights. And for many communities noncommercial broadcasting often seemed to replicate and extend, rather than correct, the problems of commercial television in terms of the politics of representation onscreen, the employment practices that structured their workforce, and the restricted understanding of the broadcasting public. Thus to understand media advocacy is to examine the on-the-ground efforts of a range of communities who saw immediate harms in the way that broadcasting operated locally and in the nation at large. The histories within *Public Interests* provide alternate ways of framing the problem of the media and speak to the urgency with which a range of communities saw in media reform part of the solution.

Broadening our view of media advocacy history expands our understanding of what media reform has been, who has participated in it, and, perhaps most important, how it has mattered to political struggles. It helps us see how broadcasting regulation has been an important site of struggle for the most important social movements of the twentieth century and opens the way for us to consider how the opportunity structure of social movements is in some ways conditioned by the structure of public culture. Thus, rather than contributing my own declension narrative, I would like to end with a consideration of how this history can inform the way we think about the politics of media advocacy, drawing four lessons from the stories of the communities at the center of *Public Interests*.

History Matters

Media advocacy fights routinely have been fought on the terrain of history. The JCET's battle for educational television relied on a scripting of radio history in which commercial interests had betrayed the public interest and educational stations were denied the support they needed to reach an audience or meet their communities' educational and informational needs. The NAACP's fight for minority media rights in the 1980s and 1990s centered on the reassertion of a history of racial discrimination, especially in the realm of broadcasting, to legitimize the need for continued reforms to bring more people of color into positions of authority within it. The PTC's efforts to combat broadcast raunch depended on a history of television's wholesome past, when the medium was, in Bozell's words, "a force for good" that inculcated strong morals rather than functioning as a powerful attack on them. To evoke the past was to recognize how, within the realm of law and policy, history is a legitimating discourse.

While narrating particular histories of media has been a critical component of advocacy campaigns, the history of media advocacy itself can function as a site of legitimacy and power. The long history of media reform efforts attests to the ways that the media, historically, has underserved the needs and infringed on the rights of diverse publics. The histories within *Public Interests* highlight, for example, long-standing feminist concerns over broadcasting's sexism, enduring arguments by Latino civil rights groups over the ownership structure of Spanish-language broadcasting companies, and consistent documentation by African American civil rights activists of media's role in perpetuating racism. Media advocacy campaigns have left a long paper trail articulating public interest grievances, demonstrating enduring concerns over the failures of media companies and their federal regulators to address multicultural and multiracial publics. Such history could serve future efforts in making the case for regulatory action, the insufficiencies of past decisions requiring redress in the present.

Identity Matters

Since the 1960s, media reform activity has been focused on destabilizing the notion of a unitary "public" with homogenous interests. Much of the work of identity-based civil rights organizations has been oriented not only toward changing law and policy but toward demonstrating how law and policy, though seemingly neutral, have been imbricated with structures of discrimination. This is one of the most important lessons to come from their advocacy efforts—that to presume a genderless, raceless public erases existing disparities in power across publics and naturalizes a system mired in and likely to perpetuate social inequality.

While insisting on the existence of multiple publics, advocacy groups long have found common cause with one another. Strategic coalitions have been a key part of media reform efforts—from the big tent of interests brought together by the JCET to advocate for educational television, to the local coalitions in which NOW chapters participated in the 1970s to pressure local stations to be more responsive to their publics, to the ideologically diverse coalition, of which the PTC was a part, to push back against greater media consolidation in the early 2000s. When these communities banded together, they were able to more forcefully exert pressure on broadcasters and policy makers alike and to more strenuously make the case for the public interest benefits of their objectives. Indeed, if there is a lesson to be learned from the history of media reform, it is that coalition building is really important.

But recognizing shared concerns is not the same thing as presuming a singular, knowable public interest. Going forward, media advocacy groups need to keep the lessons of the past in sight and to challenge, rather than replicate, the notion of a single, knowable public, one that has the potential to efface the continuing discrepancies in power among citizens even as it highlights those between the public and media corporations. While the rhetorical power of fighting for *the* public is highly important, we should not mistake the power of rhetoric for realities on the ground or be inattentive to the myriad needs of publics vis-à-vis media and communications.

Capital Matters

In perhaps expected ways, capital matters greatly to media reform struggles. Of the disadvantages media advocacy groups face in battles for media reform, one of the largest is having to fight highly resourced, and highly politically connected, media corporations. In addition, as critics of the political economy of the media long have illustrated, as commercial media structure the possibilities of what can be said and what can be known, and as they accordingly filter out dissenting or radical views, they deploy powerful instruments of persuasion to cultivate a worldview hospitable to the interests of business and political elites, one that can work against the aims of social justice organizations seeking to reform and regulate industry to better serve the needs of the public.[8]

Yet access to capital also determines who can participate in media advocacy itself. While all citizens can participate in media reform—by filing comments with the FCC, inspecting the public records of local broadcasters, writing to a member of Congress—sustained media advocacy campaigns take a good deal of sustained labor. Frequently, they have relied on the volunteer labor of members of organizations—such as the women who sat in Sandee Cohen's living room monitoring WABC broadcasts in 1972. Or they have relied on the work of public interest law firms, like the Citizens Communication Center, a Ford Foundation–supported firm that helped greatly with the filing of petitions to deny for participants in the broadcast reform movement. Yet to level an effectual media advocacy campaign, and to engage in a continued effort to reform the media, often has required infrastructural support and a dedicated, paid staff. And that requires money.

Access to financial support is a critical, if often underdiscussed, facet of media advocacy. This was true for the JCET, whose mission was radically curtailed after the Ford Foundation ceased to provide its funding. And since what McChesney has labeled the "uprising of 2003," the wide-ranging media reform effort to push back against media consolidation, media reform has been seen as an increasingly urgent area of public policy advocacy for a range of communities. As a result there has been competition over precious foundation support for progressive media reform groups. Thus, a number of groups have turned to corporate donations as a means to fund their reform activity. The NHMC, for example, relied at first on volunteer labor. As it has expanded its scope of activity, the NHMC has received funding from the Ford Foundation but also from media companies such as Univision, Entravision, Disney/ABC, and Comcast/NBCUniversal, as well as from the National Association of Broadcasters. This support is critical to the NHMC to pursue the range of campaigns and issues at the core of its mission.[9] Yet the NHMC has taken positions on policy issues contrary to those of its funders and has worked to distance itself from other advocacy groups seen as compromised by their acceptance of corporate money, most notably David Honig's Minority Media Telecommunications Council.[10] This perception of independence has been crucial not only to its own mission but also to its standing among its community and across media advocacy groups.

Accordingly, part of media advocacy work is not only to secure money to support one's labor but also to shore up one's reputational capital to make sure that one's group is seen as a legitimate advocate for the community it represents. Before turning to the import of reputational capital, though, it is important to underline that the ability to engage in media advocacy has required either access to capable volunteer labor, to people who have the time to dedicate to reform activity, or to financial support to fund one's activities. This has placed limitations on who has been able to participate in media reform, to have their agendas considered by policy makers and the public broadly, and to be visible as stakeholders in the process.

In addition to acquiring financial support to level media reform campaigns, media advocacy groups also have to secure reputational capital within the community they seek to represent, with the policy-making community whom they wish to persuade, and with the media companies whose practices they seek to alter. Thus some of the work that media advocacy groups do is in the service of their reputational capital. NOW's first two petitions to deny against flagship network-owned and -operated stations positioned NOW as a credible media reform group on feminist issues. The PTC's securing of allies in Congress for its family-hour campaign, and especially the advertisements it took out in trade and mainstream newspapers that paraded the support lent to the group by politicians and celebrities, established the group as a powerful advocate that claimed to speak on behalf of heterosexual American families. The NHMC has taken on a number of campaigns, like that to sanction *Jose Luis sin Censura*, in response to community complaints over the deleterious impact of local programming, shoring up its reputation with its own community as a capable advocate for its interests.

Furthermore, through continued advocacy efforts, groups gain the informational literacies requisite to be seen as credible stakeholders in the policy-making process. As Becky Lentz has illustrated, media policy advocacy requires learning the grammars and genres of policy making, as well as gaining insights into tactics and strategies to make an impactful intervention. The accumulation of this informational capital, gained from continuous engagement in advocacy, is also a key part of reform efforts.[11] This has been a clear component of past advocacy campaigns, emblematized by the training provided by media reform groups—via newsletters, broadcast reform tool kits, websites, and so on—to instruct others in their rights as members of the public and to inform them about how media policy issues bear on these rights. The acquisition and spread of informational capital consistently has been critical to galvanize support and to illuminate how policy decisions presumed to be of little import to anyone outside of policy makers and regulated industries, in fact, hold great consequence for a range of political struggles.

Losing Matters

Losing, though logically taken as a marker of defeat, also matters. It matters, of course, as an opportunity to learn from past mistakes for future campaigns. The failures of educational radio advocates in the 1930s proved highly instructive for the JCET and its allies in their fight for educational television in the 1950s, the inability of educators to present a united front to the commission a well-heeded cautionary tale. Though NOW's petitions did not result in a singular license revocation, they did lead to the recognition of women as a class within broadcast regulation, at least for a time, and to substantial concessions from local broadcasters. The PTC's inability to persuade broadcasters to bring back the family hour flagged the group's miscalculations in its approach to reforming broadcast programming and led it to pursue a more fruitful course in which it directly engaged with broadcasting regulations.

Yet losing can also be strategic. As Jessica Gonzalez, executive vice president and general counsel at the NHMC, put it, "sometimes you lose to win."[12] In other words, there can be a difference between short-term efforts and long-term objectives, losing in the immediate part of a broader strategy for larger scale reform. Engaging in efforts presumed even by the group itself to be futile can establish its reputational capital, especially with the community it represents as it takes action to address the community's concerns. Such efforts also can introduce legal arguments into a docket that can be fruitful down the road, even if they prove unpersuasive in the short term. In addition, advocacy campaigns can function as tools to persuade media companies to act, rather than deal with a lengthy legal process, and thus to address the needs of the group outside of official regulatory channels.

Recognizing that "losing matters" can help, perhaps paradoxically, to decenter the question of success or failure from our study of media reform and the declension narratives that so often structure how we look back on the advocacy campaigns of the past. In so doing, we can see how media advocacy is a long-haul effort, one that has coexisted with broadcast media themselves, in which advocacy groups routinely have hewed to aspirational visions of what media could be while pragmatically determining what they could achieve given the vagaries of the system which they have sought to reform.

Notes

Abbreviations for Archives

ADA   Alabama Department of Archives and History, Montgomery

BH   Burt Harrison Collection, National Public Broadcasting Archives, University of Maryland, College Park

BPL   Birmingham Public Library, Birmingham, AL

DA   Dolores Alexander Papers, Schlesinger Library, Radcliffe Institute for Advanced Study, Harvard University, Cambridge, MA

DAP   Donna Allen Papers, State Historical Society of Missouri, Columbia

DCN   National Organization for Women DC Chapters Records, Gelman Library, George Washington University, Washington, DC

IKT   I. Keith Tyler Papers, Ohio State University Archives, Columbus

JD   James Day Collection, National Public Broadcasting Archives, University of Maryland, College Park

JR   Jim Robertson Collection, National Public Broadcasting Archives, University of Maryland, College Park

KB   Kathy Bonk Papers, Schlesinger Library, Radcliffe Institute for Advanced Study, Harvard University, Cambridge, MA

NAA   National Association for the Advancement of Colored People Records, Library of Congress, Washington, DC

NET   National Educational Television Collection, Wisconsin Historical Society, Madison

NHM   National Hispanic Media Coalition Papers, University of California, Los Angeles

NOW   National Organization for Women Records, Schlesinger Library, Radcliffe Institute for Advanced Study, Harvard University, Cambridge, MA

NYN   National Organization for Women New York City Chapter Records, Tamiment Library, New York University, New York

RH   Raymond Hurlbert Collection, National Public Broadcasting Archives, University of Maryland, College Park

RS   Ralph Steetle Collection, National Public Broadcasting Archives, University of Maryland, College Park

Introduction

1 T. H. Marshall, *Citizenship and Social Class and Other Essays* (Cambridge: Cambridge University Press, 1950).

2 See Nancy Fraser, "Rethinking Recognition," *New Left Review* 3 (May-June 2000): 107–120.

3 David A. Hollinger, "How Wide the Circle of the 'We'? American Intellectuals and the Problem of Ethnos Since World War II," *American Historical Review* 98, no. 2 (1993): 313–337.

4 Quoted in Bob Ostertag, *People's Movements, People's Press: The Journalism of Social Justice Movements* (Boston: Beacon, 2006), 29.

5 This quotation appeared at the start of a Smithsonian Museum of American History exhibit on African Americans and television. It appears in Charlie Reilly, ed., *Conversations with Amiri Baraka* (Jackson: University Press of Mississippi, 1994), 18.

6 Susan Douglas, *Inventing American Broadcasting, 1899–1922* (Baltimore: Johns Hopkins University Press, 1989), chap. 7.

7 Federal Communications Commission, "Minority Ownership of Broadcasting Facilities: Statement of Policy," *Federal Register* 43 (June 9, 1978): 25189.

8 The literature on the politics of broadcast policy making in the United States has been especially attentive to the power dynamics among Congress, the FCC, the courts, broadcasters, and citizens' groups. See, e.g., James L. Baughman, *Television's Guardians: The FCC and the Politics of Programming, 1958–67* (Knoxville: University of Tennessee Press, 1985); Des Freedman, *The Politics of Media Policy* (Cambridge: Polity, 2008); Robert B. Horwitz, *The Irony of Regulatory Reform: The Deregulation of American Telecommunications* (New York: Oxford University Press, 1989); Edwin G. Krasnow, Lawrence D. Longley, and Herbert A. Terry, *The Politics of Broadcast Regulation* (New York: St. Martin's, 1982).

9 Joanna Grisinger, "Law in Action: The Attorney General Committee on Administrative Procedure," *Journal of Policy History* 20, no. 3 (2008): 379–416.

10 Thomas Streeter, *Selling the Air: A Critique of the Policy of Commercial Broadcasting in the United States* (Chicago: University of Chicago Press, 1996); Thomas Streeter, "Beyond Freedom of Speech and the Public Interest: The Relevance of Critical Legal Studies to Communications Policy," *Journal of Communication* 40, no. 2 (1990): 42–63; Thomas Streeter, "Policy, Politics, and Discourse," *Communication, Culture and Critique* 6, no. 4 (2013): 488–501; Steven Douglas Classen, "Standing on Unstable Grounds: A Reexamination of the WLBT-TV Case," *Critical Studies in Mass Communication* 11, no. 1 (1994): 71–91; John McMurria, "Regulation and the Law: A Critical Cultural Citizenship Approach," in *Media Industries: History, Theory, Method*, ed. Jennifer Holt and Alisa Perren (Malden, MA: Wiley-Blackwell, 2009), 171–183.

11 Freedman, *The Politics of Media Policy*, 3.

12 See, e.g., Robert W. McChesney, *Telecommunications, Mass Media, and Democracy:*

The Battle for Control of U.S. Broadcasting, 1928–1935 (New York: Oxford University Press, 1993); Elizabeth A. Fones-Wolf, *Waves of Opposition: Labor and the Struggle for Democratic Radio* (Urbana: University of Illinois Press, 2006); Victor Pickard, "Reopening the Postwar Settlement for U.S. Media: The Origins and Implications of the Social Contract between Media, the State, and the Polity," *Communication, Culture and Critique* 3, no. 2 (2010): 170–189; Victor Pickard, "'Whether the Giants Should Be Slain or Persuaded to Be Good': Revisiting the Hutchins Commission and the Role of Media in a Democratic Society," *Critical Studies in Media Communication* 27, no. 4 (2010): 291–311.

13 Steven D. Classen, *Watching Jim Crow: The Struggles over Mississippi TV, 1955–1969* (Durham, NC: Duke University Press, 2004); Chon A. Noriega, *Shot in America: Television, the State, and the Rise of Chicano Cinema* (Minneapolis: University of Minnesota Press, 2000); Kay Mills, *Changing Channels: The Civil Rights Case That Transformed Television* (Jackson: University Press of Mississippi, 2004).

14 Nicholas Johnson, *How to Talk Back to Your Television Set* (Boston: Little, Brown, 1970), 187.

15 On "constitutive moments" see Paul Starr, *The Creation of the Media: Political Origins of Modern Communication* (New York: Basic Books, 2005), 7, 362.

16 See Robert W. McChesney, *Communication Revolution: Critical Junctures and the Future of Media* (New York: New Press, 2006).

17 Mark S. Fowler and Daniel L. Brenner, "A Marketplace Approach to Broadcast Regulation," *Texas Law Review* 60, no. 2 (1982): 207–257.

Chapter 1   The Battle for Educational Television

1 Jack Gould, "Television: Boon or Bane?" *Public Opinion Quarterly* 10 (August 1946): 320.

2 See Tim Brooks and Earle March, *The Complete Directory to Prime Time Network and Cable Shows, 1946–Present* (New York: Ballantine, 1999), 1151 (for the prime-time schedule of networks in 1946).

3 Thomas Hutchinson, *Here Is Television, Your Window to the World* (New York: Hastings House, 1946), ix–xi; Lynn Spigel, *Make Room for TV: Television and the Family Ideal in Postwar America* (Chicago: University of Chicago Press, 1992), 36–72.

4 Gould, "Television," 318.

5 Ibid., 319–320.

6 For an excellent discussion of education radio programming see Hugh Richard Slotten, *Radio's Hidden Voice: The Origins of Public Broadcasting in the United States* (Urbana: University of Illinois Press, 2009), 23–39.

7 See Richard Hull, interview by Burt Harrison, 8, Box 5, Folder 16, BH.

8 See "The Great Lakes Statement," in *Documents of American Broadcasting*, ed. Frank Kahn (Englewood Cliffs, NJ: Prentice-Hall, 1984), 64–68.

9 Ralph Engelman, *Public Radio and Television in America: A Political History* (Thousand Oaks, CA: Sage, 1996), 24.

10 Ibid., 23–25.

11 Robert W. McChesney, *Telecommunications, Mass Media, and Democracy: The Battle for the Control of U.S. Broadcasting* (New York: Oxford University Press, 1995).

12 Hugh Slotten, *Radio's Hidden Voice: The Origins of Public Broadcasting in the*

United States (Urbana: University of Illinois Press, 2009), chap. 6; Josh Shepperd, "Infrastructure in the Air: The Office of Education and the Development of Public Broadcasting in the U.S., 1934–1944," *Critical Studies in Media Communication* 31, no. 3 (2014): 230–243.

13 Jerome G. Kerwin, *The Control of Radio* (Chicago: University of Chicago Press, 1934).

14 James Rorty, *Order on the Air!* (New York: John Day, 1934).

15 Morris L. Ernst, *The First Freedom* (New York: Macmillan, 1946).

16 Richard J. Meyer, "The Blue Book," *Journal of Broadcasting* 6, no. 3 (1962): 197–207; Victor Pickard, "The Battle over the FCC Blue Book: Determining the Role of Broadcast Media in a Democratic Society," *Media, Culture and Society* 33, no. 2 (2011): 171–191.

17 See Victor Pickard, *America's Battle for Media Democracy: The Triumph of Corporate Libertarianism and the Future of Media Reform* (New York: Cambridge University Press, 2015); see also Victor Pickard, "Whether the Giants Should Be Slain or Persuaded to Be Good: Revisiting the Hutchins Commission and the Role of Media in a Democratic Society," *Critical Studies in Media Communication* 27, no. 4 (2010): 391–411; Elizabeth Fones-Wolf, *Waves of Opposition: Labor and the Struggle for Democratic Radio* (Urbana: University of Illinois Press, 2006).

18 For a discussion of the technical aspects of the freeze, especially the issue of UHF allocations, see William Boddy, *Fifties Television: The Industry and Its Critics* (Urbana: University of Illinois Press, 1990), chap. 3. For a discussion of the role of the freeze in determining how to interconnect stations, see Jonathan Sterne, "Television under Construction: American Television and the Problem of Distribution, 1926–62," *Media, Culture and Society* 21, no. 4 (1999): 503–530.

19 See the recollections of Robert B. Hudson, Ralph Steetle, and Harold B. "Mac" McCarty in Jim Robertson, *TeleVisionaries* (Charlotte Harbor, FL: Tabby House Books, 1993), 53–55.

20 National Education Association to Educational Institutions and Organizations, memorandum, Oct. 8, 1950, Record Group 40/62/5/2, IKT.

21 The four major networks were NBC, ABC, CBS, and DuMont. DuMont would fold in 1955.

22 Hull interview, 5.

23 Hugh Slotten, "'Rainbow in the Sky': FM Radio, Technical Superiority, and Regulatory Decision-Making," *Technology and Culture* 37, no. 4 (1996): 686–720.

24 Ibid., 688.

25 Amy L. Toro, "Standing Up for Listeners' Rights: A History of Public Participation at the Federal Communications Commission" (PhD diss., University of California, Berkeley, 2000), 68.

26 Ibid., 68–69.

27 W. Wayne Alford, *National Association of Educational Broadcasters History*, vol. 2, *1954–1965* (Urbana: National Association of Educational Broadcasters, 1966), 8.

28 Richard Hull to NAEB Members Concerned with TV Hearings, memorandum, Oct. 7, 1950, Record Group 40/62/5/2, IKT.

29 Special Meeting on TV Allocation Hearings, Box 1, Folder 1, RS.

30 JCET Meeting Notes, April 23, 1951, Box 1, Folder 1, RS.

31 I. Keith Tyler, interview by Jim Robertson, 5–10, Box 3, Folder 12, JR; Theresa R. Richardson and Erwin V. Johanningmeier, "Educational Radio, Childhood, and Philanthropy: A New Role for the Humanities in Popular Culture, 1924–1941," *Journal of Radio Studies* 13, no. 1 (2006): 12–13.

32 JCET Meeting Notes, Dec. 7, 1950, 2, Box 1, Folder 2, RS.

33 Special Meeting on TV Allocation Hearings Notes, Box 1, Folder 1, RS. The meeting was held on Oct. 16, 1950, in Washington, DC.

34 JCET Meeting Notes, Dec. 7, 1950, 4, Box 1, Folder 2, RS.

35 JCET Meeting Notes, June 4, 1951, 5–6, Box 1, Folder 5, RS.

36 JCET Meeting Notes, Dec. 7, 1950, 2, Box 1, Folder 2, RS.

37 "Educators Take Up Torch for TV Channels," *Broadcasting, Telecasting*, Dec. 4, 1950, 55, 96.

38 "VHF-UHF Channels: Educators Ask in Petition," *Broadcasting, Telecasting*, Nov. 27, 1950, 77. "Educational TV—'Hell Hath No Fury,'" *Television Digest*, Dec. 2, 1950, 7–8; "Educators Take Up Torch."

39 Quoted in "Educators Take Up Torch."

40 "Educator's Bid: FCC Hears Endorsements," *Broadcasting, Telecasting*, Dec. 11, 1950, 74.

41 Murray Schumach, "15 Women Know They Hate TV: Took It 12 Hours a Day for a Week," *New York Times*, Jan. 11, 1951, 27.

42 Ibid.

43 "Monitors Criticize Seven TV Stations," *New York Times*, Jan. 24, 1951, 29; "To Probe 'Anatomy' of TV Programs," *Television Digest*, Jan. 27, 1951, 2–3.

44 "TV Survey Shows Little Educational, FCC Told," *Los Angeles Times*, Jan. 25, 1951, 26.

45 Seymour N. Siegel, "From the Mailbag," *New York Times*, Feb. 4, 1951, 91.

46 Morris Novik, interview by Burt Harrison, 29, Box 6, Folder 4, BH; Hull interview, 20; Tyler interview, 22, Box 6, Folder 16, BH.

47 Tyler interview, 27.

48 Susan L. Brinson, *Personal and Public Interests: Frieda B. Hennock and the Federal Communications Commission* (Westport, CT: Praeger, 2002), chap. 5; see also Susan L. Brinson, "Missed Opportunities: FCC Commissioner Frieda Hennock and the UHF Debacle," *Journal of Broadcasting and Electronic Media* 44 (Spring 2000): 249.

49 The National Association of Broadcasters (NAB) was founded in 1922. It operated as the primary trade organization for broadcasters.

50 "Two Years of Color Controversy . . . ," *Broadcasting, Telecasting*, June 4, 1951, 62.

51 "Educators' Bid: FCC Hears Endorsements," *Broadcasting, Telecasting*, Dec. 11, 1950, 100; and "Educators Make Hay in VHF-UHF Hearing," *Television Digest*, Dec. 9, 1950, 5.

52 For example, Bricker introduced a resolution in Congress to investigate ETV reservations. "Educators Take Up Torch for TV," *Broadcasting, Telecasting*, Dec. 4, 1950, 55; "Channels Study Requested by Bricker," *Broadcasting, Telecasting*, Feb. 5, 1951, 75.

53 On Bricker's background in educational broadcasting see Tyler's interview with Harrison, 13.

54 "Bricker Plan: Wants Educational TV Probe," *Broadcasting, Telecasting*, Dec. 4, 1950, 54.

55 Robert O. Davies, *Defender of the Old Guard: John Bricker in American Politics* (Columbus: Ohio State University Press, 1993).

56 Testimony of Kenneth Baker, 7, RG 40/62/5/4, IKT.

57 Testimony of Frank Stanton, 3–5, RG 40/62/5/4, IKT.

58 "Educators' Proposal Called Wasteful," *Television Digest*, Jan. 27, 1951, 3–4; "Educators' Survey: Highlights JCET Testimony," *Broadcasting, Telecasting*, Jan. 29, 1951,

88–89; "Miller, Stanton Testify on Educational Video," *Broadcasting, Telecasting*, Jan. 29, 1951, 90.

59 *Third Report of Commission*, repr. in *Television Digest*, March 24, 1951, 4.

60 JCET Meeting Notes, June 4–5, 1951, 5–6, Box 1, Folder 5, RS; JCET Meeting Notes, Sept. 10, 1951, 3, Box 1, Folder 8, RS.

61 Ralph Steetle, interview by Jim Robertson, 10, Box 3, Folder 8, JR.

62 JCET Meeting Notes, July 16, 1951, 1, Box 1, Folder 7, RS.

63 Ibid., 5.

64 Burton Paulu, "The Challenge of 242 Channels: Part I," *Quarterly Review of Film, Radio, and Television* 7 (Autumn 1952): 5.

65 Brief of the Joint Committee on Educational Television, 130, Box 4, Folder 1, RS.

66 Ibid., 189.

67 Ibid., 278.

68 Ibid., 16.

69 Ibid., 291–292.

70 Federal Communications Commission, *Sixth Report and Order* 41 FCC 148, 160.

71 Ibid., 161.

72 Ibid., 160.

73 Ibid., 166.

74 Ibid.

75 Robert Blakely, *To Serve the Public Interest: Educational Broadcasting in the United States* (Syracuse, NY: Syracuse University Press, 1979); Streeter, *Selling the Air*, 187–190.

76 Laurie Ouellette, *Viewers Like You? How Public TV Failed the People* (New York: Columbia University Press, 2002), 41–44; Glenda Balas, *Recovering a Public Vision for Public Television* (Lanham, MD: Rowman and Littlefield, 2003), chap. 4.

77 Educational Television: Hearing Before the Committee on Interstate and Foreign Commerce, United States Senate, 83rd Cong., 1st sess., April 21, 1953 (testimony of Frieda Hennock).

78 See, e.g., JCET Meeting Notes, July 15, 1953, 2–4, Box 1, Folder 24, RS; JCET Meeting Notes, Sept. 25, 1953, 2–4, Box 1, Folder 25, RS; JCET Meeting Notes, May 14, 1954, 7–8, Box 1, Folder 30, RS; JCET Meeting Notes, Jan. 5, 1955, 7–8, Box 1, Folder 35, RS.

79 Blakely, *To Serve*, 92–93; *Educational Television: Factsheet and Box Score*, Nov. 1956, 2–7, Box 5, Folder 8, RS; *Educational Television: Factsheet and Box Score*, Feb. 1958, 6–7, Box 5, Folder 8, RS; *Educational Television: Factsheet and Box Score*, Nov. 1958, 5, Box 5, Folder 8, RS.

80 JCET Meeting Notes, June 3, 1953, 6, Box 1, Folder 43, RS. The JCET voted at this meeting to send a letter of appreciation to the NARTB to thank and congratulate it for this support.

81 JCET Meeting Notes, Feb. 14, 1954, 2, Box 1, Folder 28, RS.

82 Alford, *National Association of Educational Broadcasters History*, 2:21–22.

83 *Educational Television: Factsheet and Box Score*, June 15, 1956, 2–3, Box 5, Folder 8, RS.

84 JCET Meeting Notes, Feb. 3, 1960, 8, Box 1, Folder 51, RS. Interview with Steetle, 43.

85 Television Inquiry, Hearings Before the Committee on Interstate and Foreign Commerce, United States Senate, 84th Cong., 2nd sess., on S. Res. 13 and 163, Authorizing Investigations of Certain Problems Relating to Interstate and Foreign Commerce, Feb. 29, 1956 (testimony of Ralph Steetle).

86 JCET Meeting Notes, Nov. 22, 1955, Box 1, Folder 40, RS.

87 Steetle to "Those Concerned with Educational Television," July 24, 1952, RG 40/62/5/9, IKT.

88 James Day, *The Vanishing Vision: The Inside Story of Public Television* (Berkeley: University of California Press, 1995), 30.

89 Steetle interview, 17.

90 Ibid.

91 JCET, "Two Years of Progress in Educational Television," Sept. 1954, Box 7, Folder 9, RS; JCET, "Four Years of Progress in Educational Television," Dec. 1956, Box 4, Folder 12, RS; JCET, "Current Developments in Educational Television," Jan. 1961, Box 5, Folder 17, RS.

92 Quoted in William J. Reese, *America's Public Schools: From the Common School to "No Child Left Behind"* (Baltimore: Johns Hopkins University Press, 2005), 221.

93 Ibid., 221–225.

94 Andrew Hartman, *Education and the Cold War: The Battle for the American School* (New York: Palgrave Macmillan, 2008).

95 JCET, "Four Years," 11.

96 Allison Perlman, "Television Up in the Air: The Midwest Program on Airborne Television Instruction, 1959–1971," *Critical Studies in Media Communication* 27, no. 5 (2010): 477–497.

97 Larry Cuban, *Teachers and Machines: The Classroom Use of Technology Since 1920* (New York: Teachers College Press, 1988), 5.

98 Ibid., passim.

99 Robertson, *TeleVisionaries*, 113.

100 The following articles appeared in the first issue of *Southern School News* 1 (Sept. 3, 1954), a monthly newsletter established by the Southern Educational Reporting Service (SERS) to chronicle what was happening in the South after *Brown*: "Arkansas," 2; "Georgia," 5; "Mississippi," 8; "North Carolina," 10; "South Carolina," 12.

101 See, e.g., "South Carolina," *Southern School News* 1 (Nov. 4, 1954): 14; "Legislatures Take Up Segregation Issue," *Southern School News* 1 (Feb. 3, 1955): 1; "Arguments on Decrees to Begin April 11," *Southern School News* 1 (April 7, 1955): 1.

102 Hull interview, 28.

103 "America's First ETV Network Is Your Alabama Educational Television Network," 3, Box 1, Folder 7, RH.

104 *Now There Are Four: Alabama Educational Television Network*, 9, Box 1, Folder 7, RH.

105 Jan Collins Stucker, "South Carolina's Educational Television Heads the Class," *New York Times*, March 2, 1975, 29.

106 "ETV in South Carolina," *New Republic*, August 31, 1963, 7.

107 "Salvation by Television," *Time*, May 25, 1962, 50.

108 *Missouri Ex Rel Gaines v. Canada* 305 U.S.337 (1938).

109 Redding S. Sugg Jr. and George Hilton Jones, *The Southern Regional Education Board: Ten Years of Regional Cooperation in Higher Education* (Baton Rouge: Louisiana State University Press, 1960).

110 For a discussion of the Southern Manifesto see Francis M. Wilhoit, *The Politics of Massive Resistance* (New York: George Braziller, 1973), 52–54.

111 Barbara Barksdale Clowse, *Brainpower for the Cold War: The Sputnik Crisis and the National Defense Education Act of 1958* (Westport, CT: Greenwood Press, 1981).

112 Alford, *National Association of Educational Broadcasters History*, 2:77, 99.

113 John Edward Burke, "An Historical Analytical Study of the Legislative and Political

Origins of the Public Broadcasting Act of 1967" (PhD diss., Ohio State University, 1971), 42–43.

114 Educational Television: Hearings Before the Committee on Interstate and Foreign Commerce, United States Senate, 86th Cong., 1st sess., on S. 12, A Bill to Expedite the Utilization of Television Transmission Facilities in our Public Schools and Colleges, and in Adult Training Programs, Jan. 27, 1959 (testimony of Ralph Steetle).

115 Educational Television: Hearings Before a Subcommittee on Communications and Power of the Committee on Interstate and Foreign Commerce, United States House of Representatives, on H.R. 132, H.R. 5099, H.R. 5536, H.R. 5602, Bills to Amend the Communications Act of 1934 to Establish a Program of Federal Matching Grants for the Construction of Television Facilities to Be Used for Educational Purposes; H.R. 645, A Bill to Amend the Communications Act of 1934 to Assist in the Establishment and Improvement of Certain Television Broadcasting Facilities; H.R. 965 and H.R. 2910, Bills to Expedite the Utilization of Television Transmission Facilities in Our Public Schools and Colleges, and in Adult Training Programs; and S. 205, An Act to Expedite the Utilization of Television Transmission Facilities in Our Public Schools and Colleges, and in Adult Training Programs, 87th Cong., 1st sess., March 22, 1961, 135 (testimony of Robert Anderson).

116 Educational Television: Hearings Before a Subcommittee on Communications and Power of the Committee on Interstate and Foreign Commerce, United States House of Representatives, 86th Cong., 1st sess., on H.R. 32, A Bill to Amend the Communications Act of 1934 to Assist in the Establishment and Improvement of Certain Television Broadcasting Facilities; H.R. 1981, H.R. 3723, H.R. 4248, H.R. 4572, Bills to Amend the Communications Act of 1934 to Establish a Program of Federal Matching Grants for the Construction of Television Facilities to Be Used for Educational Purposes; S. 12, An Act to Expedite the Utilization of Television Transmission Facilities in Our Public Schools and Colleges and in Adult Training Programs, 86th Cong., 1st sess., May 12, 1959, 71–72 (testimony of William G. Harley).

117 W. Wayne Alford, "The Educational Television Facilities Act of 1962," *AV Communication Review* 15, no. 1 (1967): 84–88.

118 See Ouellette, *Viewers Like You?*

119 Joint Council on Educational Broadcasting, *Statement of Function and Organization*, Feb. 2, 1961, Series 5B, Box 12, Folder 1, NET.

120 In 1966 the JCEB became the Joint Council on Educational Telecommunications and would assure policies regarding communication technologies beyond broadcasting—cable, satellite, and so on—considered their educational applications. This final iteration of the original JCET dissolved in 1982.

Chapter 2   The Black Freedom Struggle and the Broadcast Reform Movement

1 B. J. Richey, "Alabama ETV under Fire for Racism, 'Censorship,'" *Mobile Register*, June 18, 1970, Hurlbert Papers, 23.1.7.10.1, BPL.

2 *In Re Application of the Alabama Educational Television Commission*, Memorandum Opinion and Order, 50 FCC 2d 461 (1975).

3 U.S. Civil Rights Commission, *Window Dressing on the Set: Women and Minorities in Television* (Washington, DC: US Government Printing Office, 1977), 62.

4 Steven Suitts, telephone interview by the author, July 14, 2011.

5   Anne W. Branscomb and Maria Savage, "The Broadcast Reform Movement: At the Crossroads," *Journal of Communication* 28, no. 4 (1978): 25–34; Robert W. McChesney, *Communication Revolution: Critical Junctures and the Future of Media* (New York: New Press, 2006), 31–34.

6   McChesney, *Communication Revolution*, 31.

7   Ronald H. Coase, "The Federal Communications Commission," *Journal of Law and Economics* 2 (Oct. 1959): 1–40; Davis A. Moss and Michael R. Fein, "Radio Regulation Revisited: Coase, the FCC, and the Public Interest," *Journal of Policy History* 15, no. 4 (2003): 389–416.

8   Steven D. Classen, *Watching Jim Crow: The Struggles over Mississippi TV, 1955–1969* (Durham, NC: Duke University Press, 2004), 42–48.

9   Ibid.

10 Robert Britt Horwitz, "Broadcast Reform Revisited: Reverend Everett C. Parker and the 'Standing' Case (*Office of Communication of United Church of Christ v. Federal Communications Commission*)," *Communication Review* 2, no. 3 (1997): 320.

11 See "Standing of Television Viewers to Contest FCC Orders: The Private Action Goes Public," *Columbia Law Review* 66, no. 8 (1966): 1511–1528; and "Administrative Law—Community Representatives Have Standing to Challenge FCC License Renewal—*Office of Communication of United Church of Christ v. FCC*," *Michigan Law Review* 65, no. 3 (1967): 518–531.

12 "Administrative Law," 520.

13 *Office of Communication of the United Church of Christ v. Federal Communications Commission* 359 F.2d 994 (1966).

14 *Office of Communication of the United Church of Christ v. Federal Communications Commission* 425 F.2d 543 (1969). For a discussion of African American control of the station see Kay Mills, *Changing Channels: The Civil Rights Case That Transformed Television* (Jackson: University Press of Mississippi, 2004), chaps. 6 and 7.

15 Laurence Laurent, "FCC Challenged on WLBT Permit," *Washington Post*, June 11, 1965, D12; "Court Rules Negroes Must Have Hearing on TV Bias," *Chicago Defender*, April 9, 1966, 7; Eileen Shanahan, "TV, Radio Stations Warned on Bias," *New York Times*, July 6, 1968, 1, 41; Christopher Lydon, "F.C.C. Is Rebuked by Appeals Court in Burger Decision," *New York Times*, June 24, 1969, 1; Thomas W. Lippman, "TV Outlet Accused of Racism Stripped of Permit by Court," *Washington Post*, June 24, 1969, A9; "Burger Blasts FCC Ruling in Bias Case," *Chicago Tribune*, B14; Paul Molloy, "Reversal for FCC: Broadcast Industry Shaken by Court," *Los Angeles Times*, July 10, 1969, C30.

16 Steven D. Classen, "Standing on Unstable Grounds: A Reexamination of the WLBT-TV Case," *Critical Studies in Mass Communication* 11, no. 1 (1994): 71–91.

17 *Office of Communication v. FCC* (1969), 550.

18 Cass Sunstein, *After the Rights Revolution: Reconceiving the Regulatory State* (Cambridge, MA: Harvard University Press, 1990).

19 Theodore J. Schneyer, "An Overview of Public Interest Law in the Communication Field," *Wisconsin Law Review*, no. 3 (1977): 623; Kathryn Montgomery, *Target: Prime Time: Advocacy Groups and the Struggle over Entertainment Television* (New York: Oxford University Press, 1989), 25.

20 "The Pool of Experts on Access," *Broadcasting*, Sept. 20, 1971, 36.

21 The "minority rights revolution" is a phenomenon discussed at length in John D. Skrentny, *The Minority Rights Revolution* (Cambridge, MA: Harvard University Press, 2002).

22 Kevin Mumford, "Harvesting the Crisis: The Newark Uprising, the Kerner Commission, and Writings on Riots," in *African American Urban History since World War II*, ed. Kenneth L. Kusmer and Joe W. Trotter (Chicago: University of Chicago Press, 2009), 210.

23 Robert Fogelson, "White on Black: A Critique of the McCone Commission Report on the Los Angeles Riots," in *The Los Angeles Riots*, ed. Robert Fogelson (New York: Arno, 1969), 114.

24 "Violence in the City—An End or a Beginning? A Report by the Governor's Commission on the Los Angeles Riots," in *The Los Angeles Riots*, ed. Robert Fogelson (New York: Arno, 1969), 92.

25 "Assess Radio-TV Role in Epidemic of Race Rioting," *Variety*, August 2, 1967, 1; "B'casting Role in Riots a Growing Issue with Solons," *Variety*, August 9, 1967, 29; "Riot Coverage 'Restrained': Magnuson," *Variety*, Sept. 9, 1967, 27.

26 *The Kerner Report: The 1968 Report of the National Advisory on Civil Disorders*, with a preface by Fred R. Harris and introduction by Tom Wicker (New York: Pantheon, 1988), 369–372. Subsequent citations of this report are referenced parenthetically in the text.

27 Aniko Bodroghkozy, *Equal Time: Television and the Civil Rights Movement* (Urbana: University of Illinois Press, 2012), 151.

28 Richard J. Meyer, "ETV and the Ghetto," *Educational Broadcasting Review*, August 1968, 19–24.

29 John Horn, "Television," *Nation*, March 18, 1968, 390.

30 Nondiscrimination Employment Practices of Broadcast Licensees, 13 FCC 2d 766 (1968), 774.

31 Ibid., 775. For affirmative action as "crisis management" see John D. Skrentny, *The Ironies of Affirmative Action: Politics, Culture, and Justice in America* (Chicago: University of Chicago Press, 1996), 67–110.

32 Federal Communications Commission, "Minority Ownership of Broadcasting Facilities: Statement of Policy," *Federal Register* 43 (June 9, 1978): 25189.

33 U.S. Civil Rights Commission, *Window Dressing on the Set*, 1.

34 Federal Communications Commission, "Minority Ownership of Broadcasting Facilities: Statement of Policy," *Federal Register* 43 (June 9, 1978): 25189; *Metro Broadcasting Inc. v. Federal Communications Commission* 497 U.S. 547 (1990).

35 John White, interview by Jim Robertson, 21, Box 3, Folder 14, JR.

36 John F. White, "Net as the Fourth Network," in *The Farther Vision: Educational Television Today*, ed. Allen E. Koenig and Ruane Hill (Madison: University of Wisconsin Press, 1967), 87–96.

37 Carolyn Brooks, "Documentary Programming and the Emergence of the National Educational Television Center as a Network, 1958–1972" (PhD diss., University of Wisconsin-Madison, 1994).

38 National Educational Television, Report of the Year, 1964, 34. Submitted to Ford Foundation, Feb. 15, 1965, Box 11, Folder 12, JD.

39 Box 11 of the James Day collection at the NPBA contains reports filed by NET to the Ford Foundation from 1965 through 1972. These reports include appendices that list, based on stations reporting back to NET, which shows affiliates refused to air and why.

40 On refusal to air the broadcast on North Vietnam see "Memorandum: Survey of NET Program Use by Affiliates during January to March 1968," 5. This memo was submitted as part of National Educational Television, Semi-annual Report,

January–June 1968, Box 12, Folder 1, JD. A discussion of the controversy around the NET broadcast on North Vietnam can be found on pages 5–6 of the report. See also Edwin R. Bayley, "An Attempt at Suppression: An Ugly Omen," *Educational Broadcasting Review* 2, no. 3 (1968): 9–11. On refusal to air the program on Fidel Castro see "Memorandum: Survey of NET Program Usage by Affiliates during October, November, December 1968," 7–8; and "Survey of NET Program Usage by Affiliates, April to June 1969, 10–11," Box 12, Folder 2, JD.

41 In, for example, the survey conducted by NET in 1967 about program usage, a number of stations indicated that they did not broadcast certain shows because of "local tensions and riots" or because of the "racial situation" in their community at the time. See Fritz Jauch, "Memorandum: Survey of NET Program Usage by Affiliates during July, August, September 1967" (December 21, 1967), 4–5, Box 11, Folder 5, JD.

42 Yolanda Branham, "A Study of the Southern Educational Communications Association in the Development of the South's Regional Public Television Network" (master's thesis, University of Georgia, 1970).

43 "SECA Board: Program Standards Resolution," adopted April 30, 1970, Alabama Governor, Administrative Assistant Files, SG019966, Folder 13, ADA.

44 White, "National Educational Television as Fourth Network," 90.

45 Tommy Lee Lott, "Documenting Social Issues: *Black Journal*, 1968–1970," in *Struggle for Representation: African American Documentary Film and Video*, ed. Phyllis R. Klotman and Janet K. Cutler (Bloomington: Indiana University Press, 1999), 71–88. See also Laurie Ouellette, *Viewers Like You? How Public TV Failed the People* (New York: Columbia University Press, 2002), 132–135; Devorah Heitner, *Black Power TV* (Durham, NC: Duke University Press, 2013), chap. 3; and Christine Acham, *Revolution Televised: Prime Time and the Struggle for Black Power* (Minneapolis: University of Minnesota Press, 2004), chap. 2.

46 Gayle Wald, *It's Been Beautiful: "Soul!" and Black Power Television* (Durham, NC: Duke University Press, 2015), 1. For a discussion of the context in which the show was produced see pages 44–56.

47 Judy Austin to William B. Ray, Jan. 28, 1970, Alabama Governor, Administrative Assistant Files, SG019966, Folder 15, ADA.

48 Spiro Agnew, "The Des Moines Speech," in *Readings in Mass Communications: Concepts and Ideas in the Mass Media*, ed. Michael C. Emery and Ted Curtis Smythe (Dubuque, IA: Wm. C. Brown, 1974), 502.

49 Rev. Eugene Farrell to Spiro Agnew, March 12, 1970, Alabama Governor, Administrative Assistant Files, SG019966, Folder 15, ADA.

50 Raymond D. Hurlbert to Robert Rawson, Feb. 25, 1970, Hurlbert Collection, 23.1.4.2.1, BPL. Hurlbert's letter was signed by the AETC's five commissioners and constituted the commission's official response to the charges. Rawson was the officer in charge of the FCC's Broadcast Bureau's Renewal and Transfer Division.

51 Ibid., 3.

52 *In Re Complaint by Faculty Senate of the College of Arts and Sciences of the University of Alabama Concerning Programming of Alabama Educational Stations,* Memorandum Opinion and Order, 25 FCC 2d 342 (1970), 343.

53 Ibid., 346.

54 Ibid., 347.

55 Barry Cole and Mal Oettinger refer to Wright as "*the* spokesman for blacks in FCC matters" in the late 1960s and early 1970s. See Barry Cole and Mal Oettinger, *Reluctant Regulators: The FCC and the Broadcast Audience* (Reading: Addison-Wesley,

1978), 67. See also Bishetta D. Merritt, "A Historical-Critical Study of a Pressure Group in Broadcasting: Black Efforts for Soul in Television" (PhD diss., Ohio State University, 1974); and Juan Gonzalez and Joseph Torres, *News for All the People: The Epic Story of Race and the American Media* (New York: Verso, 2012), 306–307.

56 Anthony Brown and William D. Wright, Petition for Reconsideration, July 28, 1970, 3, Alabama Governor, Administrative Assistant Files, SG019966, Folder 14, ADA.

57 Steven Suitts to John Mitchell, August 5, 1970, Hurlbert Papers, 23.1.4.2.1, BPL.

58 Rev. Eugene Farrell to Vice President Spiro Agnew, March 12, 1970, Alabama Governor, Administrative Assistant Files, SG019966, Folder 14, ADA.

59 Linda Edwards, Eugene Farrell, Steven Suitts, Petition for Reconsideration, July 28, 1970, 19–20, Alabama Governor, Administrative Assistant Files, SG019966, Folder 14, ADA.

60 Opposition of Alabama Educational Television Commission to Petition for Reconsideration, submitted Sept. 14, 1970, Alabama Governor, Administrative Assistant Files, SG019966, Folder 13, ADA.

61 Ibid., 13.

62 Ibid., 22.

63 See Appendix in the AETC's Opposition of Alabama Educational Television Commission to the Petition for Reconsideration.

64 Whitney Strub, "Black and White and Banned All Over: Race, Censorship, and Obscenity in Postwar Memphis," *Journal of Social History* 40, no. 3 (2007): 685–715.

65 Opposition of Alabama Educational Television Commission to Petition for Reconsideration, 24–25. This call for a code of standards for public broadcasting was repeated throughout the early years of the AETC license battle.

66 Ibid., 31.

67 Kerner Report, 1.

68 For discussions of *Black Journal*'s politics see Devorah Heitner, *Black Power TV* (Durham, NC: Duke University Press, 2013), chap. 3; and Christine Acham, *Revolution Televised: Prime Time and the Struggle for Black Power* (Minneapolis: University of Minnesota Press, 2004), chap. 2.

69 Opposition of Alabama Educational Television Commission to Petition, 22.

70 Ibid., 31.

71 *In Re Application of the Alabama Educational Television Commission*, Memorandum Opinion and Order, 33 FCC 2d 495 (1972).

72 Raymond D. Hurlbert to Governor Albert Brewer, Sept. 8, 1970, Alabama Governor, Administrative Assistant Files, SG019966, Folder 13, ADA.

73 "Buchanan Backs ETV in Dispute," *Birmingham News*, August, 12, 1970, Hurlbert Papers, 23.1.7.10.1, BPL.

74 Senator James Allen to Raymond Hurlbert, Oct. 12, 1970, Hurlbert Papers, 23.4.1.2.1, BPL.

75 Steven Suitts, interview by the author, July 14, 2011; H. C. Rice, Jr., to Governor George Wallace, Feb. 11, 1972, Administrative Files, Alabama Governor, SG022683, Folder 7, ADA.

76 Raymond D. Hurlbert to Robert E. Smith, Assistant Director for Public Affairs, Office of Civil Rights, Department of Housing, Education, and Welfare, Jan. 19, 1972, Hurlbert Papers, 23.4.1.2.1, BPL.

77 Wright, incidentally, had been president of Samford University in Alabama and had worked to prevent desegregating the school. See Marvin J. Diamond to William A. Jackson, Nov. 16, 1973, Administrative Files, Alabama Governor, SG022683, Folder

7, ADA; Steven Suitts to George Wallace, Nov. 27, 1973; and Steven Suitts to Robert Dod, Nov. 27, 1973, Hurlbert Papers, 23.4.1.2.1, BPL.

78 "Wallace Selects Black Professor for Membership on ETV Commission," *Montgomery Advertiser*, June 28, 1974, Hurlbert Papers, 23.1.7.13.1, BPL.

79 *Alabama Educational Television Commission et al.*, Memorandum Opinion and Order, 50 FCC 2d 461 (1975), 470.

80 Ibid., 473.

81 David Greenberg, "The Idea of 'The Liberal Media' and Its Roots in the Civil Rights Movement," *The Sixties: A Journal of History, Politics and Culture* 1, no. 2 (2008): 167–186.

82 Jack Coggins, "Alabama's ETV Rights in Danger," *Birmingham News*, Dec. 14, 1974, Hurlbert Papers, 23.1.7.14.1, BPL.

83 "FCC: Bureaucratic Stupidity," *Birmingham News*, Dec. 26, 1974, Hurlbert Papers, 23.1.7.14.1, BPL.

84 "Sen. Allen Says FCC Denial 'Slap in the Face,'" *Demopolis Times*, Jan. 16, 1975, Hurlbert Papers, 23.1.7.14.1, BPL.

85 "Carpetbagger Justice," *Montgomery Advertiser*, Jan. 10, 1975, Hurlbert Papers, 23.1.7.14.1, BPL.

86 *Alabama Educational Television Commission*, 1975, 477.

87 Suitts interview.

88 Devorah Heitner, "Performing Black Power in the 'Cradle of Liberty': *Say Brother* Envisions New Principles of Blackness in Boston," *Television and New Media* 10, no. 5 (2009): 392–415; Devorah Heitner, "The Good Side of the Ghetto: The Case of *Inside Bedford Stuyvesant*," *Velvet Light Trap* 62 (Fall 2008): 48–61. See also Heitner, *Black Power TV*; and Wald, *It's Been Beautiful*.

89 See Bodroghkozy, *Equal Time, chaps. 2–5*.

Chapter 3   Feminists in the Wasteland Fight Back

An earlier version of this chapter was published as Allison Perlman, "Feminists in the Wasteland: The National Organization for Women and Television Reform," in "Feminist Contributions to Cultural Policy," special issue, Feminist Media Studies 7, no. 4 (2007): 413–431.

1 See "Image of Women in the Mass Media," Statement of Jean Faust at the New York City Commission on Human Rights, Hearings on "Women's Role in Contemporary Society," Sept. 25, 1970, 3–4, Box 56, Folder 5, NOW.

2 Anne Hall, Coordinator of Image of Women Task Force, to NOW President, Chair-One, Officers, Board, and Members of the Image of Women Task Force, National Project on *Sesame Street*, memorandum, March 15, 1972; and Jo Ann Gardner to Jean Cooney, Dec. 12, 1969, Box 47, Folder 4, NOW. NOW chapters in the D.C. Metro Area contacted the local PBS station, WETA, regarding its disapproval of sex role stereotypes on *Sesame Street*, as reported in *Vocal Majority: A National Organization for Women (NOW) Newsletter*, "NOW FCC Task Force," April 1972, 7, Box 2, Folder 4, DCN.

3 The New York chapter, through NOW's Legal Defense and Education Fund, created five print and two television ads that mocked how the media prescribed narrow roles for women and advocated for more liberated views of women's capabilities. The project began in 1971, and the ads hit magazines in 1972, broadcast outlets in 1973. For materials related to this effort see the contents of Box 15, Folder 8, NYN.

4 The Image of Women Committee of the New York chapter spearheaded this strategy of providing awards to agencies whose representations of women relied on sex-role stereotypes. See, e.g., "Image of Women Committee Events, August 1970–June 1971," Box 15, Folder 3, NYN; or Press Release, "National Organization for Women Media Awards Dramatize Good and Bad Portrayals of Women," August 26, 1974, Box 15, Folder 9, NYN.

5 See "Action Alert—*3's a Crowd*," Dec. 1979; and "*3's a Crowd*—A Detroit Success Story," n.d., Box 48, Folder 5, NOW.

6 Serena Mayeri, *Reasoning from Race: Feminism, Law, and the Civil Rights Revolution* (Cambridge, MA: Harvard University Press, 2011).

7 John D. Skrentny, *The Minority Rights Revolution* (Cambridge, MA: Harvard University Press, 2002).

8 See, e.g., Bonnie J. Dow, *Prime Time Feminism: Television, Media Culture, and the Women's Movement since 1970* (Philadelphia: University of Pennsylvania Press, 1996); Patricia Bradley, *Mass Media and the Shaping of American Feminism, 1963–1975* (Jackson: University Press of Mississippi, 2003); Elana Levine, *Wallowing in Sex: The New Sexual Culture of 1970s American Television* (Durham, NC: Duke University Press, 2007); Ruth Rosen, *The World Split Open: How the Modern Women's Movement Changed America* (New York: Penguin, 2006); Susan J. Douglas, *Where the Girls Are: Growing Up Female with the Mass Media* (New York: Three Rivers, 1994); Kirsten Marthe Lentz, "Quality versus Relevance: Feminism, Races, and the Politics of the Sign in 1970s Television," *Camera Obscura* 15, no. 1 (2000): 45–93; Bonnie J. Dow, "Fixing Feminism: Women's Liberation and the Rhetoric of Television Documentary," *Quarterly Journal of Speech* 90 (Feb. 2004): 53–80; Bernadette Barker-Plummer, "Producing Public Voice: Resource Mobilization and Media Access in the National Organization for Women," *Journal of Mass Communication Quarterly* 79 (Spring 2002): 188–205.

9 For a discussion of the *Maude* episode and NOW's support of it, see Kathryn C. Montgomery, *Target: Prime Time: Advocacy Groups and the Struggle over Entertainment Television* (New York: Oxford University Press, 1989), 43.

10 Kathy M. Newman, *Radio Active: Advertising and Consumer Activism, 1935–1947* (Berkeley: University of California Press, 2004).

11 Donald Guimary, *Citizens' Groups and Broadcasting* (New York: Praeger, 1975), 19–32.

12 In its original Statement of Purpose, NOW is characterized as a civil rights organization for women, analogous to those for African Americans. As such, and since, NOW has been referred to as an "NAACP for women." See "The National Organization for Women's 1966 Statement of Purpose," National Organization for Women website, http://now.org/about/history/statement-of-purpose/; Maren Lockwood Cohen, *The New Feminist Movement* (New York: Russell Sage Foundation, 1974), 104; Maryann Barasko, *Governing NOW: Grassroots Activism in the National Organization for Women* (Ithaca, NY: Cornell University Press, 2004), 21–22; Flora Davis, *Moving the Mountain: The Women's Movement in America since 1960* (New York: Touchstone, 1991), 53.

13 Davis, *Moving the Mountain*, 53–59; Winifred D. Wandersee, *On the Move: American Women in the 1970s* (Boston: Twayne, 1988), 17–18.

14 Barasko, *Governing NOW*, 33.

15 Bradley, *Mass Media*, 44; Mayeri, *Reasoning from Race*.

16 Pauli Murray and Mary O. Eastwood, "Jane Crow and the Law: Sex Discrimination and Title VII," *George Washington Law Review* 34, no. 2 (1966): 232–256.

17 Quoted in Skrentny, *Minority Rights Revolution*, 243–244.

18 Bonnie J. Dow, *Watching Women's Liberation 1970: Feminism's Pivotal Year on the Network News* (Urbana: University of Illinois Press, 2014).

19 Midge Kovacs and Muriel Fox, for example, worked in advertising; Dolores Alexander was a magazine editor and journalist.

20 The chapter held a feminist conference in 1971 for advertising heads, met with the American Association of Advertising Agencies, met with representatives from a number of prominent agencies in New York (BBDO, Benton and Bowles, for example). The chapter committee also created, c. 1973, presentations for the *New York Times* and the *New York Daily News* in which they compiled and annotated articles and ads and described why they were offensive to women. Press Release, NY Image of Women of NOW "Dialogue with Women," n.d., Box 47, Folder 4, NOW; "Image of Women Committee Events," Box 15, Folder 3, NYN; Midge Kovacs, "NOW Image of Women Committee, Standing Committee to Improve the Image of Women in the Media," Box 15, Folder 4, NYN; "Image of Women in the Mass Media" brochure, Box 15, Folder 9, NYN.

21 NOW protested feminine hygiene sprays, which went on the market in 1966, both for their advertising (which created an anxiety over "feminine odor" and promised benefits of dubious merit) and for the health problems they posed to women. Anne Hall to NOW President, Chairperson of the Board, Officers, Board of Directors, Chapter Presidents, Members of Image of Woman Task Force, Re: National Boycott Against All Feminine Hygiene Deodorant Sprays Commencing August 26, 1972, memorandum, August 5, 1972, Box 7, Folder 5, NYN; The Dade County NOW chapter filed an official complaint against National Airlines for its campaign, which included photos of female flight attendants with the tagline, "I'm Cheryl . . . Fly Me." Elizabeth Antigaglia to Midge Kovacs, Nov. 9, 1971; Midge Kovacs, Letter to the Editor, *Marketing/Communications*, Nov. 9, 1971, 5, Box 15, Folder 3, NYN. NY NOW countered with its own ad, of a burly man in front of a truck with the line, "I'm Marvin . . . Truck Me." "Fly Me Department," *Vocal Majority*, May 1972, 10, Box 1, Folder 2, DCN.

22 "Task Force on Image of Women in Mass Media," n.d., Box 4, Folder 6, DA.

23 Cherie Sue Lewis, "Television License Renewal Challenges by Women's Groups" (PhD diss., University of Minnesota, 1986), 60–63.

24 Lucy Komisar, "How to Challenge Sexism in Broadcasting," unpublished document (1978), 4, Box 1, Folder 2, KB.

25 There were a number of chapters in the D.C. metro area that frequently collaborated during this era, including chapters in the District of Columbia, Montgomery County (MD), Northern Virginia, Arlington (VA), Alexandria (VA), Lower Prince Georges County (MD), and Upper Prince Georges County (MD).

26 "A Victory," *Vocal Majority*, Feb. 1971, 6; Whitney Adams, "Your Image on TV: The Feminine Look? Results of the April Monitoring in Washington," *Vocal Majority*, June 1971, 19; Whitney Adams, "Our TV Report Goes to the FTC," *Vocal Majority*, Nov. 1971, 7; "Maybe We'll See Anchorwomen," *Vocal Majority*, Jan. 1972, 9, all in Box 1, Folder 1, DCN; "Wash. Area Television Stations Are Bad on Women," *Vocal Majority*, March 1972, 10; "NOW FCC Task Force," *Vocal Majority*, April 1972, 7; Marj Cingan, "NOW FCC Task Force—Monitoring," *Vocal Majority*, May 1972, 4; Whitney Adams, "Women in the Wasteland Fight Back!" *Vocal Majority*, July 1972, 7, all in Box 1, Folder 2, DCN; Whitney Adams, "Feminists v. WRC-TV: The Task Has Just Begun," *Vocal Majority*, Oct. 1972, 5, Box 1, Folder 3, DCN.

27 Nancy Stanley, "Federal Communications Law and Women's Rights: Women in the Wasteland Fight Back," *Hastings Law Journal* 22 (Nov. 1971): 15–53.

28 Newton Minow, "Television and the Public Interest," speech delivered May 9, 1961, to the National Association of Broadcasters. Full text available at www.american-rhetoric.com/speeches/newtonminow.htm.

29 Stanley, "Federal Communications Law and Women's Rights," 17–18.

30 Ibid., 75; "Women in the Wasteland Fight Back," *Vocal Majority*, May 1972, Box 1, Folder 2, DCN.

31 Stanley, "Federal Communications Law and Women's Rights," 42.

32 Ibid., 23.

33 Ibid., 27.

34 Ibid., 29. For example, in a 1968 article, Friedan referred to a woman who insisted that women get more satisfaction from domestic labor than professional work an "Aunt Tom." Friedan is quoted in Martha Weiman Lear, "The Second Feminist Wave," *New York Times*, March 10, 1968, 50.

35 Stanley, "Federal Communications Law and Women's Rights," 45.

36 See *Friends of the Earth v. FCC*, 449 F.2d 1164 (1971). For Stanley's discussion of the application of the Fairness Doctrine to all programming see Stanley, "Federal Communications Law and Women's Rights," 45–49.

37 Komisar, "How to Challenge," 6–14.

38 National Organization for Women, *Women in the Wasteland Fight Back: A Report on the Image of Women Portrayed in TV Programming; Survey of WRC-TV Public Affairs and News Programming since February, 1972* (Washington, DC: NOW, 1972), 18–19.

39 Ibid., title page.

40 Jon Wiener, *Come Together: John Lennon in His Time* (Urbana: University of Illinois Press, 1984), 212–215; Robert Hilburn, "Lennon, Yoko Back in the News," *Los Angeles Times*, April 22, 1972, B6; "John Lennon's at It Again; Pete Bennett's Trying Again, but It May Not Fly," *Broadcasting*, May 8, 1972, 57; Linda Winer, "The Fact, Fantasy of John and Yoko," *Chicago Tribune*, July 2, 1972, L8.

41 "NOW Pans, Applauds the Media," *Los Angeles Times*, August 28, 1972, F9.

42 U.S. Civil Rights Commission, *Window Dressing on the Set: Women and Minorities in Television* (Washington, DC: US Government Printing Office, 1977), 134; Whitney Adams, "Women Win First Round of Fight," *Vocal Majority*, Dec. 1971, 11, Box 1, Folder 1, DCN.

43 See the commission's ruling in *Cosmos Broadcasting Corp.*, 21 FCC 2d 729, 747 (1970).

44 In Re: Application of AMERICAN BROADCASTING CO., Licensee of WABC-TV New York, New York; For: Renewal of License: Petition-to-Deny, Folder 229, 23, DAP.

45 Ibid., 83.

46 Ibid., 94.

47 Ibid., 55.

48 Ibid., 95.

49 "Challenges from All Sides in New York Renewals: For First Time Women's Lib Appears in New Wave of Coalitions and Causes Opposing Applications of 26 Stations," *Broadcasting*, May 8, 1972, 34.

50 "Two of Networks' O&O's Sign with N.Y. Coalition," *Broadcasting*, May 22, 1972, 8.

51 "WMAL-TV Called 'Supreme Racist' as Black United Front Challenges License

Renewal in Plea to FCC," *Variety*, Sept. 3, 1969, 33; "BEST, Soul Group Hits WMAL-TV On 'Fairness' Grounds," *Variety*, Jan. 21, 1970, 35.

52 *In Re Application of American Broadcasting Co., Inc.*, Memorandum Opinion and Order (MO&O), 52 F.C.C. 2d 98 (1975), 99–104 (hereafter WABC MO&O); *In Re Application of the National Broadcasting Co, Inc.*, Memorandum Opinion and Order (MO&O), 52 F.C.C. 2d 273 (1975), 273–276 (hereafter WRC MO&O).

53 WABC MO&O, 110–11; WRC MO&O, 284–287.

54 WRC MO&O, 282.

55 WABC MO&O, 120–123; WRC MO&O, 292–293. The "zone of reasonableness" standard was established in *Stone v. FCC*, a federal appeals case initiated in response to the FCC's renewal of WMAL-TV's license, which had been challenged by members of the African American community in Washington, DC *Stone v. FCC 466 F.2d 316 (1972)*, 332.

56 WABC MO&O, 100–101.

57 Ibid., 103, 107.

58 WABC MO&O, 123–124; WRC MO&O, 295–296.

59 WABC MO&O, 125; WRC MO&O, 300.

60 WRC MO&O, 298.

61 Ibid., 299.

62 Ibid., 299.

63 Nicholas Johnson, *How to Talk Back to Your Television Set* (Boston: Little, Brown, 1970), 187.

64 *National Organization for Women, New York City v. Federal Communications Commission 555 F.2d 1002 (1977).*

65 FCC Press Release, "Broadcast Action: FCC Rejects NOW's Petition to Deny License Renewal of WABC-TV, New York City," March 21, 1975, 3, Box 48, Folder 16, NOW.

66 Whitney Adams, Report on the F.C.C. Task Force, Oct. 15, 1972, Box 48, Folder 4, NOW; Eleanor Smeal to Kathy Bonk, Jan. 3, 1978, Box 48, Folder 5, NOW.

67 "N.O.W. Media Project: An Action Plan to Create a Feminist Media," May 1974, Box 48, Folder 16, NOW; Whitney Adams and Kathy Bonk, "Fairness for Feminism on the Broadcast Airwaves: NOW Guidelines on the FCC Fairness Doctrine," May 1974, Box 210, Folder 26, NOW; "Model Agreement between NOW Chapter and KPIG-TV (AM-FM)," n.d., Box 48, Folder 17, NOW; "Ascertainment of N.O.W. Chapters by Radio and Television Stations," n.d., Box 48, Folder 17, NOW; Joyce Snyder and Kathy Bonk, "Welcome to the Feminist Media Revolution," n.d. (c. 1975), Box 48, Folder 17, NOW.

68 Duncan Brown and Jeffrey Layne Blevins focus on the significant role of "epistemic communities" in media policy battles, defining them as professionals with expertise in a particular area who share a set of beliefs about the nature of the problem and its remedy. See Duncan H. Brown and Jeffrey Layne Blevins, "Can the FCC Still Ignore the Public? Interviews with Two Commissioners Who Listened," *Television and New Media* 9, no. 6 (2008): 447–470.

69 Lewis, "Television License Renewal Challenges," 54–55; Robert Lewis Shayon, "Parties in Interest: A Citizens Guide to Improving Television and Radio," 8–9, Box VIII.404, Folder 5, NAA.

70 NOW National FCC Task Force, "On Monitoring Television," Fall 1972, Box 48, Folder 10, NOW.

71 James King to Kathy Bonk, June 29, 1972, outlining agreement between Pittsburgh

NOW and KDKA-TV; Leonard Swanson to Members of NOW, July 12, 1972, outlining agreement between the chapter and WIIC-TV; WTAE-TV to Pittsburgh NOW, July 3, 1972, outlining agreement with WTAE-TV, Box 48, Folder 4, NOW.

72 Whitney Adams, "NOW Action to Create a Feminist Broadcast Media: A Report on the National Broadcast Media (FCC) Task Force," April 1974, 4–9, Box 48, Folder 16, NOW; "Update on the NOW National F.C.C. Task Force," 3–4, Box 210, Folder 29, NOW; James Osborn to Joan Israel, letter of agreement, August 7, 1973, Box 31, Folder 33, NOW; Whitney Adams, "NOW FCC Task Force," Nov. 1973, Box 48, Folder 16, NOW; NOW FCC Task Force, "On Monitoring Television," Fall 1972, Box 48, Folder 20, NOW.

73 Adams, "NOW Action," 5.

74 Ibid., 5–9.

75 Snyder and Bonk, "Welcome to the Feminist Media Revolution."

76 Kathy Bonk, "NOW Media Project: An Action Plan to Create a Feminist Media," May 1974, 7, Box 1, Folder 5, KB.

77 Detroit NOW was part of the Detroit Media Coalition, which, in September 1973, filed a petition against WJBK-TV. Press Release, issued by the Office of Communication of the United Church of Christ; In Re: Application of Storer Broadcasting Company for Renewal of License of WJBK-TV, Petition to Deny Renewal, Box 31, Folder 33, NOW.

78 Adams, "NOW Action," 8.

79 In 1973 the House held hearings on a number of very similar bills that would have extended the license term to five years and made it easier for incumbents to get renewal. This language is taken from the wording of bills H.R. 3854 and H.R. 1066, though twelve nearly identical bills were under consideration. H.R. 1066, United States House of Representatives, 93rd Cong., 1st sess., Jan. 3, 1973, 2; H.R. 3854, United States House of Representatives, 93rd Cong, 1st sess., Feb. 6, 1973, 2.

80 "The FCC and Broadcasting License Renewals: Perspectives on *WHDH*," *University of Chicago Law Review* 36, no. 4 (1968–69): 872–984; Hyman H. Goldin, "'Spare the Golden Goose'—The Aftermath of *WHDH* in License Renewal Policy," *Harvard Law Review* 83, no. 5 (1969–70): 1023–1024.

81 "Pendulum Swings on License Renewal," *Broadcasting*, April 23, 1973, 17–19.

82 Broadcast License Renewal Act: Hearings Before the Subcommittee on Communications of the Committee on Commerce, United States Senate, 93rd Cong., 2nd sess., on S. 16, S. 247, S. 272, S. 613, S. 822, S. 844, S. 849, S. 851, S. 1311, S. 1589, S. 1870, S. 3637, and H.R. 12993, Miscellaneous Broadcast License Renewal Legislation, June 26, 1974, 250 (testimony of Judith Hennessee).

83 Broadcast License Renewal: Hearings Before the Subcommittee on Communications and Power of the Committee on Interstate and Foreign Commerce, 93rd Cong., 1st sess., on H.R. 5546, H.R. 3854, H.R. 370, H.R. 565, H.R. 1066, H.R. 1864, H.R. 2011, H.R. 2349, H.R. 2355, H.R. 3551, HR. 6319, H.R. 6320, Bills to Amend the Communications Act of 1934 with Regard to Renewal of Broadcast Licenses, March 27, 1973, 408 (testimony of Jan Crawford).

84 Broadcast License Renewal Act, Senate Hearings, June 26, 1974, 251 (testimony of Anne Lang) (see note 82 above for full citation).

85 Broadcast License Renewal, House Hearings, March 29, 1973, 522 (testimony of Whitney Adams) (see note 83 above for full citation).

86 Broadcast License Renewal Act, Senate Hearings, 253 (testimony of Ann Lang).

87 Broadcast License Renewal Act, Senate Hearings, 260–264 (testimony of Ann Lang and Kathy Bonk).

88 Cass Sunstein, *After the Rights Revolution: Reconceiving the Regulatory State* (Cambridge, MA: Harvard University Press, 1990).

89 Robert Britt Horwitz, *The Irony of Regulatory Reform* (New York: Oxford University Press, 1989).

90 Snyder and Bonk, "Welcome to the Feminist Media Revolution."

91 "Top of the Week: And It Is from the Basement to the Attic," *Broadcasting*, June 12, 1978, 29, 34, 36, 38–39; "Top of the Week: Rewrite II More Radical Than Its Predecessor," *Broadcasting*, April 2, 1979, 29–32. See also Nicholas Johnson, CRPB [Coalition for Public Rights in Broadcasting] Update: Good News/Bad News, July 23, 1979; CRPB Report to Members, Feb. 16, 1979, Folder 48, Box 11, NOW.

92 "Telecommunications Consumer Coalition: An Information Clearinghouse for Telecommunications Concern," Nov. 1978, Box 48, Folder 10, NOW; Coalition for Public Rights in Broadcasting, form letter, August 1978, Box 48, Folder 11, NOW.

93 Quoted in Stuart Mieher, "Broadcast Amendments Attacked by Coalition," *Washington Post*, July 21, 1979, C1.

94 Volume V—Part I: The Communications Act of 1978: Hearings Before the Subcommittee on Communications of the Committee on Interstate and Foreign Commerce, United States House of Representatives, 95th Cong., 2nd sess., on H.R. 1305, Field Hearings, August 22, 1978, 336 (testimony of Karen Boehning).

95 Kathleen Bonk, Testimony on HR 3333, Before House Subcommittee on Communications, May 16, 1979, 7 Schlesinger, Box 48, Folder 17, NOW.

96 Federal Communications Commission, *Primer on Ascertainment of Community Problems*, Federal Register 41, Jan. 7, 1976, 1384.

97 Federal Communications Commission, "In Re Applications of Mid-Florida Television Corporation," 70 F.C.C. 2d 281, 326.

98 Whitney Adams, "Now Action to Create a Feminist Broadcast Media: Report on the National Broadcast Media (FCC) Task Force," April 1974, 12, Box 48, Folder 16, NOW; Long-Range Financing for Public Broadcasting: Hearings Before the Subcommittee on Communications of the Committee on Interstate and Foreign Commerce, 94th Cong., 1st sess., on H.R. 4563, A Bill to Amend Certain Provisions of Communications Act of 1934 to Provide Long-Term Financing for the Corporation of Public Broadcasting and Other Purposes, April 9, 1975, 353–358 (testimony of Kathy Bonk and Cathy Irwin).

99 Bonk testimony, Public Broadcasting Hearings, 356.

100 NOW LDEF supported Christine Craft, who sued the Metromedia Group on sexual discrimination grounds, and Cecily Coleman, who sued ABC for sexual harassment. On Craft see Box 2, Folder 8, KB; on Coleman see Box 1, Folder 17, KB.

Chapter 4   Diversity and Deregulation

1 Minority Participation in the Media: Hearings Before the House Subcommittee on Telecommunications, Consumer Protection and Finance of the Committee on Energy and Commerce, U.S. House of Representatives, 98th Cong., 1st sess., Sept. 19, 1983, 3 (opening statement of Mickey Leland). Testifying at these hearings were representatives from a range of advocacy groups, including the NAACP, National

Black Media Coalition, Black Citizens for a Fair Media, Action for Children's Television, and LULAC. For an important rejoinder to politics of representation on *Gimme a Break*, see Jennifer Fuller, "*Gimme a Break!* and the Limits of the Modern Mammy," in *Watching While Black: Centering the Television of Black Audiences*, ed. Beretta E. Smith-Shomade (New Brunswick, NJ: Rutgers University Press, 2012), 105–120.

2 Minority Participation in the Media: Hearings Before the House Subcommittee (see previous note); see, e.g., 20–22 (testimony of Raul Yzaguirre); 46–47 (testimony of Willis Edwards); 153–154 (testimony of Pluria Marshall).

3 Janet Staiger, *Blockbuster TV: Must-See Sitcoms in the Network Era* (New York: New York University Press, 2000), chap. 5.

4 Herman Gray, "Remembering Civil Rights: Television, Memory, and the 1960s," in *The Revolution Wasn't Televised: Sixties Television and Social Conflict*, ed. Lynn Spigel and Michael Curtin (New York: Routledge, 1997), 349–358.

5 Herman Gray, *Watching Race: Television and the Struggle for "Blackness"* (Minneapolis: University of Minnesota Press, 1995), esp. chap. 5; Sut Jhally and Justin Lewis, *Enlightened Racism: "The Cosby Show," Audiences, and the Myth of the American Dream* (Boulder, CO: Westview Press, 1992).

6 Kimberlé Williams Crenshaw, "Race, Reform, and Retrenchment: Transformation and Legitimation in Antidiscrimination Law," *Harvard Law Review* 101, no. 7 (May 1988): 1336–1341.

7 Robert Britt Horwitz, "The First Amendment Meets Some New Technologies: Broadcasting, Common Carriers, and Free Speech in the 1990s," *Theory and Society* 20, no. 1 (1991): 22.

8 David Honig, "The FCC and Its Fluctuating Commitment to Minority Ownership of Broadcast Facilities," *Howard Law Journal* 27 (1984): 869.

9 Federal Communications Commission, "Minority Ownership of Broadcasting Facilities: Statement of Policy," *Federal Register* 43 (June 9, 1978): 25189.

10 Ibid., 980–981.

11 For a detailed discussion of the messiness of the *Bakke* decision see Howard Ball, *The "Bakke" Case: Race, Education, and Affirmative Action* (Lawrence: University Press of Kansas, 2000), chap. 6.

12 *Regents of the University of California v. Bakke*, 438 U.S. 265 (1978).

13 Ibid., 387.

14 Quoted in Merrill Brown, "Fowler: FCC Is No Censor," *Washington Post*, June 27, 1981, D7.

15 Mark S. Fowler and Daniel L. Brenner, "A Marketplace Approach to Broadcast Regulation," *Texas Law Review* 60 (1981): 210.

16 Ibid., 226.

17 See Derek Kompare, *Rerun Nation: How Repeats Invented American Television* (New York: Routledge, 2006), chap. 7.

18 Andrew Hartman, *A War for the Soul of America: A History of the Culture Wars* (Chicago: University of Chicago Press, 2015), 7.

19 Daniel T. Rodgers, *The Age of Fracture* (Cambridge, MA: Belknap, 2011), chap. 4.

20 Quoted in Terry H. Anderson, *The Pursuit of Fairness: A History of Affirmative Action* (New York: Oxford University Press, 2004), 185, 184.

21 Ibid., 193–197.

22 Arthur Lennig, "Myth and Fact: The Reception of *Birth of a Nation*," *Film History* 16, no. 2 (2004): 117–141.

23 Thomas Cripps, "*Amos 'n' Andy* and the Debate over American Racial Integration," in *American History/American Television: Interpreting the Video Past*, ed. John E. O'Connor (New York: Frederick Ungar, 1983), 33–54; Melvin Patrick Ely, *The Adventures of Amos 'n' Andy: A Social History of an American Phenomenon* (New York: Free Press, 1991), 223–237; and Leonard Courtney Archer, *Black Images in the American Theatre: NAACP Protest Campaigns—Stage, Screen, Radio, and Television* (New York: Pageant, 1973), 233–259.

24 Executive director Roy Wilkins was especially upset about a CBS series on the history of "the Negro in America," which according to Wilkins privileged "the contemporary left-of-center black militant minority view, liberally garnished with the thrust for a new apartheid." For more on this campaign see Roy Wilkins to Frank Stanton, Jan. 8, 1969; and Henry Lee Moon to NAACP Branch Presidents, Regional and Field Directors, memorandum, July 8, 1969, Box VIII 403, Folder 11, NAA.

25 Kathryn Montgomery provides a solid overview of this controversy in *Target: Prime Time: Advocacy Groups and the Struggle over Entertainment Television* (New York: Oxford University Press, 1989), 123–153. Key documents related to this campaign are in Box VIII 404, Folder 4, NAA.

26 Amy L. Toro, "Standing Up for Listeners' Rights: A History of Public Participation at the Federal Communications Commission" (PhD diss., University of California, Berkeley, 2000), 51–54.

27 David Honig to Colleagues Supportive of Minority Broadcast Ownership, memorandum, March 2, 1992, Box V 2716, Folder 7, NAA.

28 Comments of NAACP and LULAC, In Matter of Amendment of Part 76, Subpart J, Section 76.501 of Commission's Rules and Regulations to Eliminate the Prohibition on Common Ownership of Cable Television Stations and National Television Networks (MM Docket No. 82–434), March 23, 1992, Box V 2716, Folder 7, NAA.

29 Norman C. Amaker, *Civil Rights and the Reagan Administration* (Washington, DC: Urban Institute, 1988).

30 Remarks of Althea T. L. Simmons, 10th Annual Convention of the Coalition of Labor Union Women, March 22, 1984, 8, Box IX 423, Folder 1, NAA.

31 Benjamin Hooks quotation from NAACP Press Release: "NAACP Sets August 26th for 'Silent March,' Urges Local Support," July 18, 1989, Box IX 424, Folder 8, NAA. For descriptions of the march see Clyde H. Farnsworth, "5,000 March to Protest Court Action on Rights," *New York Times*, August 27, 1989, sec. 1, 20.

32 David Honig to Pluria Marshall et al., memorandum, June 1, 1983, Box VIII 493, Folder 3, NAA.

33 David Honig to Dennis Courtland Hayes, Re: FCC Sanctions for Broadcast EEO Violations, memorandum, March 15, 1993, Box V 315, Folder 6, NAA.

34 For representative memoranda outlining this process see David Honig to Dennis Courtland Hayes, and Everald Thompson, Re: Justification Memorandum for Proposed Petitions to Deny License Renewal of Three Television Stations in Kentucky, memorandum, May 26, 1992; and David Honig to William Cofield, Norman Bartleson, Shelby Lanier, Michael Lowrey, Re: Proposed Petitions to Deny the FCC License Renewal Applications of Three Television Stations in Kentucky, memorandum, June 12, 1992, in Box V 319, Folder 7, NAA.

35 *In re Applications of Certain Broadcast Stations Serving Communities in the State*

of South Carolina, Memorandum Opinion and Order and Notices of Apparent Liability, Box V 316, Folder 8, NAA.

36 Jube Shiver Jr., "Bias Challenges against Stations' Licenses Soaring," *Los Angeles Times,* July 16, 1990, D1.

37 Draft, David Honig to Suzanne M. Perry, Re: WIOD/WZTA, Box V 224, Folder 3, NAA.

38 Letter from Everald Thompson et al. to Tylin Smith, July 1, 1992, Box V 319, Folder 17, NAA.

39 In Re: Applications for Renewal of Licenses of the Following Missouri Stations: KFUO-AM-FM, Clayton; KARO-FM, Columbia; KRJY-FM, St. Louis, Jan. 2, 1990, 3, Box V 325, Folder 4, NAA.

40 "NAACP Files Petition to Deny Missouri Radio Licenses," NAACP News Press Release, Jan. 24, 1990, Box V 325, Folder 4, NAA.

41 Glenn A. Wolfe to Paul DeVantier, Jan. 4, 1990, Box V 325, Folder 4, NAA.

42 Opposition to Petition to Deny and Response to Inquiry, Lutheran Church, Feb. 23, 1990, 7, Box V 325, Folder 4, NAA.

43 Ibid., 10.

44 Ibid., 11–13.

45 *In Re Applications of the Lutheran Church/Missouri Synod,* Initial Decision of Administrative Law Judge, Released Sept. 15, 1995, 10 FCCR 9880 (1995), 9921.

46 David Honig, "The FCC and Broadcast EEO Enforcement," paper presented at the NAACP Sixth Annual Lawyers CLE Seminar, July 6, 1990, 13, Box V 315, Folder 9, NAA.

47 *In Re Applications of The Lutheran Church/Missouri Synod,* Memorandum Opinion and Order, Released January 31, 1997, 12 FCCR 2152 (1997), 2156.

48 Ibid., 2168–2169.

49 Members of the Lutheran Church Missouri Synod to FCC, March 8, 1994, Box V 325, Folder 7, NAA. The letter was signed by twenty-nine members of the congregation.

50 Richard A. Roth to the FCC, Feb. 28, 1994; Douglas J. Gill to FCC, March 4, 1994, Box V 325, Folder 7, NAA.

51 David N. Wexler to FCC, March 3, 1994, Box V 325, Folder 7, NAA.

52 *Lutheran Church-Missouri Synod v. Federal Communications Commission,* 141 F.3d 344 (1998), 354.

53 Ibid., 355.

54 Ibid., 356.

55 Federal appellate courts first review cases by three-judge panels. After a ruling the losing party can appeal to have the case heard "en banc," or by all ten judges sitting on the court.

56 *Mid-Florida Television Corp.* 33 FCC 2d 34 (1970).

57 *TV9, Inc. v. FCC,* 495 F.2d 929 (1973), 936.

58 Michael Isikoff and Art Harris, "PTL Fund Raising: A Tangled Saga," *Washington Post,* May 23, 1987, A1.

59 FCC News, "FCC Instructs Staff to Apprise Justice Department of Investigation Involving PTL," Dec. 8, 1982, Box V 370, Folder 8, NAA.

60 Joint Dissenting Statement of Commissioners Joseph R. Fogarty and Henry M. Rivera, In Re: Application for Assignment of License of UHF Television Station WJAN, Canton, Ohio, 7, Dec. 8, 1992, Box V 370, Folder 8, NAA.

61 If a party wants the Supreme Court to hear its case, it must file a writ of certiorari with the Court, which will then decide whether it will hear the case.

62 David Honig to Pluria Marshall et al., Re: PTL Settlement, memorandum, August 23, 1985, 2, Box V 371, Folder 5, NAA.

63 See, e.g., *Wygant v. Jackson Board of Education*, 476 U.S. 267 (1986); *City of Richmond v. J. A. Croson*, 488 U.S. 469 (1989); *Martin v. Wilks*, 490 U.S. 755 (1989).

64 Julian N. Eule, "Promoting Speaker Diversity: *Austin* and *Metro Broadcasting*," *Supreme Court Review* (1990): 121.

65 *Garrett v. FCC*, 513 F.2d 1056 (1975); *West Michigan Broadcasting v. FCC*, 735 F.2d 601 (1984).

66 *Steele v. Federal Communications Commission*, 770 F.2d 1192 (1985), 1198.

67 Ibid., 1198–99.

68 In *Wygant* the Court, in a 5–4 decision, ruled that race-based policies must be rooted in established findings of discrimination, and general societal discrimination was not a sufficient rationale for race-based policies.

69 Minority-Owned Broadcast Stations: Hearing Before the Subcommittee on Telecommunications, Consumer Protection and Finance of the Committee on Energy and Commerce, U.S. House of Representatives, 99th Cong., 2nd sess., on H.R. 5373, a Bill to Amend the Internal Revenue Code of 1954 to Deny Deductions for Expenses of Advertising to Persons Who Discriminate against Minority Owned or Formatted Communications Entities in the Purchase or Placement of Advertisements, and to Permit Persons Aggrieved by Such Discrimination to Bring Civil Actions to Recover Lost Profits and Other Appropriate Damages, Oct. 2, 1986, 99th Cong. (1987), esp. 17–21, and the Q&A that follows (33–58) (testimony of Mark Fowler).

70 Notice of Inquiry in the Matter of Reexamination of the Commission's Comparative Licensing, Distress Sales and Tax Certificate Policies Premised on Racial, Ethnic, or Gender Classifications, Released Dec. 30, 1986, 1 FCCR 1315 (1986).

71 Associated Press, "F.C.C. to Revive Minority-Help Policies," *New York Times*, Jan. 6, 1988, C22.

72 *Winter Park Communications, Inc. v. Federal Communications Commission*, 873 F.2d 347 (1989).

73 *Shurberg Broadcasting of Hartford, Inc. v. Federal Communications Commission*, 876 F.2d 902 (1989), 915–919.

74 Ibid., 921–923.

75 In *Fullilove v. Klutznick*, 448 U.S. 448 (1980) the Supreme Court affirmed the constitutionality of the Public Works Employment Act, which required that 10 percent of federal funds of public works projects go to minority-owned companies. In *City of Richmond v. J. A. Croson*, 488 U.S. 469 (1989), the Court ruled unconstitutional a city plan that required contractors with city contracts to subcontract 30 percent of their business to minority businesses since it violated the Fourteenth Amendment. The case affirmed that "general society discrimination" cannot justify race-conscious policies.

76 See, e.g., the following briefs, submitted for *Metro Broadcasting v. FCC* 49 U.S. 547 (1990) (applies to notes 77–86), accessed via LexisNexis. Brief for the Pacific Legal Foundation as Amicus Curiae, 23–24; Brief for the Mountain States Legal Foundation and Anti-defamation League of B'nai Brith as Amicus Curiae, 14–16; Brief of Washington Legal Foundation as Amicus Curiae, 33–41; Brief for the United States

as Amicus Curiae Supporting Petitioner, 21–23; Brief of Galaxy Communications Inc. as Amicus Curiae, 7–13; Brief for the Petitioner Metro Broadcasting, 68–72.

77 Brief of Galaxy Communications, 17–18; Brief of Cook Inlet Region Inc. and Granite Broadcasting Corporation as Amicus Curiae, 53–56; Brief for Petitioner Metro Broadcasting, 43–44; Brief for Mountain States, 16–17; Brief for Washington Legal, 42–43

78 Brief for the Petitioner Metro Broadcasting Inc., 43.

79 Brief of Pacific Legal Foundation, 30, 67–68; Brief of Mountain States, 8–10; Brief for Respondent Shurberg Broadcasting of Hartford, 32–34; Brief of the United Sates as Amicus Curiae Supporting Respondent Shurberg, 42–43.

80 Brief of Associated General Contractors of America Inc. as Amicus Curiae, 6–16; Brief of Southeastern Legal Foundation as Amicus Curiae, 3–8.

81 Language is from Brief for Mountain States, 7.

82 Brief of the National Bar Association as Amicus Curiae, 9–36; Brief of the National Association of Black Owned Broadcasters Inc. and Congressman Edolphus Towns as Amicus Curiae, 21–30; Brief of Capital Cities/ABC Inc. as Amicus Curiae, 14–16.

83 Brief of the American Civil Liberties Union, the New York City Commission on Human Rights, and the NOW Legal Defense and Education Fund as Amicus Curiae, 11–18, 21; Brief of the National Association of Black Owned Broadcasters, 39–40; Brief of Capital Cities, 17–20.

84 Brief of Congressional Black Caucus, the National Association for the Advancement of Colored People, National Black Media Coalition, and the League of United Latin American Citizens as Amicus Curiae, 17.

85 Ibid.

86 Brief of NAACP Legal Defense and Education Fund Inc. as Amicus Curiae, 40–41.

87 *Metro Broadcasting, Inc. v. Federal Communications Commission*, 497 U.S. 547 (1990), 567. Subsequent quotations from this case are cited parenthetically in the text.

88 "The Strange Career of Jim Crow," *Washington Times*, July 5, 1990, D2. For similar responses see Bruce Fein, "Choosing by Race Is Doing the Wrong Thing," *USA Today*, June 29, 1990, 10A; and James J. Kirkpatrick, "Supreme Court Term Was a Stinker," *St. Petersburg Times*, July 18, 1990, 13A.

89 Patricia J. Williams, "*Metro Broadcasting, Inc. v. FCC*: Regrouping in Singular Times," *Harvard Law Review* 104, no. 2 (1990): 543.

90 *Lamprecht v. FCC*, 958 F.2d 382 (1992).

91 Ibid., 404.

92 Laurie Thomas and Barry R. Litman, "Fox Broadcasting Company, Why Now? An Economic Study of the Rise of the Fourth Network," *Journal of Broadcasting and Electronic Media* 35 (Spring 1991): 146.

93 Ibid., 146–149.

94 Marc L. Herskovitz, "The Repeal of the Financial Interest and Syndication Rules: The Demise of Program Diversity and Television Network Competition?" *Cardozo Arts and Entertainment Law Journal* 15, no. 1 (1997): 195–196; William T. Bielby and Denise D. Bielby, "Controlling Prime-Time: Organizational Concentration and Network Television Programming Strategies," *Journal of Broadcasting and Electronic Media* 47 (Dec. 2003): 576.

95 Petition to Deny Request for Waiver, In the Matter of Fox Television Stations Inc. for Permanent Waiver of the Newspaper-Broadcast Cross Ownership Rule, May 10,

1993, Box V 326, Folder 12, NAA; Petition to Deny, In Re: Application of Combined Broadcasting Inc. WGBS-TV for Transfer of Control of Combined Broadcasting of Philadelphia to FTS Philadelphia, Sept. 20, 1993, Box V 326, Folder 14, NAA.

96 James G. Ennis and David N. Roberts, "Foreign Ownership in US Communications Industry: The Impact of Section 310," *International Business Lawyer* 19 (May 1991): 243–246; Vincent M. Paladini, "Foreign Ownership Restrictions under Section 310(B) of the Telecommunications Act of 1996," *Boston University International Law Journal* 14 (Fall 1996): 341–373.

97 Quoted in Edmund L. Andrews, "The Media Business: Fox TV Deal Seems to Face Few Official Barriers," *New York Times*, May 25, 1994, D6.

98 NBC rescinded its petition in February 1995 in exchange for an agreement with Murdoch in which two NBC-owned cable channels would be distributed over the Star Television system. See Bill Carter, "NBC Agrees to End Its Attempt to Block Fox TV Expansion," *New York Times*, Feb. 18, 1995, 1.

99 In Re Application of Combined Broadcasting Inc. and FTS Philadelphia Inc., Response to "Supplement" to Petition to Deny, Dec. 2, 1993, Box V 326, Folder 14, NAA.

100 Petition to Deny Request for Waiver, 45.

101 Petition to Deny WGBS-TV, 25.

102 Edmund L. Andrews, "The Media Business: Fox TV Deal Seems to Face Few Official Barriers," *New York Times*, May 25, 1994, D6; "NAACP Hits Fox on Ownership," *Television Digest*, June 20, 1994, 3.

103 Krystal Brent Zook, *Color by Fox: The FOX Network and the Revolution in Black Television* (New York: Oxford University Press, 1999), 4.

104 Zook specifically examines the production conditions and textual practices of a series of shows that aired on Fox, including *Martin, Living Single, The Sinbad Show, South Central, Roc,* and *New York Undercover.*

105 Response to Supplement to Petition to Deny, Dec. 2, 1993, 12, Box V 326, Folder 14, NAA.

106 Depositions of Murdoch, Diller, and Herwitz are in Box 1, Folders 31–32, NHM.

107 Marvin Kitman, "Murdoch Triumphant: How We Could Have Stopped Him—Twice," *Harper's Magazine*, Nov. 2010, 32.

108 "The Gingrich-Murdoch Two-Fer," *Washington Times*, Jan. 20, 1995.

109 Further Supplement to Petition to Deny: Fox's Misconduct in Connection with Gingrich Book Deal, filed by NY State Branches of the NAACP and Metro Council of NAACP Branches, Jan. 27, 1995, Box 2, Folder 1, NHM.

110 *Metropolitan Council of NAACP Branches v. Federal Communications Commission,* 46 F.3d 1154 (1995).

111 *In Re Applications of Fox Television Stations Inc.,* Memorandum Opinion and Order, 16 FCCR 8452 (1995). See also Amelia Arsenault and Manuel Castells, "Switching Power: Rupert Murdoch and the Global Business of Media Politics: A Sociological Analysis," *International Sociology* 23, no. 4 (2008): 503–504; Dennis Wharton, "Escape Hatch for Fox: Net Foreign-Owned but Waiver Seems Assured," *Daily Variety*, May 5, 1995, 1.

112 Kitman, "Murdoch Triumphant," 29.

113 See Dennis Wharton, "Author! Author! Fox Claims Old Document Ties CBS to FCC Probe," *Variety*, June 8, 1994, 1; Joe Flint and Dennis Wharton, "Weblet Sez CBS behind NAACP Charges; Fox-y Maneuvers Stir B'Cast Flap," *Variety*, June 13, 1994, 33.

Chapter 5   Fighting for a Safe Haven

1 Robert Bork, *Slouching toward Gomorrah: Modern Liberalism and American Decline* (New York: Regan Books, 1996), 139.

2 Michael Medved, *Hollywood vs. America* (New York: HarperCollins, 1992), 10.

3 Robert Bianco, "Invasion of the Family Hour: Adult Entertainment Wouldn't Be There If We Didn't Want It," *Pittsburgh Post Gazette*, Dec. 3, 1995, G5.

4 Fowler and Brenner gesture to this in their important "A Marketplace Approach" article. See Mark S. Fowler and Daniel L. Brenner, "A Marketplace Approach to Regulation," *Texas Law* Review 60 (1981): 227–229, 237–239, 244–245. See also Marjorie Heins, *Not in Front of the Children: "Indecency," Censorship, and the Innocence of Youth* (New Brunswick, NJ: Rutgers University Press, 2007), chap 5.

5 Robert O. Self, *All in the Family: The Realignment of American Democracy since the 1960s* (New York: Hill and Wang, 2012), 311.

6 Donald Wildmon, one of the most prominent figures battling prime-time content, entitled his book *The Home Invaders* (Wheaton, IL: Victor Books, 1985).

7 Debates over the Fairness Doctrine exemplify tensions among conservatives over the efficacy of broadcast regulation. Some saw the Fairness Doctrine as a means to diversify the perspectives circulating on the air; others saw its intention and enforcement as a means to silence conservative voices. Reed Irvine's *Accuracy in Media* used the Fairness Doctrine to get conservative perspectives on the air. See "Accuracy in Media Humbles NBC," *Human Events*, Dec. 8, 1973, 33, 49. Edith Efron, in her study of news bias during the 1968 election, similarly positions use of the Fairness Doctrine as a means to combat the networks' liberalism. See Edith Efron, *The News Twisters* (Los Angeles: Nash Publishing, 1971), 217. For examples of how conservatives interpreted the Fairness Doctrine as a means to silence conservative voices, see Heather Hendershot, "God's Angriest Man: Carl McIntire, Cold War Fundamentalism, and Right-Wing Broadcasting," *American Quarterly* 59, no. 2 (2007): 373–396; Heather Hendershot, *What's Fair on the Air? Cold War Right-Wing Broadcasting and the Public Interest* (Chicago: University of Chicago Press, 2011), chap. 4; Nicole Hemmer, "Conservative Media, Liberal Bias, and the Origins of Balance" (presentation, Annual Meeting of the American Historical Association, Washington, DC, Jan. 4, 2014). Fred Friendly argues that the Kennedy administration explicitly pressured the FCC to use the Fairness Doctrine to silence conservative speech. See Fred W. Friendly, *The Good Guys, the Bad Guys, and the First Amendment: Free Speech vs. the Fairness Doctrine* (New York: Random House, 1976), chap. 3.

8 For representative articles that perform this sort of nostalgia, see Mike Duffy, "8–9PM 'Family Hour' Is Fading Away on TV," *Philadelphia Inquirer*, April 5, 1995, G01; Ed Bark, "ABC Tackles Teen Angst: *My So-Called Life* Is a Stark View of Being 15," *Dallas Morning News*, August 21, 1994, 1C; Phil Kloer, "It's 8 P.M.: Do You Know What Your Kids Are Watching?" *Atlanta Journal and Constitution*, Oct. 23, 1995, 1D; and Tom Hopkins, "Fall Evening TV Not-So-Family Affair," *Dayton (OH) Daily News*, July 23, 1995, 1C.

9 Ann Hodges, "What Family Hour? En Route to Ratings, Networks Take Low Road," *Houston Chronicle*, August 13, 1995, 12.

10 See Heins, *Not in Front of the Children*, chap. 4.

11 *Red Lion Broadcasting Co. Inc. v. Federal Communications Commission*, 395 U.S. 367 (1969), 400.

12 This provision was part of H.R. 15572 (adopted August 15, 1974), which was the 1975 Appropriations Bill.

13 Sander Vancour, "Sometime between Daylight and Dark, There's the 'Family Hour,'" *Washington Post*, August 17, 1975, 147.

14 Mara Einstein, *Media Diversity: Economics, Ownership, and the FCC* (Mahwah, NJ: Lawrence Erlbaum, 2004), chap. 2.

15 Jane Feuer, "MTM Enterprises: An Overview," in *MTM: "Quality Television,"* ed. Jane Feuer, Paul Kerr, and Tise Vahimagi (London: British Film Institute, 1984), 1–4.

16 Jane Feuer, "The MTM Style," in *MTM: "Quality Television,"* ed. Jane Feuer, Paul Kerr, and Tise Vahimagi (London: British Film Institute, 1984), 56; Janet Staiger, *Blockbuster TV: Must-See Sitcoms in the Network Era* (New York: New York University Press, 2000), chap. 3.

17 Quoted in *Writers Guild of America West, Inc. v. Federal Communications Commission*, 423 F. Supp. 1064 (1976), 1127.

18 Quoted in ibid., 1126.

19 Ibid., 1072.

20 Ibid., 1076.

21 Norman Black, "FCC Denies Coercion in TV 'Family Hour' Policy," *Associated Press*, Sept. 12, 1983.

22 The NAB Code's restrictions on commercials were the particular target of the antitrust investigation, interpreted as an illegal restraint on trade. The Justice Department initiated investigations in 1979, primarily focusing its limits on the sale of advertising time. The NAB lost an appellate court case, *U.S. v. N.A.B.*, in which it had tried to defend its Code by appeals to the benefits of self-regulation as a mode of public interest service; in 1982 the NAB signed a consent decree in which it agreed to remove its advertising provisions, and in 1983 it abandoned its radio and television codes altogether. See Val E. Limburg, "The Decline of Broadcast Ethics: *U.S. v. NAB*," *Journal of Mass Media Ethics* 4, no. 2 (1989): 214–231. On the FCC ruling on the WGA family-hour challenge see Black, "FCC Denies Coercion."

23 Lili Levi, "The Hard Case of Broadcast Indecency," *New York University Review of Law and Social Change* 20 (1992–93): 86–88.

24 Ibid., 89.

25 Quoted in ibid., 89.

26 Memorandum Opinion and Order, In the Matter of a Citizen's Complaint against Pacifica Foundation WBAI, 56 FCC 2d 94, 98.

27 Ibid., 97.

28 Ibid., 98.

29 *Federal Communications Commission v. Pacifica Foundation et al.*, 438 U.S. 726 (1978), 748.

30 Ibid., 749.

31 Ibid., 750.

32 Brennan dissent, *Federal Communications Commission v. Pacifica Foundation et al.*, 438 U.S. 726 (1978), 775.

33 Ibid., 766.

34 Levi, "The Hard Case," 91.

35 See Elana Levine, *Wallowing in Sex: The New Sexual Culture of 1970s American Television* (Durham, NC: Duke University Press, 2007).

36 Quoted in Harry F. Waters et al., "The New Right's TV Hit List," *Newsweek*, June 15, 1981, 101.

37 Quoted in Patrick M. Fahey, "Advocacy Group Boycotting of Network Television Advertisers and Its Effects on Programming Content," *University of Pennsylvania Law Review* 140, no. 2 (1991): 658.

38 Michael Hill, "Crusader Rakolta Still Has a Lot to Learn," *Baltimore Sun*, July 26, 1989, D07; Fahey, "Advocacy Group Boycotting," 676.

39 Patrick Buchanan, "A Conservative Makes a Final Plea," *Newsweek*, March 30, 1987, 23, 26.

40 John Crigler and William J. Byrnes, "Decency Redux: The Curious History of the New FCC Broadcast Indecency Policy," *Catholic University Law Review* 38, no. 2 (1988–89), 344.

41 Heins, *Not in Front*, 113–119; Levi, "The Hard Case," 91–112.

42 Brent Baker, telephone interview by the author, Jan. 11, 2005; John Carmody, "Now Here's the News," *Washington Post*, June 6, 1983, B9; Chuck Conconi, "Personalities," *Washington Post*, June 9, 1983, C3; Sandra Gregg, "'The Africans': The Calm behind PBS' Stormy Series," *Washington Post*, Oct. 5, 1986, Y7; John Carmody, "The TV Column," *Washington Post*, Nov. 3, 1986, B8; Robin Toner, "The White House Crisis: Got No Iran Funds, Conservative Says," *New York Times*, Dec. 17, 1986, A18; "Conservative Official Resigns," *New York Times*, Sept. 1, 1987, A12; Thomas B. Edsall, "Head of Conservative PAC Quits in Dispute with Board," *Washington Post*, Sept. 1, 1987, 28.

43 Joe Queenan, "The Media's Wacky Watchdogs," *Time*, August 5, 1991, 54.

44 Baker interview.

45 Ann Coulter, *Slander: Liberal Lies about the American Right* (New York: Three Rivers Press, 2002), x.

46 Kathleen Hall Jamieson and Joseph N. Cappella, *Echo Chamber: Rush Limbaugh and the Conservative Media Establishment* (New York: Oxford University Press, 2008).

47 Baker interview.

48 Allison Perlman, "Whitewashing Diversity: Conservatives and the 'Stealth Fairness Doctrine,'" *Television and New Media* 13, no. 4 (2012): 353–373.

49 "Keeping an Eye on the Left," *Broadcasting*, June 5, 1989, 73.

50 Glenn Simpson and Craig Winneker, "Leather, Lingerie, Hair-Tossing, Loud Music, and HUAC," *Roll Call*, March 26, 1990, www.lexisnexis.com/hottopics/lnacademic/?shr=t&sfi=AC00NBGenSrch&csi=3624.

51 Quoted in "Conservative Spotlight: Media Research Center," *Human Events*, Nov. 11, 1994, 14.

52 Baker interview.

53 L. Brent Bozell III, "Pro-Life Forces and Their Foes," *Washington Times*, July 24, 1994, B4. See also L. Brent Bozell III, "TV's Insistent Storyline on Abortion," *Washington Times*, July 12, 1992, B4; L. Brent Bozell III, "TV's Warped Way of Looking at Life," *Washington Times*, June 13, 1993, B4; L. Brent Bozell III, "Good News and Bad News," *Washington Times*, June 4, 1994, D3.

54 L. Brent Bozell III, "Offering Parents a New Resource for TV Choices," *Washington Times*, Dec. 3, 1994, D3.

55 Parents Television Council, *10th Anniversary*, 14.

56 Tina Fetner, *How the Religious Right Shaped Lesbian and Gay Activism* (Minneapolis: University of Minnesota Press, 2008), 102.

57 Martha C. Nussbaum, *From Disgust to Humanity: Sexual Orientation and Constitutional Law* (New York: Oxford University Press, 2010).

58 For discussions of gay media activism see Kathryn C. Montgomery, "Special

Interest Citizen Groups and the Networks: A Case Study of Pressure and Access," in *Telecommunications Policy Handbook*, ed. Jorge Reina Schement, Felix Gutierrez, and Marvin A. Sirbu Jr. (New York: Praeger, 1982): 441–254; Larry Gross, *Up from Invisibility: Lesbians, Gay Men, and the Media in America* (New York: Columbia University Press, 2001), 43–55; Kathryn C. Montgomery, *Target: Prime Time: Advocacy Groups and the Struggle over Entertainment Television* (New York: Oxford University Press, 1989), chap. 5.

59 Thomas Johnson, *A Vanishing Haven: The Decline of the Family Hour*, released Feb. 8, 1996, 1–2. Many thanks to PTC Director of Communications and Education Melissa Henson for providing me with a copy of this report.

60 Tim Brooks and Earle March, *The Complete Directory to Prime Time Network and Cable Shows, 1946–Present* (New York: Ballantine, 1999), 120.

61 For prime-time schedules see ibid., 1151–1203.

62 This insight is Benjamin Alpers's.

63 Chris Roberts, "Violence Is Up in 'Family Hour,'" *Associated Press*, May 9, 1980; Seymour Feshbash, "TV View Mixing Sex with Violence—A Dangerous Alchemy," *New York Times*, August 3, 1980, sec. 2, 29; Mike Robinson, "Violence Raging on Prime Time's 'Family Hour,' Study Says," *Associated Press*, Sept. 10, 1986; Matt Roush and Jefferson Graham, "TV 'Family Hour' Is Fading to Black," *USA Today*, July 19, 1990, 1D; Robert P. Laurence, "Fall TV: Let's Talk Dirty: Raunch Comes to the Family Hour," *San Diego Union-Tribune*, Sept. 2, 1990, E1; Tom Shales, "Fall's Off-Color: Ruder, Cruder Talk for the New Season," *Washington Post*, Sept. 4, 1990, C1.

64 Johnson, *A Vanishing Haven*, 2–3.

65 Ibid.

66 Ibid., 4–6.

67 Thomas Johnson, *A TV Ratings Report Card: F for Failure*, released Feb. 11, 1997, 3. My thanks to Melissa Henson for providing me with a copy of this report.

68 See "Top 10 Best & Worst Family Shows on Television: 1996–1997 Season," Parents Television Council, n.d., www.parentstv.org/PTC/publications/reports/top10bestandworst/97top/main.asp.

69 See "Top 10 Best & Worst Family Shows on Television: 1998–1999 Season," Parents Television Council, n.d., www.parentstv.org/PTC/publications/reports/top10bestandworst/99top/main.asp.

70 Complete lists of worst shows from 1996 to 2008 can be found at www.parentstv.org/PTC/publications/reports/welcome.asp.

71 Self, *All in the Family*, 247.

72 Johnson, *A Vanishing Haven*, 6.

73 Ron Becker, *Gay TV and Straight America* (New Brunswick, NJ: Rutgers University Press, 2006); David Brooks, *Bobos in Paradise: The New Upper Class and How They Got There* (New York: Simon and Schuster, 2000); Richard Florida, *The Rise of the Creative Class: And How It's Transforming Work, Leisure, Community, and Everyday Life* (New York: Basic Books, 2003).

74 For excellent analyses of gay representation during prime time in the 1990s, see the final two chapters of Becker, *Gay TV and Straight America*.

75 Eric O. Clarke, *Virtuous Vice: Homoeroticism and the Public Sphere* (Durham, NC: Duke University Press, 2000).

76 Julia Duin, "Network TV Affiliates Won't Air Ads for Converting Gays: Campaign's Sponsors Decry 'Hypocrisy,' Censorship," *Washington Times*, March 12,

1999, A2; Julia Duin, "In Media Circles, GLAAD Flexes Its Pro-Gay Muscles: Activist Group Influences Print, Broadcast Portrayals," *Washington Times*, Nov. 16, 1999, A2; Joyce Howard Price, "Paramount Allays Fears of Gays: Dr. Laura to Offer 'Many Points of View' on Homosexuals," *Washington Times*, Feb. 17, 2000, A9; Julia Duin, "Gays Vow to Keep Heat on TV Host," *Washington Times*, March 15, 2000, A10.

77 See, e.g., "NewsBites: PC Protestors," *MediaWatch*, Oct. 1991, www.mediar-esearch.org/mediawatch/1991/watch19911001.asp#NewsBites; "Janet Cooke Award: *NBC*: Is It *Today* or *Toady*?" *MediaWatch*, August 1992, www.mediar-esearch.org/mediawatch/1992/watch19920801.asp#Award; "NewsBites: Gay Backlash," *MediaWatch*, Oct. 1992, www.mediaresearch.org/mediawatch/1992/watch19921001.asp#NewsBites; "NewsBites: Crying over Colorado," *MediaWatch*, Dec. 1992, www.mediaresearch.org/mediawatch/1992/watch19921201.asp#NewsBites; "Networks Ignore Protest Platform, Explicit Sex Talk, and Hate Speech," *MediaWatch*, May 1993, www.mediaresearch.org/mediawatch/1993/watch19930501.asp; "Study: Networks Rarely Cover Church News, Ignore Religious Concerns on Social Issues," *MediaWatch*, March 1994, www.mediaresearch.org/mediawatch/1994/watch19940301.asp#6; "Study: Unlike Religious Right, Gay Left Goes Label-Free," *MediaWatch*, Sept. 7, 1998, www.mediaresearch.org/mediawatch/1998/watch19980907.asp#.

78 William Hoynes, "Public Television and the Culture Wars," in *The American Culture Wars: Current Contests and Future Prospects*, ed. James L. Nolan Jr. (Charlottesville: University Press of Virginia, 1996), 61–87.

79 Brian Lowry, "Bozell, Riggs Square Off at Sesh on Public TV Funding," *Daily Variety*, July 16, 1992, 3; Downsizing Government and Setting Priorities of Federal Programs: Hearings Before the Subcommittees of the Committee on Appropriations, U.S. House of Representatives, 104th Cong., 1st sess., Jan. 19, 1995, 948 (testimony of L. Brent Bozell III). For a discussion of responses to *Tales* see David R. Craig, "Coming Out of the Television: LGBT-Themed Made-for-Television Movies as Critical Pedagogy" (PhD diss., University of California, Los Angeles, 2014), 140–141.

80 James R. Bennett, "Perspectives: The Public Broadcasting Service: Censorship, Self-Censorship, and the Struggle for Independence," *Journal of Popular Film and Television* 24, no. 4 (1997): 177–181.

81 Government and Television: Improving Programming without Censorship: Hearings Before the Subcommittee on Oversight of Government Management, Restructuring and the District of Columbia of the Committee on Governmental Affairs, U.S. Senate, 105th Cong., 1st sess., April 16, 1997, 53 (testimony of L. Brent Bozell III).

82 Richard Maltby, "The Production Code and the Hays Office," in *Grand Design: Hollywood as a Modern Business Enterprise, 1930–1939*, ed. Tino Balio (Berkeley: University of California Press, 1995), 37–72; Kevin Sandler, *The Naked Truth: Why Hollywood Doesn't Make X-Rated Movies* (New Brunswick, NJ: Rutgers University Press, 2007), chap. 1.

83 Patricia Aufderheide, *Communications Policy and the Public Interest* (New York: Guilford, 1999), 78.

84 L. Brent Bozell III, "Chip/Con," *Dallas Morning News*, March 17, 1996, 1J.

85 Alan Bash, "Senator Aims to Clean Up Prime-Time's Family Hour," *USA Today*, Feb. 8, 1996, 3D; Dennis Wharton, "Primetime Sex under Fire," *Daily Variety*, Feb. 9, 1996, 46; Julia Duin, "Broadcasters Urged to Save Family Hour: Congressional Intervention Threatened," *Washington Times*, Feb. 9, 1996, A2.

86 Dennis Wharton, "Lawmakers Urge Return to Family Viewing Hour," *Daily Variety*, May 1, 1996, 30; Julia Duin, "Hill Tells Networks to Revive Family TV: Published Letter Urges Responsibility," *Washington Times*, A2.

87 Christopher Stern, "The Newt-ered TV Era: Speaker Joins Crusade for Hour without Sex, Violence," *Daily Variety*, May 9, 1997, 1; John Carmody, "Gingrich Calls for New 'Family Hour,'" *Washington Post*, May 9, 1997, D01.

88 Quoted in Christopher Stern, "Call for Family Hour: Congress Members Ask Nets to Reserve Airtime," *Daily Variety*, July 19, 1996, 35.

89 Joseph Lieberman, "Why Parents Hate TV," *Policy Review* 77 (May-June 1996): 18–23.

90 Johnson, *A TV Ratings*, 1.

91 Ibid., 10.

92 Ibid., 3.

93 Quoted in "Culture, et cetera," *Washington Times*, August 1, 1997, A2.

94 Johnson, *The "Family Hour."*

95 Joe Flint and Dennis Wharton, "Censors to Networks: Gotcha! Content Rating Could Wreak Havoc for TV," *Variety*, Feb. 19–25, 1996, 61–62; Christopher Stern, "Senate Panel Chair Takes Poke at Biz," *Variety*, April 21–27, 1997, 34.

96 Bozell testimony, 54 (see note 79 above).

97 L. Brent Bozell III, "Dialing T for Trash on Tube," *Washington Times*, Feb. 28, 1998, C3.

98 L. Brent Bozell III, "Family Values According to L.A.," *Washington Times*, Jan. 24, 2000, A15.

99 L. Brent Bozell III, "Bad Teen Choices: Who's to Blame," *Washington Times*, Sept. 4, 2000, A15.

100 Quoted in Clay Calvert and Robert D. Richards, "The Parents Television Council Uncensored: An Inside Look at the Watchdog of the Public Airwaves and the War on Indecency with Its President, Tim Winter," *Hastings Communication and Entertainment Law Journal* 333 (Spring 2011): 307.

101 Melissa Henson, telephone interview by the author, Oct. 11, 2010.

102 Ibid., 295–296.

103 Testimony of L. Brent Bozell III, "'Can You Say That on TV?': An Examination of the FCC's Enforcement with Respect to Broadcast Indecency," Subcommittee on Telecommunications and the Internet, House of Representatives, Jan. 28, 2004, 26, 28.

104 Frank Ahrens, "Unlikely Alliances Forged in Fight over Media Rules," *Washington Post*, May 20, 2003, E01.

105 Testimony of L. Brent Bozell III, FCC Public Hearing on Media Ownership Rules, Richmond, VA, Feb. 27, 2003.

106 *Prometheus Radio Project v. Federal Communications Commission*, 373 F.3d 372 (2004).

Chapter 6   The National Hispanic Media Coalition, Spanish-Language Broadcasting, and Latino Media Advocacy

1 Public Hearing on Media Ownership, University of Texas at Austin, Jester Auditorium, Sept. 19, 2006. The evening's panel included Adelstein, Rosa Rosales (LULAC), Ann Toback (Writers Guild of America), Mariana Piñeda (Univision), Tony Tafoya (*Musica*), Jerry Davila, Federico Subervi (Texas State University), and

Gonzales Barrientos (Texas state senator) and was moderated by Marcelo Tafoya (LULAC). I was in attendance at the event.

2 See Hector Amaya, *Citizenship Excess: Latinas/os, Media, and the Nation* (New York: New York University Press, 2013), esp. 142–156.

3 Decision of Administrative Law Judge John Conlin, released Jan. 8, 1986, 13, Box 35, Folder 5, NHM.

4 Amaya, *Citizenship Excess*, 140.

5 Juan Gonzalez, *Harvest of Empire: A History of Latinos in America* (New York: Penguin, 2011), 227.

6 See, e.g., William V. Flores and Rina Benmayor, eds., *Latino Cultural Citizenship: Claiming Identity, Space, and Rights* (Boston: Beacon, 1997); Cristina Beltran, *The Trouble with Unity: Latino Politics and the Creation of Identity* (New York: Oxford University Press, 2010); Suzanne Oboler, "The Politics of Labeling: Latino/a Cultural Identities of Self and Others," *Latin American Perspectives* 19, no. 4 (1992): 18–36; America Rodriguez, *Making Latino News: Race, Language, Class* (Thousand Oaks, CA: Sage, 1999); and Arlene Davila, *Latinos, Inc.: The Marketing and Making of a People* (Berkeley: University of California Press, 2001).

7 Craig A. Kaplowitz, *LULAC, Mexican Americans, and National Policy* (College Station: Texas A&M University Press, 2005), 171–183.

8 Dolores Inés Casillas, *Sounds of Belonging: U.S. Spanish-Language Radio and Public Advocacy* (New York: New York University Press, 2014), 29–35.

9 America Rodriguez, "Creating an Audience and Remapping a Nation: A Brief History of U.S. Spanish-Language Broadcasting, 1930–1980," *Quarterly Review of Film and Video* 16, no. 3/4 (1999): 359–361.

10 For an excellent discussion and critique of the FCC's format policy see Theodore L. Glasser, "Competition and Diversity among Radio Formats: Legal and Structural Issues," *Journal of Broadcasting and Electronic Media* 28, no. 2 (1984): 127–142.

11 Amy Jo Coffee and Amy Kristin Sanders, "Defining a Product Market for Spanish-Language Broadcast Media: Lessons from *United States v. Univision Communications, Inc.* and Hispanic Broadcasting," *Communication Law and Policy* 15 (Winter 2010): 70–74. In particular, Coffee and Sanders note that the FCC had distinguished Spanish-language media for antitrust purposes, had identified in 1972 a public interest obligation of audience comprehension (here tied to language), and had waived since 1978 its National Spot Sales Rule (which had prohibited networks from negotiating spot ad sales for its affiliates) for Spanish-language broadcasters.

12 Alex Nogales, interview by the author, July 10, 2013, Offices of National Hispanic Media Coalition, Pasadena, CA.

13 Chon A. Noriega, *Shot in America: Television, the State, and Chicano Cinema* (Minneapolis: University of Minnesota Press, 2000), 174–181.

14 "TV and Video," *Los Angeles Times*, April 21, 1987, 2; Dennis McDougal and Victor Valle, "Tom Van Amburg Resigns Post at KCBS-TV, Channel 2," *Los Angeles Times*, April 23, 1987, H1, H12; Victor Valle, "Latino Wins Key Job at Channel 2," *Los Angeles Times*, May 30, 1987, E1, E11; Victor Valle, "Latino Group Challenges TV Licenses," *Los Angeles Times*, Nov. 2, 1988, 1; Victor Valle, "Latino Coalition's Bid for KTTV: Full Assault, Long Odds," *Los Angeles Times*, Nov. 10, 1988, H1, H13.

15 Victor Valle, "Latinos Claim Job Bias at KCBS," *Los Angeles Times*, Dec. 31, 1986, J1, J2; McDougal and Valle, "Tom Van Amburg Resigns"; Valle, "Latino Wins Key Job."

16 Press release, NHMC Signs Landmark Agreement with KABC-TV, Nov. 11, 1993, Box 7, Folder 1, NHM.

17 Declaration of Ana Barbosa, NHMC Supports Petition to Deny Application Field by Edward Gonzales, Box 29, Folder 7, NHM.

18 Armando Durón to Board of Directors, Reliance, Telemundo, Estrella, June 22, 1989; Donald Raider to Armando Durón, July 25, 1989; Armando Durón to Henry Silverman, August 9, 1989; Henry Silverman to Armando Durón, August 10, 1989; Press release, "National Hispanic Media Coalition to 'Educate' KVEA Advertisers," Sept. 6, 1989; Armando Durón to KVEA Advertiser, Sept. 7, 1989, Box 29, Folder 7, NHM.

19 The NHMC files also include transcripts of depositions of the FCC's investigation into Fox's ownership structure. See Box 1, Folder 31, NHM.

20 Dennis Wharton, "NAACP Opposes Murdoch's Post Bid," *Daily Variety*, May 13, 1993, 6.

21 Initial Decision of Administrative Law Judge John H. Conlin, 6.

22 Ibid., 8.

23 Rodriguez, *Making Latino News*, 38.

24 Ibid., 38–40.

25 See In the Matter of Amendment of Section 3.658 to the Commission's Rules and Regulations, 27 FCC 697 (1959).

26 Nicole Serratore, "How Do You Say 'Big Media' in Spanish? Spanish-Language Media Regulation and the Implications of the Univision-Hispanic Broadcasting Merger on the Public Interest," *Fordham Intellectual Property Media and Entertainment Law Journal* 15, no. 1 (2004): 223–227.

27 Ibid., 224.

28 G. Christina Mora, "Regulating Immigrant Media and Instituting Ethnic Boundaries—The FCC and Spanish Language Television: 1960–1990," *Latino Studies* 9, no. 2 (2011): 242–262.

29 Initial Decision of Administrative Law Judge John H. Conlin, 37.

30 Ibid., 39.

31 Ibid.

32 Ibid., 40–41.

33 Quoted in *Coalition for the Preservation of Hispanic Broadcasting v. FCC*, 893 F.2d 1349 (1990), 1352.

34 Petition to Intervene and Objections to Proposed Settlement, *In Re Applications of SICC for Renewal*, Sept. 25, 1986, Box 35, Folder 6, NHM.

35 See *Jefferson Radio Company v. FCC*, 340 F.2d 781 (1964).

36 The rationale here was that creditors would be unduly harmed should the commission prevent sales when a licensee had filed for bankruptcy. For a discussion of these exceptions see Philip H. Lebowitz, "FCC Minority Distress Sale Policy: Public Interest v. the Public's Interest," *Wisconsin Law Review*, no. 2 (1981): 365–397.

37 Petition to Intervene and Objections to Proposed Settlement, filed Sept. 25, 1986, by Armando Durón, Box 35, Folder 6, NHM.

38 Armando Durón to Eli Sandoval, Oct. 17, 1986, Box 36, Folder 9, NHM.

39 Memorandum Opinion and Order, released June 2, 1987, Box 34, Folder 3, NHM.

40 Memorandum Opinion and Order, released June 23, 1987, 5, Box 34, Folder 3, NHM.

41 See Stephen F. Sewell, "Assignments and Transfers of Control of FCC Authorizations under Section 310(d) of the Communications Act of 1934," *Federal Communications Law Journal* 43, no. 3 (1991): 277–389, esp. 285–288.

42 Memorandum Opinion and Order, June 2, 1987, 7, Box 34, Folder 3, NHM.

43 Consolidated Opposition to Applications for Petition for Review, filed August 19,

1987; Reply to Opposition to Petition for Reconsideration, filed by TVL, July 31, 1987, Box 34, Folder 1, NHM.

44 See *Coalition for the Preservation of Hispanic Broadcasting v. FCC* 893 F.2d 1349 (1990).

45 *Coalition for the Preservation of Hispanic Broadcasting v. FCC*, 931 F.2d 73 (1991), 79.

46 Jeffrey Daniels, "Univision to Perenchio Group: Spanish-Language TV Net Sold by Hallmark for $550 Million," *Hollywood Reporter*, April 9, 1992; Richard W. Stevenson, "Company News: Hallmark to Sell Its Univision TV Group," *New York Times*, April 9, 1992, D1.

47 American G.I. Forum, Petition for Denial of Transfer of FCC Licensee Univision Television Network to Applicants Perenchio Communications, Inc., Grupo Televisa, and Venevisión, June 16, 1992; American G.I. Forum, First Amended Petition for Denial of Transfer of Control of FCC Licensee Univision Television Network to Applicants Perenchio Communications, Inc., Grupo Televisa, and Venevisión, July 14, 1992, both in Box 30, Folder 5, NHM; Nora Hamerman, editor of Executive Intelligence Review, to Donna Searcy, Secretary of FCC, June 18, 1992; Petition to Deny filed by the National Hispanic Media Coalition, the U.S. Hispanic Chamber of Commerce, and the National Puerto Rican Coalition, Inc., June 17, 1992, both in Box 30, Folder 7, NHM. Reply Oppositions to Petition to Deny and for Other Relief, filed by Eduardo Pena and David Honig, July 14, 1992, Box 28, Folder 9, NHM. Reply to Consolidated Oppositions, filed on behalf of Telemundo Group Inc. by William S. Reyner Jr., Marvin J. Diamond, David J. Saylor, Susan Wing, July 14, 1992, Box 28, Folder 8, NHM.

48 LULAC, Reply to Oppositions to Petition to Deny, July 14, 1992, 14, Box 28, Folder 9, NHM.

49 Consolidated Opposition filed on behalf of Perenchio Television Inc. by Grover C. Cooper, Clifford M. Harrington, and Scott R. Flick, July 1, 1992, 4, Box 28, Folder 10, NHM.

50 Ibid., 61.

51 Memorandum Opinion and Order, released Sept. 30, 1992, 13, Box 28, Folder 9, NHM.

52 Ibid., 20.

53 Ibid., 20–21.

54 Ibid., 23.

55 Notice of Appeal, NHMC v. FCC, filed Oct. 20, 1992; Notion of Intention to Intervene, NHMC v. FCC, filed Nov. 5, 1992, Box 32, Folder 2, NHM; Settlement Agreement, Entered into between National Hispanic Media Coalition and the Univision Television Group, Inc., May 20, 1994; Enrique Baray to Armando Durón, Oct. 18, 1995, Box 31, Folder 3, NHM.

56 Justin Oppelaar and Paula Bernstein, "NBC Habla Telemundo," *Daily Variety*, Oct. 12, 2001, 1.

57 Ibid.; Andrew Ross Sorkin, "NBC Is Paying $1.98 Billion for Telemundo," *New York Times*, Oct. 12, 2001, C1; David Lieberman, "NBC to Buy Telemundo in $2B Deal," *USA Today*, Oct. 12, 2001, 2B.

58 The other groups were Puerto Rican Legal Defense and Education Fund Inc.; National Council of La Raza; LULAC; NOSOTROS; Mexican American Grocers Association; National Puerto Rican Coalition; and the National Association of Hispanic Publications.

59 Petition to Deny and Motion to Dismiss, filed Dec. 3, 2001, 7, http://transition .fcc.gov/transaction/nbc-telemundo/nosotros_petdeny120401.pdf.

60 Andrew Ross Sorkin, "NBC Is Paying $1.98 Billion for Telemundo," *New York Times*, Oct. 12, 2001, C1.

61 Ibid., 9.

62 Ibid., 10–14.

63 *In the Matter of Telemundo Communication Groups*, Memorandum Opinion and Order, released April 10, 2002, 19, https://apps.fcc.gov/edocs_public/attachmatch/ FCC-02-113A1.pdf.

64 Mimi Whitefield, "Univision Said to Be Buying Hispanic Broadcasting Corp.," *Houston Chronicle*, June 12, 2002, Business Section, 1; David Kaplan, "A Niche No More: Spanish-Language Networks Are Becoming Media Titans," *Houston Chronicle*, June 23, 2002, A1.

65 Quoted in Sanford Nowlin, "Spanish TV Giant Will Move into Radio: Univision's Parent Firm to Buy Hispanic Broadcasting Corp.," *San Antonio Express News*, June 13, 2012, 1A.

66 For example, rival Spanish-language radio network SBS filed a lawsuit against Clear Channel, one of HBC's biggest shareholders, for allegedly using illegal means to depress SBS's stock prices to acquire the company and to sabotage its merger with a third company. See Dan Cox and Erica Copulsky, "Spanish Broadcast Deal Snag," *New York Post*, June 13, 2012, 5.

67 Letters filed on behalf of the merger can be found at http://hraunfoss.fcc.gov/ edocs_public/attachmatch/FCC-02-113A1.pdf. Representatives from approximately eighty-five organizations filed the same essential form letter and included individuals from Hispanic Chambers of Commerce in cities across the nation, LULAC chapters, Mexican American community service organizations, Latino cultural centers, and Latino professional organizations.

68 Alex Nogales to Michael Powell, n.d., http://hraunfoss.fcc.gov/edocs_public/ attachmatch/FCC-02-113A1.pdf.

69 See Jennifer Holt, *Empires of Entertainment: Media Industries and the Politics of Deregulation* (New Brunswick, NJ: Rutgers University Press, 2011), 169–177.

70 For a history of this see Robert W. McChesney, "Media Policy Goes to Main Street: The Uprising of 2003," *Communication Review* 7, no. 3 (2004): 223–258.

71 Esther Renteria to Michael Powell, Dec. 6, 2002, http://apps.fcc.gov/ecfs/ document/view?id=6513582880.

72 Ibid.

73 Petition to Deny, filed by Arthur Belendiuk, counsel for the National Hispanic Policy Institute, Sept. 3, 2002, http://apps.fcc.gov/ecfs/document/ view?id=6513290709.

74 Martin Frost to Michael Powell, May 20, 2003, http://apps.fcc.gov/ecfs/ document/view?id=6514783893.

75 Lee Terry, Roy Blunt, Nathan Deal, Ed Whitfield, Barbara Cubin, John Shinkus, Charles W. "Chip" Pickering, Joe Barton, Steve Buyer, George Radanovich, Mary Bond, Mike Ferguson, Darrell E. Issa, and C. L. "Butch" Otter to Michael Powell, June 19, 2003, http://apps.fcc.gov/ecfs/document/view?id=6514783898.

76 Jose E. Serrano to Michael Powell, August 8, 2003, http://apps.fcc.gov/ecfs/ document/view?id=6514783988.

77 Bill Richardson to Tom Daschle and Nancy Pelosi, repr. in *Business Wire*, June 4,

2003; Steve Terrell, "Legislator Critical of Merger," *Santa Fe New Mexican*, June 7, 2003, B1.

78 Glen Justice, "Private Political Donations Can Carry a Business Price," *New York Times*, Oct. 28, 2004, A22.

79 Ted Kennedy, Richard Durbin, John Conyers Jr., Robert C. Scott, Mel West, Maxine Waters, William D. Delahunt, and Linda Sanchez to Michael Powell, May 15, 2003, http://apps.fcc.gov/ecfs/document/view?id=6514182974.

80 Hillary Clinton to Michael Powell, May 7, 2003, http://apps.fcc.gov/ecfs/document/view?id=6514182728.

81 Nancy Pelosi to Michael Powell, May 16, 2003, http://apps.fcc.gov/ecfs/document/view?id=6514783901.

82 See, e.g., Thomas B. Edsall and Sarah Cohen, "Broadcasters Bank on a Combination of Interests: Parties Seeking FCC Approval of Hispanic Broadcasting Merger Are Big Donors to Bush Campaign," *Washington Post*, August 10, 2003, A07.

83 Quoted in Anne C. Mulkern and John Aloysius Farrell, "Univision Deal Arouses D.C. Ire for Dems Fear Non-Hispanic, Conservative Control in Spanish-Media Merger Plan," *Denver Post*, June 2, 2003, A01.

84 Memorandum Opinion and Order, released Sept. 22, 2003, 25, http://hraunfoss.fcc.gov/edocs_public/attachmatch/FCC-03-218A1.pdf.

85 Ibid., 27.

86 Ibid., 37.

87 For a discussion of these practices see Kofi Ofori's study for the FCC, "When Being No. 1 Is Not Enough: The Impact of Advertising Practices on Minority-Owned and Minority-Formatted Broadcast Stations," Jan. 1999, www.fcc.gov/Bureaus/Mass_Media/Informal/ad-study/adstudy01.pdf.

88 Nogales interview.

89 Allison Perlman and Hector Amaya, "Owning a Voice: Broadcasting Policy, Spanish-Language Media, and Latino Speech Rights," *Communication, Culture and Critique* 6, no. 1 (2013): 145–147.

90 Rincon and Associates, Petition to Deny, *In Re Application Univision Communications*, http://transition.fcc.gov/transaction/univision.html.

91 Nogales Interview.

92 Nogales interview; FCC, *Shareholders of Univision Communication Inc.*, Memorandum Opinion and Order, released March 27, 2007, 22, FCC Rcd 5842.

93 FCC News Release, "FCC Approves Transfer of Univision Communications Inc., and Enters into $24 Million Consent Decree with Univision Concerning Children's Programming Requirements," March 27, 2007, http://transition.fcc.gov/transaction/univision.html#timeline.

94 Letter filed in the Matter of Implementation of the Child Safe Viewing Act, by Jessica Gonzalez, counsel for the NHMC, April 16, 2009, http://apps.fcc.gov/ecfs/comment/view?id=5515358414.

95 The complaint can be found at www.nhmc.org/wp-content/uploads/2011/02/Jose-Luis-Sin-Censura-Liberman-Complaint.pdf; Meg James, "Company Town: 'Jose Luis Sin Censura' Protest Building Steam; Show Seen as Raunchy Spanish-Language 'Jerry Springer,' Loses Two Big Advertisers," *Los Angeles Times*, June 3, 2011, B3; Meg James, "Broadcaster Crops Talk Show Targeted by Gay Activists," *Los Angeles Times*, August 11, 2012, B3; "Liberman Broadcasting to Pay $110,000 to Resolve FCC Indecency Investigation," Nov. 14, 2013, http://hraunfoss.fcc.gov/edocs_public/attachmatch/DOC-324171A1.pdf.

Conclusion

1 Kathryn Montgomery, *Target: Prime Time: Advocacy Groups and the Struggle over Entertainment Television* (New York: Oxford University Press, 1989), 219–224.
2 Elizabeth Fones-Wolf, *Waves of Opposition: Labor and the Struggle for Democratic Radio* (Urbana: University of Illinois Press, 2006), 242–243; Victor Pickard, *America's Battle for Media Democracy: The Triumph of Corporate Liberalism and the Future of Media Reform* (New York: Cambridge University Press, 2015), chap. 7.
3 Robert Britt Horwitz, "Broadcast Reform Revisited: Reverend Everett C. Parker and the 'Standing' Case (*Office of Communication of the United Church of Christ v. Federal Communications Commission*)," *Communication Review* 2, no. 2 (1997): 344.
4 Robert W. McChesney, *Telecommunications, Mass Media, and Democracy: The Battle for the Control of U.S. Broadcasting* (New York: Oxford University Press, 1995), 37.
5 Willard Rowland, "The Illusion of Fulfillment: The Broadcast Reform Movement," *Journalism Monographs* 79 (Dec. 1982): 2, 41.
6 Thomas Streeter, "What Is an Advocacy Group, Anyway?" in *Advocacy Groups and the Entertainment Industry*, ed. Michael Suman and Gabriel Rossman (Westport, CT: Praeger, 2000), 81.
7 Quoted in Timothy Shenk, "Booked #3: What Exactly Is Neoliberalism?" *Dissent Magazine Blog*, April 2, 2015, www.dissentmagazine.org/blog/booked-3-what-exactly-is-neoliberalism-wendy-brown-undoing-the-demos.
8 See, e.g., Robert W. McChesney, *Rich Media, Poor Democracy: Communication Politics in Dubious Times* (Urbana: University of Illinois Press, 1999); Edward S. Herman and Noam Chomsky, *Manufacturing Consent: The Political Economy of the Mass Media* (New York: Pantheon, 1988); and Herbert I. Schiller, *Culture, Inc.: The Corporate Takeover of Public Expression* (New York: Oxford University Press, 1989).
9 Jessica Gonzalez, interview by the author, April 17, 2014, Offices of National Hispanic Media Coalition, Pasadena, CA.
10 Allison Perlman, "The Precarity and Politics of Media Advocacy," in *Precarious Creativity: Global Media, Local Labor*, ed. Michael Curtin and Kevin Sanson (Berkeley: University of California Press, forthcoming); Jason McLure, "Civil Rights Group's FCC Positions Reflect Industry Funding, Critics Say," Center for Public Integrity, June 6, 2013, www.publicintegrity.org/2013/06/06/12769/civil-rights-groups-fcc-positions-reflect-industry-funding-critics-say; James Rucker, "Net Neutrality, Civil Rights, and Big Telecom Dollars," *Huffington Post*, Sept. 10, 2014, www.huffington-post.com/james-rucker/net-neutrality-civil-rights-orgs_b_5796944.html.
11 Becky Lentz, *Docket Politics: Genres of Participation in Policy Change* (New York: Fordham University Press, forthcoming).
12 Gonzalez interview.

Index

About the Author

ALLISON PERLMAN is an assistant professor in the Department of Film and Media Studies and the Department of History at the University of California, Irvine.